The Forging
of an Aristocracy

The Forging
of an Aristocracy

Harvard & the Boston Upper Class,
1800–1870

Ronald Story

WESLEYAN UNIVERSITY PRESS

MIDDLETOWN, CONNECTICUT

Library of Congress Cataloging in Publication Data

Story, Ronald.
    The forging of an aristocracy.

    Includes bibliographical references and index.
        1. Elite (Social sciences)—Massachusetts—Boston—
History—19th century. 2. Harvard University—History
—19th century. 3. Boston—Social life and customs.
4. Elite (Social sciences)—New England—History—19th
century. I. Title.
HN80.B7S76   305.5′2′09   80–460
ISBN 0–8195–5044–2

Designed by Joe Freedman

Distributed by Columbia University Press
136 South Broadway, Irvington, N.Y. 10533

Manufactured in the United States of America
First edition

To my
mother & father

Contents

Preface

THIS book had its genesis some years ago in a study of the cultural and intellectual aspects of social reform movements in antebellum Massachusetts: penal and asylum improvement, women's rights, the common school revival, free incorporation, equitable taxation, workers' benefits, and electoral participation. This work was progressing satisfactorily when two influences conspired to divert it from its original channel. The first influence was intellectual. It involved a growing recognition that many of the reformist movements seemed to share a common foe, or at least a common obstacle or underlying cause — namely, the group of shippers, textile manufacturers, and railroad promoters whose exploits once preoccupied New England scholars and whose activities and, indeed, very existence appeared more and more to be intertwined with virtually all of the period's mass movements, whether meliorist or egalitarian.

The second influence was professional, involving mainly the appearance of the very exciting early work of the new quantitative social and urban historians, much of it dealing with stratification in urban-industrial areas and tending, on the whole, to underscore the immense (if somewhat vague) importance of the antebellum elites, including that of Boston. This second influence fused almost ineluctably with the first to determine both the subject and the methods of the present work, which is now, for better or worse, quite different from what had originally been anticipated.

As far as the work may have drifted from its initial emphases, however, it still remains informed by them, most evidently in conception and to a considerable degree in execution as well. There is, first, its cultural focus, which derives from a particular concept of the relationship between consciousness and social class and also from the search for a procedure capable of tracing the cultural predilections and participation of elite Bostonians.

The concept comes in part from work on mass movements in antebellum New England and elsewhere. The procedure comes in part from the examples of business history, with its attention to who governs whom to what purpose, and urbanology, with its sensitivity to institution-building and associational life.

Except incidentally, the term "culture" as used here means neither "high" culture in the sense traditionally associated with elite studies nor "national" or "community" culture in its conventional anthropological meaning. It means rather that body of perceptions, attitudes, and values, whether cognitive or stylistic, coherent or incongruous, rich or sparse, which are instrumental in the evolution of a social class. "Institutional culture" means simply the cultural work, both intellectual and social, that took place in and around the civic institutions discussed in the body of the text. "Culture" obviously has very wide and important meanings, as all students of Kluckhohn and Kroeber will appreciate, and may be used in diverse ways. As employed in this book, it is hardly narrow or unimportant and needs, therefore, no apology.

This approach to the question of the social functions of culture has shaped what educational historians will almost certainly consider the somewhat unorthodox treatment of Harvard University in the text. Educational institutions are commonly considered in three ways: as autonomous administrative entities ruled by presidents and other chief officers within a practically nonexistent social context; as houses of intellect whose main raison d'etre is the scholarship of its faculty, the context here being usually the history of ideas; and as "typical" educational institutions from which information may be drawn as needed to indicate trends in higher education in the nation (or sometimes the region) as a whole, the context now being The College, as it were, in abstracto. In this book the college, Harvard, has been placed as firmly as possible within the dual contexts of elite evolution on the one hand and civic entrepreneurship on the other — within the two contexts, that is, suggested by modern social history generally and urban stratification studies specifically. Hence the initial discussion of the institutional network of antebellum Boston, with which Harvard may be compared and within which it may be located. Hence, too, the recurring analysis of the various constituencies of the university, admittedly pursued with some doggedness but always as the best means to a particular end: the revelation of the social characteristics and relationships essential to the purpose of this study.

The preoccupation with culture and insurgency which was once my primary concern has, along with the recent discoveries about urban development and social stratification, played an important role in shaping the concept of class which informs the book. The role of culture is crucial because of the assumption that the processes of cohesion, continuity, and differentiation which characterize a social class are cultural as well as economic and political and that a class cannot be said to exist until it becomes consciously aware of itself as a distinctive stratum of society and acquires the style, perspective, and symbolic attachments that would mold and sustain that distinctiveness. Hence, for example, the importance of chapter 7, "Harvard Students and the Class Ideal," where the issues of class objectives and cultural attainment are addressed somewhat more explicitly than elsewhere. Insurgency, in turn, plays its part because true class status derives not merely from stylistic uniformities or similarity of life chances over time, but also from struggle, sometimes covert but sometimes not, with antagonistic social groups over the access to and control of valued resources, whether economic or cultural. Hence the importance of chapter 8, "Mid-century Crisis and the Shock of Recognition," which becomes, in a real sense, the climax of the half-century of development analyzed in the preceding sections of the book.

That these assumptions concerning culture and confrontation are valid for the situation at hand will be a portion of the book's burden of proof. For the present it may suffice to emphasize how these two factors, plus other scholars' findings as to rising concentrations of wealth and residential propinquity, suggest a sharp shift in the character of New England's higher circles from 1800 to 1860. The shift would seem to have been so dramatic, indeed, as to warrant the replacement of the view that class is a more or less constant condition to a view of class as an achieved condition. In this sense the upper class of antebellum New England would not be a Schumpeterian "bus" merely shuffling its passengers periodically irrespective of broader social forces, as even some of the best contemporary students would have it. It would be rather a stratum which emerges from a prior condition of *less* economic control, residential concentration, cultural conditioning, and social confrontation to one of *more* of these, the former condition being insufficient, the latter sufficient, to the attainment of class stature.

The term "upper class" thus denotes a social elite which has achieved a singularly high degree of control, consciousness, and resolution, as had the higher circles of the Boston area by 1870. "Elite," according to this usage, signifies not simply the top people of any particular group (which is a reasonable and common usage) but rather what came before the class, i.e., the economically low-grade, territorially disparate, culturally unfinished yet aspiring elements *in process of becoming* an upper class. These definitions are employed partly for the sake of convenience — there must be something to call the earlier elements and the later that will distinguish between the two — but they are also analytically coherent and conform closely to historical reality. In any case the terms are never used interchangeably. "Elite" stands for what existed before mid-century; "class," for what emerged thereafter. The precise character of the change is partly, of course, a matter for correct measurement, to which this study will perhaps make some minor contribution. It is also, however, a matter of the proper perception of changing social attitudes and relationships, to which this study will, I hope, make a major contribution.

Certain other terms may also require a word of comment. Prominent Bostonians are commonly called "Brahmins" by historians. Actually (as noted in chapter 1) the employment of this term before mid-century is an anachronism, for it did not enter the lexicon until about the time of the Civil War, its appearance being one indication that the elite had transcended its antecedents at last. The term is used here, therefore, only with reference to the period after the 1850s. "Brahmin," moreover, also at times

connotes an ineffectual literati, alienated from the economic barons of the realm. But by 1870 the term meant the rich and
well-born as well as the cultivated; was used interchangeably
with "upper class"; and was a sign, accordingly, of distinctiveness as well as attainment, the achievement of a degree of security, cultivation, and arrogance that struck observers as noteworthy, if not unique. This book should help to explain both how
the Boston upper class came to be and how it came to be
Brahmin.

As for the term "aristocracy" there is little excuse save
rhetoric. An aristocracy enjoys privileges which stem not from
possession but from law, though wealth may of course be its
ultimate base. The United States has had no aristocracy but,
instead, an ascriptive upper class exerting influence and control
through a combination of wealth and culture (a point evident to
the Bostonians themselves, as chapter 7 reveals). But since the
word "aristocracy" suggests to the vulgar ear nothing if not inordinate hauteur and durability, it has seemed not wholly in-
applicable to the Brahmin upper class. The fusion of the two
terms, as in "Brahmin aristocracy," doubtless gilds the lily a
bit — for which the writer begs indulgence. As an alternative,
finally, the term "patriciate," meaning families possessing
wealth, status, and culture for at least two generations, periodically recurs in place of "upper class," as does "Proper Bostonians," a phrase vague enough, to be sure, but nonetheless serv-
iceable if stripped of its connotations of eccentric and harmless
caricature. Indeed, in the interests of euphony if not strict logic,
the Bostonians have been considered "Proper," be they elite or
upper class.

The use of both "patriciate" and "Proper Bostonian" serves to
underscore the essentially cultural reputation of the Boston
upper class and the essentially cultural preoccupation of this
analysis of its emergence. This said, however, it should be explained that the underlying philosophy of the work is dialectical
materialism. Culture may have class functions, but the culture
itself and the institutions which embody and support it are
products of economic forces — capital accumulation, industrial

entrepreneurship, economic coordination and control — which in turn feed upon the resources and perspectives engendered in the cultural sphere. Equally, it is entrepreneurship and accumulation and their impact that generate those social forces — disgruntled religious and political dissidents, hard-pressed farmers and artisans, exploited factory workers and day laborers — which are antagonistic to the dominant elements and whose antagonism precipitates a transforming leap forward in elite consciousness. While most of the book thus concentrates on the origins and development of cultural institutions, it expends much effort in illustrating their material underpinnings and class functions, as in the initial chapters on funding and control. Similarly, while most of the book stresses developments internal to the elite, a bruising confrontation with opposing forces lies waiting at the end. It is hoped that the result will be to erase the line so often drawn between culture and economics and highlight the fact that class is a matter of process and relationship. In any event the study, more than many in American history, moves with a rhythm of thesis, antithesis, and synthesis to which the reader might be sensitized from the outset.

This book will undoubtedly appeal most strongly to students of antebellum elites, urban institutions, and higher education, all of which are treated in detail and from somewhat novel vantage points. But the ramifications of the study, as the general reader will perceive, are not thereby exhausted. It relates, for example, more or less directly (and as anticipated) to New England intellectual and labor history, helping to depict both the institutionalism to which transcendentalism was in part a reaction and the oppressive socioeconomic innovations to which the workingmen of Lynn, Waltham, and elsewhere were responding. It bears, too, upon long-standing historiographical questions concerning the Middle Period — the extent, for instance, to which the North was throwing up a bourgeois upper class as counterpart to the South's planter caste and the degree to which the fragmentation of the Whig party in the 1850s was paralleled by fragmentation in the economic and cultural areas as well, thus producing what might well have been a "general crisis" of the

mid–nineteenth century. Finally, it provides some clues as to
the roots of the cultural gulfs of post–Civil War urban society
and the institutional sources of the twentieth-century ruling
class. Some of these suggestions are broached more fully in the
text. Whether they, or perhaps others unbroached, bear actual
scholarly fruit is, of course, for later scholars to determine.

I wish to thank the *Journal of Social History*, the *History of Education
Quarterly*, and the *American Quarterly* for permission to reproduce
certain materials which previously appeared in the pages of those
journals. I also wish to thank the Harvard University Archives
and the Massachusetts Historical Society for granting permission
to quote from documents contained in their vast and invaluable
collections.

The Forging
of an Aristocracy

The Boston Elite

THE concept of a Jacksonian "Age of the Common Man" is, at last, no more. The complex forces of individualism, social mobility, and economic opportunity notwithstanding, it is crystal clear that the concentration of wealth, status, and political power persisted in the hands of small local elites throughout the decades between the Revolution and the Civil War. "Any notion," now writes a historian,

> that the Jacksonian era was a kind of socially democratic interim between the aristocratic characteristics of earlier generations and the admittedly great inequalities of the industrial era of the late nineteenth century, is largely undermined by the evidence. The political representation of poorer men increased in the latter part of the period. But the portion of wealth they held, the standing they commanded, the actual opportunities to rise that were available to them [reflected] a continuation or even a worsening of inegalitarian tendencies that had commenced in the colonial era.[1]

"The generation before the Civil War," says another student, "witnessed the emergence of a class of wealthy persons set apart quite clearly from the rest of society."[2] The evidence suggests, in fact, that the concentration of wealth and prestige — the long march toward inequality and stratification — may have been more intense in these years than at any other time in American history.[3]

New England conformed thoroughly to this trend. In Massachusetts the elite was more exclusive and well defined and owned a larger share of total assets in 1870 than in 1780. In Boston the top 1 percent of the adult population owned two-fifths of the taxable wealth of the city in 1860 as compared to about one-fourth before 1800. For Massachusetts as a whole the top 1 percent, mainly Bostonians, may have owned half the total wealth by mid-century, when the concentration of wealth and economic power reached such "heroic proportions" that the Bostonians "broadened themselves from an economic elite into an urban upper class."[4] The displacement by the 1860s of the terms "Federalist (or Whig) Aristocracy" and "Boston Associates," which were political and business references, respectively, by the more general "Boston Brahmins," may be taken to symbolize the attainment of modern upper-class stature and distinction. Never before, says a recent scholar, were the rich "so rich" or the poor "so plentiful."[5]

How did such inchoate, dispersed, preindustrial elites, bobbing uncomfortably in the restive middle-class democracy of the late eighteenth century, achieve an ascendance which stood so dramatically athwart the egalitarian, individualistic, democratizing tendencies which were once thought, with some justification, to have characterized the age? One investigator records his "amazement" at the evidence of "great inequality at such an early stage of development" and wonders "how this might have happened in a land of opportunity."[6] Another registers with exclamation points his astonishment that 10 percent of the population of a northern city owned 90 percent of the wealth by 1860.[7] A student of the wealthy families of antebellum Boston finds some modest representation from the pre-Revolutionary years but very striking persistence in the post-Revolutionary era.[8]

For Boston, at least, sufficient monographic and other literature exists to permit a brief summary of some of the key processes of elite development. Entrepreneurship, first of all, was manifestly important in a group so defined in the beginning by the sheer accumulation of wealth. As a contemporary merchant wrote, "A man without money is like a body without a soul — a walking dead man."[9] Bostonians pioneered in maritime commerce, textile manufacturing, and eastern railroads. They acquired additional wealth from real estate and lesser industrial ventures and from the development of great financial institutions: Boston's oldest, largest, and most influential commercial banks; its major insurance and trust companies; its biggest savings institution; and the American headquarters of the largest British investment house. Interlocking directorates linked one financial institution to another and the financial institutions themselves to the various industrial concerns, which were in turn controlled and capitalized by the great banks.[10] By mid-century, the Boston elite controlled commercial, financial, and manufacturing enterprises which held sway throughout New England, generated wealth at an unprecedented rate, and thus contributed to the establishment and maintenance of Brahmin prominence and identity in the decades to come.[11]

This entrepreneurial wealth was combined and consolidated, secondly, through kinship. Family ties facilitated the acquisition of capital, provided reliable business associates in an age of imperfect communications and supervisory methods, and served as a cushion in economic difficulties.[12] Marriage between friends and relatives, including first cousins, was common, with the result, according to a close student of such marital patterns, that "property was not dissipated in alien hands."[13] As early as 1818 a Boston lawyer provided this striking assessment of the family role:

> It is an obvious advantage to the young folks to grow up in the midst of a respectable family connection. Weight of character and success are frequently promoted by the *esprit de corps* or *de famille*. Uncles and cousins are frequently of service to each other in a great variety of relations. . . . You are now in the midst of *a clan;* and the children of brothers and sisters are growing up together in habits of friendship, with the probability of "dwelling together in unity," and the certainty of the confidence and complacency which are derived from feeling that one is not alone in the world.[14]

Increasingly, a chief function of such clannishness was the mingling and preservation of entrepreneurial fortunes.[15]

To accumulating wealth through business and consolidating it through kinship may be added, thirdly, protecting it through politics. This was a matter of some moment, of course, in view of the broad suffrage and intense competition of the American party system and the ominous ultimate sovereignty of the state; for in this combination lurked a potential "anarchy" which could reduce "the rich to poverty" and rich and poor alike to "starva-

tion and extinction."[16] Elite political organizations thus became
here what they were throughout the nineteenth-century
world — "agents of class unification" as well as instruments of
public influence. The actual identity of the Bostonians' party
changed from Federalism in the early years of the century to
Whiggery between 1830 and the 1850s to Republicanism by the
1860s. At any given point, however, loyalty was generally high,
so that, for example, some 90 percent of the wealthy Bostonians
of the 1840s were Whigs, a figure undoubtedly approximating
that for the Federalists of 1815 or the Republicans of 1870.[17]

Attitudes toward gevernment itself naturally shifted with
need and circumstances. As politics became more competitive
and popular in the Federalist era, elite party leaders became
suspicious of government's capacity for mischief; as the economy
advanced, on the other hand, the Whigs found it expedient to
seek government aid for economic or cultural projects which
would serve as social overhead capital. Yet despite this fundamental and lasting ambivalence toward governmental authority,
the elite parties commonly promoted policies with regard to certain matters — law and constitutionality, the rights and preroga-
tives of property, the efficacy and privileges of large-scale
enterprise, the importance of stabilizing philanthropic and educational measures — which were, as a rule, sufficient to preserve
the fruits of past entrepreneurial accumulation and prepare the
vineyards for future harvests.[18]

The accumulation of entrepreneurial wealth and its preservation
by kinship and politics are so palpably important in the evolution
of capitalist social classes that cultural factors have been comparatively neglected as agents of elite development, particularly
in the formless years of the early nineteenth century. Yet the
emergence of a viable upper class quite obviously entails more
than economic activity. At the very least it involves such factors
as the modification of individualistic or acquisitive behavior in
the interest of a larger group; the integration of potentially rival
families and factions; the harmonizing of business and nonbusi-

ness, particularly cultural, elements; the acculturation and absorption of new members; the elaboration and adoption of a distinctive value system; and the provision of social models to which the group may aspire.[19]

These developments would seem to involve considerations of culture as much as of accumulation and to deserve commensurate attention. In Boston, moreover, such considerations are especially relevant, for what most distinguished the "Proper Boston" of pre–Civil War days from its New York or Philadelphia counterparts was precisely its singular cultural sheen — its clannishness and exclusiveness, to be sure, but also its "spirit of Patronage" and "ethic of stewardship," its pronounced Anglophilia, its taste for literature and tone of cultivation.[20] An Englishman observed of the emergent upper class in 1871 that "Boston is the one place in America where wealth and knowledge of how to use it are apt to coincide."[21] It was probably also the place in America where the early elite had achieved the most finished and resolved class stature. By 1870 the term "Brahmin" signified not merely an upper class, but one of considerable distinctiveness. Hence the cultural sources of this distinctiveness and the role of culture generally in the formation of the Brahmin upper class — and therefore of upper classes generally — are matters of some moment.

Religion, to be sure, was a factor in the development of a culturally coherent Boston elite, which seems to have been so overwhelmingly "liberal" (Arminian until about 1815, Unitarian thereafter) in affiliation and outlook that contemporaries referred to Unitarianism as "the Boston religion." That they did so in the face of a far vaster increase in the number of area Methodists, Baptists, and Catholics only underscores the class dimension of this elite attachment to the "liberal" faith, an attachment which persisted, as will be seen, well into the twentieth century. By 1850 approximately two-thirds of the wealthiest Bostonians were Unitarians; by 1870 the average Unitarian was thirteen times richer and twenty times more likely to be a lawyer or businessman than was a member of any other denomination.[22] By mid-century only about a tenth of Boston's rich families adhered to Orthodox Congregationalism, whose archaic cosmology was less naturalistic than that of the Unitarians and whose doctrines involved more theological constraints on worldly success. Like all classes seeking a devotional pattern consonant with their status and occupations, entrepreneurial families flocked readily to a creed which contained no other-worldly or antiegoistic doctrines whatever.[23]

The evidence, however, also suggests large cultural and civic concerns extending beyond religion or kinship or politics. A leading theorist of antebellum entrepreneurship thus describes the parallel creation of "social organizations, clubs, . . . and educational and recreational institutions" which tended to channel oncoming generations into given slots in an "increasingly hierarchical structure."[24] A student of nineteenth-century elites discusses the proliferation of "voluntary philanthropic associations" as corollaries to urban living and political participation.[25] The chronicler of New England's literary "flowering" notes the appearance of cultural institutions as accompaniments to the growth and ferment of the Boston area.[26]

Philanthropy is difficult to trace in the best of times, but it is especially so in the antebellum era, when the keeping of records on charitable bequests failed to keep pace with the bequests themselves. It would appear, however, that Bostonians expended at least ten million dollars in charitable funds between 1800 and 1860, approximately 70 percent of it on more or less permanent, endowed institutions and societies.[27] It is not clear that this sum surpassed the total philanthropy of, say, Philadelphia. But it is clear that this charity was very heavily concentrated. A full third of the total funds went to a mere handful of cultural and medical institutions in amounts roughly as follows:

Harvard University	$1,180,000
Massachusetts General Hospital/McLean Asylum	1,000,000
Boston Athenaeum	320,000
Lowell Institute	240,000
Perkins Institution for the Blind	150,000
Massachusetts Eye and Ear Infirmary	90,000
Boston Dispensary	80,000
Boston Lying-In Hospital	40,000

Boston Society of Natural History	40,000
Massachusetts Historical Society	40,000
Massachusetts Horticultural Society/ Mount Auburn Cemetery	30,000
American Academy of Arts and Sciences	30,000

One of these institutions, Harvard, was founded before 1700. Three others — the Boston Dispensary, the Massachusetts Historical Society, and the American Academy of Arts and Sciences — appeared in the immediate post-Revolutionary era. The rest, however, emerged between 1805 and 1840. Along with such unendowed but significant and durable entities as the *North American Review* and the Handel and Haydn Society, the group as a whole formed a virtual "new wave" of civic institutional development, a medico-cultural counterpart of the great economic enterprises of the business entrepreneurs.[28]

Fewer studies in the cultural than in the economic area manage to transcend the merely institutional, biographical, or evocative; fewer still treat institutional culture within the context of elite evolution. One reason, presumably, is that philanthropy and civic institution-building were common nineteenth-century urban phenomena, and Boston's development of them was in itself unremarkable, save perhaps in magnitude: it spawned its charities and organizations as did other cities, and little more need be said. Also, scholars have felt that business and culture are — or at least ought to be — essentially antithetical, even in Boston. If both flourish, they need do so separately or at odds rather than as complementary supports of a single group. Moreover, if the group does contain both, it tends to be enervated and in decline, as the Proper Bostonians and their forebears have often appeared to be. From the standpoint of either urban or cultural history, therefore, Boston cultural institutions, especially if they lie outside the realms of religion and politics, have seldom received their due as agents of class development or class maintenance.[29]

Yet the modern city, as recently noted, has been the *via regis* of the modern social class, and urban institutions are thus inevitably bound up with the development of class relations.[30] In addition, scholars as diverse as W. K. Jordan, Edward Thompson and E. Digby Baltzell stress the role that culture, especially institutional culture, has played in shaping the social classes of three centuries. Jordan writes that the philanthropic benefactions of the merchants and professional men of sixteenth and seventeenth-century England induced a sense of "class solidarity" not only because of their "enormous scale" but because "they were . . . so perfectly ordered and disposed as . . . permanent institutions." Baltzell notes the manner in which the exclusive colleges, schools, and clubs of late nineteenth-century America facilitated the consolidation of a national ruling class.[31] Such analogies point suggestively in the direction of Boston.

A look at some of these key Boston institutions should serve to establish some of the dimensions of their relationship to the elite. The most important medical institution was the Massachusetts General Hospital, incorporated in 1811 and opened just north of Beacon Hill in a building designed by Charles Bulfinch and constructed by convict labor. The only medical facility in the area to attract a million dollars in charity funds, the Massachusetts General (whose trustees also administered the McLean Asylum in nearby Somerville) was renowned for its pioneer use of ether and antiseptics, its great size — 1,500 admissions and a budget of a hundred thousand dollars by 1860 — and the eminence of its physicians, most of whom had studied abroad.[32]

Around it were clustered the other large institutions: the Massachusetts Eye and Ear Infirmary and the Boston Lying-In Hospital on the same street, the Perkins Institution for the Blind and the Boston Dispensary center a few blocks away. The complex — which ministered to the ambulatory or shut-in outpatient; the nonterminal and noncontagious injured or ill who required hospitalization; the pregnant, the insensate, and the insane — was also clustered administratively. Massachusetts General doctors had easy access to the four lesser institutions, especially the Dispensary, where most of them practiced before or during their Massachusetts General years. Almost 90 percent of the trustees of the other institutions also served as Massachusetts General trustees. Some individuals served on all five boards at various times; a few were on two or more boards simultaneously.[33]

Massachusetts General officials were almost uniformly from the elite families. Of the twenty-three officers of the hospital from 1820 to 1850, the names of all but four appear on available lists of Boston's wealthiest 200 individuals; all but three were directors of the Suffolk Bank, the Provident Institution for Savings, or the Massachusetts Hospital Life Insurance Company, Boston's most important financial institutions. Hospital trustees included an ambassador, a lieutenant governor of the state, six Boston mayors, two "fathers of American manufactures," and "many of our wealthiest and most liberal merchants." Of the twenty-one attending physicians and surgeons from 1817 to 1851, sixteen were officers or the sons of officers of the Massachusetts Medical Society, the region's leading professional organization, and eight of the attending doctors came from the same families as the trustees. The median wealth of Massachusetts General physicians was $88,000; their average wealth was $151,000.[34]

Like medical facilities in other American cities, this massive Boston complex arose from a variety of interests, including civic pride, the desire to foster scientific progress, and a reformist idealism which led the Perkins Institution director to believe he could teach "an oyster" to read and speak. Many officials, moreover, while dutifully catering to the well-to-do, acted also out of genuine concern for the poor, particularly at the Dispensary and Lying-In Hospital and the Massachusetts General, where by 1850 Irish men and women comprised a substantial proportion of admissions.[35]

Interestingly enough, this charitable function actually served to underscore the extent of elite control over the complex in two respects. First, there was an insistence among donors and officers on the nongovernmental, nonofficial character of the facilities. A Dispensary patron and manager wrote, for instance, that private charity "induces gratitude, while public charity is often demanded as a right."[36] A Massachusetts General trustee wrote similarly that private benevolence produced an "active sympathy" between donor and recipient rather than the "convulsions" which conflicting claims upon government might engender.[37] Accordingly, while the Massachusetts General Hospital and the Perkins Institution expended some $200,000 in public funds from 1820 to 1860, the disposition of this and all other institutional largesse remained entirely in private hands out of an essentially "Whiggish" ambivalence toward popular political authority and a concern to make the recipients of medical care grateful for a privilege rather than insistent upon a right.

But simultaneously, according to a contemporary source,

> among the crude and popular, perhaps natural, expressions of distrust and opposition to the first planning and the supposed subsequent administration of the [Massachusetts General] Hospital, this was prominent — namely, that poor patients were to be enticed within its walls that they might be made the subjects of experiments in surgical processes or in the trial of drugs, chemicals, and medicines; so that this gratuitous practice might fit new young doctors and surgeons for safer and well-remunerated professional work for the rich in their luxurious chambers.[38]

The allegation of such a nefarious desire for "clinical material" has been strongly denied and the dedication of the early doctors emphasized. Observers did note, however, the "strong prejudice of the deserving poor" against entering the new institutions, and later scholars have marked the "practical competition for business and money" which attended the establishment of the medical complexes of Boston and elsewhere.[39] In any case the private control of the institution and the great wealth, status, and ambition of the doctors made such a suspicion of exploitation, in the word of the contemporary, "natural."

In the cultural realm one encountered far more variety than in the medical. The Boston area included a majority of antebellum New England's fourteen organizations for the promotion of science. It also contained numerous social libraries, musical organizations, art associations, historical societies, and educational es-

tablishments, most appearing, or growing rapidly, after 1800.
Private institutional culture per se was, in fact, a greater object of
philanthropy than institutional medicine, attracting some 20
percent of the total charity funds of the era as opposed to 14
percent for medicine.[40] But the list of endowments indicates that
the cultural funds, too, went to a comparatively small number of
institutions, most of them creations of the antebellum years.
Three cultural institutions alone, for instance, received more
funds than the medical complex as a whole and three-fourths of
all the cultural funds. Thus, a preliminary look at the governance and operation of two of these, the Boston Athenaeum and
the Lowell Institute, might help to suggest again, as with the
medical facilities, the extent of their relationship with the elite
and with the various components of the large constellation of
civic institutions.

The Boston Athenaeum was a private gentlemen's library
founded in 1807. It offered the "prosperous and educated
families" of Boston access to collections of books, periodicals,
paintings, and sculpture. At a time when such things were still
quite rare, the Athenaeum's holdings expanded so rapidly that
one new building was acquired in the 1820s and then a larger,
more elegant one in 1849. The price of a share was $300, much
the highest of any American proprietary library.[41] Membership,
which was strictly limited even at mid-century to only a
thousand, was therefore exclusive. By one account, two-thirds of
the first 150 subscribers were businessmen, the rest professionals. By another, a third of the last 400 subscribers were in
maritime commerce, investment banking, or domestic merchan-
dising. Among the shareholders, in fact, could be found the
following:

90 percent of the sixty-one directors of the largest mills in seven
   New England textile towns;

65 percent of the forty-two commercial bank presidents in Boston
   in 1850;

88 percent of the forty-eight wealthiest Bostonians in 1848;

96 percent of the approximately two dozen millionaires of antebellum Boston.[42]

The mid-century Athenaeum subscription list, then, was virtually coterminous with the Boston elite. Its constituency by the post war era was "practically a family," and its hereditary shares were handed from generation to generation like "family silver."[43]

The same was true of the Athenaeum directors. Of the twenty-six original organizers, incorporators, and trustees, two-thirds left estates of $25,000 or more, which placed them in roughly the top 2 percent of the Massachusetts population; almost 40 percent left $100,000 or more, thus ranking in the top 0.3 percent. In spite of the "belletristic" tone of the early Athenaeum, a half-dozen of these men were in business, while many of the ministers, doctors, and lawyers had business interests or catered to the business establishment. Of the officers and trustees elected by the proprietors from 1816 to 1830, almost 90 percent left estates of $100,000, ranking in the top 0.6 percent of the population; two-thirds left $200,000, placing them in the top 0.2 percent; five were millionaires. Some 70 percent of this group were in business; most of the rest were lawyers.[44] These figures for wealth and occupation held roughly constant for the remainder of the antebellum period, with the board of trustees absorbing parvenu businessmen in the 1820s and periodically thereafter but with representatives of five more or less distinct, established clans filling most of the principal administrative offices from 1807 to 1860.[45]

The Lowell Institute, in turn, was endowed in 1836 through a bequest from industrialist John Lowell, Jr., and opened in 1840 as a free lecture organization for the Boston public. The lecturers were selected by the Institute's lone trustee, who was always a member of the Lowell family, and spoke, as stipulated in the founder's will, on science and technology, liberal religion, and literature and the social sciences. The original endowment increased rapidly to several hundred thousand dollars, enabling the Institute to attract prominent speakers and rent elegant quarters; from 1840 to 1860 some sixty lecturers gave over a hundred courses of lectures to several hundred thousand listeners. By 1845 the Lowell Institute was a major component of the New England cultural complex. It exercised a formidable influence over the region's thriving lyceum movement. And by 1860 it had displaced or absorbed most of the competing lecture organizations in the Boston area.[46]

The Lowell Institute was seen, quite properly, as a "monument" to the Lowell family. No fewer than seven male Lowells were connected with it in some capacity from 1835 to 1870, including a lawyer, a minister, a man of letters, and four businessmen. Four of them were officers of leading Boston financial institutions; five were officers of large textile companies. All left estates of $50,000 or more; five left $200,000 and two more than a million. By marriage they were connected directly with at least ten other leading Boston families; by residence they were associated with the broader Beacon Hill community. All were subscribers to the Athenaeum; all were Unitarian; and all belonged, with a single brief exception, to the conservative wings of the Federalist, Whig, or Republican parties.[47]

While the Institute trustees — first John Amory Lowell, the founder's cousin, and then John Amory's son, Augustus — exerted what an observer termed "a silent authoritative control" over the Institute's proceedings, they did not operate wholly in splendid family isolation. John Amory Lowell consulted with numerous friends and associates on the selection of speakers and hired a small staff to handle the details of the courses. Other affluent men contributed funds or equipment for particular presentations. Also, from 1840 to 1860 almost half the lecturers themselves came from the various branches of the Boston elite. Before the Civil War, in fact, an Institute lectureship sometimes helped to recruit a promising intellectual into the ranks of the elite or, later, launch the career of a promising young Brahmin.[48] Even the audiences, though sizeable, were kept largely "fashionable" — filled with businessmen, politicians, and intellectuals and their families — by the location and appointments of the hall and the strictures on propriety and attentiveness laid down by founder and trustees.[49] Formal responsibility for the Institute thus lay with a single broad clan; practical supervision and participation, with a broader but still exclusive elite spectrum.

The Athenaeum and the Lowell Institute were strongly

linked. One link was through a proviso in the will of the Institute founder giving the Athenaeum trustees a "visitation" authority over the Institute with regard to finances and administration. A second link was through the joint leadership of the Lowell family. John Lowell, Jr., was himself an Athenaeum trustee; John Amory Lowell was the seventh Athenaeum president; other Lowells were Athenaeum officers and trustees. Noting this "corporate relation" between Institute and Athenaeum, a historian observes that "no other family has had so large a representation in the management of the Library."[50]

Mutual officers linked these institutions in turn with their lesser counterparts. The Lowell family alone held office in all the most heavily endowed of them, as did the five clans — Quincys, Perkinses, Appletons, Grays, Higginsons — which dominated the Athenaeum. Other linkages completed this remarkable bonding. The American Academy of Arts and Sciences, the Massachusetts Historical Society, and the Society of Natural History presented lectures under Institute auspices. The Academy of Arts and Sciences had offices in the Athenaeum. The historical and the natural history societies shared offices in the building of the Provident Institution for Savings. The Horticultural Society sponsored and profited from the Mount Auburn Cemetery.[51]

These interrelationships make it all the more appropriate to consider the cultural organizations as a cohesive group, comparable by mid-century to the medical complex clustered round the Massachusetts General Hospital and possessing many of the same postures toward the public. The proprietors of the Athenaeum, for example, opposed a move by the municipal authorities of Boston to appropriate its collections for public use on the ground that the Athenaeum should have "a permanent, independent existence" as a memorial to "those who created and those who endowed it," and should not be "surrendered up . . . to the care of a political body." Even though one of the objectives of forming a public library in the first place was to civilize the masses and moderate their political inclinations, members of the

Athenaeum nonetheless voted in March, 1853, in a "patriotic glow" not to "throw open the doors to the many-headed."[52]

Similarly, the Lowell Institute, with its single trustee and strict lecture format, did not, like the lyceum and other small lecture organizations which dotted New England during the 1830s, allow for democratic control or audience participation. The programs, said trustee John Amory Lowell, "had always to be acceptable to me." In the turbulent 1850s, when relatively neutral scientific lectures gave way increasingly to conservative social ones inveighing against the "tumult and violence" of "excessive liberty," this was even more clearly the case.[53] At the Mount Auburn Cemetery a move in 1856 to lessen the cost of burial plots and democratize the decision-making process was decisively rejected.[54]

The popular response to the cultural institutions was an echo of the response to the medical complex. Observers contrasted the "republican liberality" of European libraries with the exclusiveness of the Athenaeum, which was "rather inclined to follow the example of Old England, and make men pay for everything."[55] A penny newspaper criticized:

> When the poor are favored with admission to study the neatly fitted up shelves of books which adorn the Athenaeum, we shall be convinced of the necessity as well as worth of it, and not before. Things are becoming quite royal in our venerable old city: money buys a ticket for the wealthy . . . while the industrious, worthy portion of the community, may intellectually starve upon a six-penny almanack.[56]

The Lowell Institute staff systematically excluded the "ignorant and critical classes of society" and the "lean, hungry, savage anti-everythings" from the environs of the lectures.[57] Henry David Thoreau wrote caustically in 1858:

> It is no compliment to be invited to lecture before the rich Institutes and Lyceums. The settled lectures are as tame as the settled ministers. . . . There is the Lowell Institute with its restrictions, requiring a certain faith in the lecturers. How can any free-thinking man accept its terms?[58]

Three characteristics of institutional development may therefore by hypothesized. First, the main era of growth was roughly the quarter-century from 1815 to 1840, during which time almost all the major institutions were either established or made financially and organizationally secure. This is, of course, coterminous with the period when urban settlement is now believed to have acquired its normative shape, into which urban elements would pour and boil for another hundred years.[59]

Second, virtually all the institutions exhibited a particular twofold relationship to the community at large as a result of the elite sources of their creation and control. On the one hand, the institutions insisted on the importance of maintaining their independence from popular control, whether governmental or otherwise and whether or not they were providing charitable public services. On the other hand, they developed an almost adversary relationship with the general public, which complained at times of the exclusiveness of their facilities, at times of the exclusiveness of their control, and at times of both.

Finally, the institutions were closely linked by structure, operations, and personnel. The evidence suggests that the medical group centered predominantly around the Massachusetts General Hospital, the cultural group predominantly around the Boston Athenaeum and Lowell Institute. Medicine and culture, moreover, were themselves closely connected. Some 46 percent of the fifty-seven Athenaeum trustees from 1820 to 1850 served also as Massachusetts General trustees; 43 percent of the eighty-two Boston Dispensary trustees between 1800 and 1860 were also members, or relatives of members, of the Massachusetts Historical Society.[60]

The linkages are suggested by the diagram on page 19. The cultural group, even as depicted here, was somewhat larger and more variegated than the medical complex and possessed, perhaps, a greater regional prestige. Certainly by 1860 it was attracting a much greater proportion of total Boston charity funds. But in a real sense it may be said that the two clusters, with mid-century assets of over two million dollars, were one.

The mere description of this interwoven cultural constellation suggests the existence of an important additional facet to the process of elite development, one potentially equivalent in significance to business, kinship, politics, and religion and relating in the most direct way to the interplay of culture and class. But the treatment is incomplete in important respects. In the first place, it is mostly structural in nature, tracing elite connections and institutional alliances. It deals inadequately, therefore, with the internal dynamics and actual social functions of the institutions — their precise role, for example, in fostering either

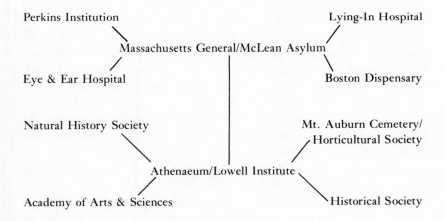

the type of elite consolidation and self-consciousness which is a precondition to class stature generally or the lofty gentility of the Brahmin upper class specifically. It is unclear how the tension between accumulation and cultivation, either in the minds of individuals or on the boards of institutions, was successfully resolved. Nor is the tension between public presence and private control satisfactorily explored, or the connection, if any, between the growth and subsequent relaxation of this tension and the appearance of a "finished Brahminism" at a particular, if not quite definable, point in the 1860s.

The second major omission is, of course, any discussion of Harvard University, which was the oldest, most prestigious, and most influential of the eastern Massachusetts cultural institutions and also the most lavishly endowed. Harvard attracted some 12 percent of total antebellum charity funds; more than a third of all funds contributed to major medical and cultural institutions; almost two-thirds of the major cultural funds; plus temporary though not insignificant grants from the Massachusetts state legislature. Its centrality is self-evident.

Historians, as might be expected, have subjected Harvard to a measure of scholarship appropriate to its august position. The most systematic and extensive of this work, however, tends to treat either the colonial era, when Harvard was a small, provincial, theology-tinged "seminary" with organic ties to church and state and commensurate service obligations to the citizenry; or else the post–Civil War era, when it was already a large, complex private university with secular concerns and a different set of obligations and responsibilities. While valuable work does now exist on Harvard in the first half of the nineteenth century, it would still not be entirely unfair to say that the antebellum era was, until very recently, Harvard's historiographical "dark age," overshadowed by studies of the colonial period on the one hand and of the modern era on the other.[61]

Students who have focused on the period from 1800 to 1870 share a propensity, moreover, to consider Harvard as a more or less typical antebellum college, whose essence may be captured through discussion of parietal regulations, town-gown problems, the progress of the curriculum, the emergence of the presidential system of governance, and the gradual growth of the institution generally.[62] Those searching for special significance find it mainly in two areas: first, in the introduction of such pedagogical reforms as lectures and electives by young professors after the War of 1812; and second, in the development of a climate of liberalism through resistance to religious fundamentalism on the one hand and outside political interference on the other.[63] Both developments are seen as harbingers of tendencies which would spread to other colleges and become still more pronounced at

Harvard under President Charles W. Eliot and his successors. They are, accordingly, portents of the academic values and environs cherished by twentieth-century historians, who commonly find them laudable for that reason.

There has in any case been little effort to relate the university's liberalism and innovativeness or even its considerable growth to the evolution of the New England social structure or to the development of the Brahmin upper class which dominated that structure. Yet the role of the burgeoning elite in the formation of other antebellum cultural and civic institutions itself suggests the likelihood of such a role at Harvard. Indeed, even the extant literature provides hints as to a special early nineteenth-century relationship: that in 1837, for example, "State Street" gained ascendance over the Harvard Corporation; that about this time "Boston society" became a "leech" on the Harvard population; that in some vague way, at some ill-defined point, Harvard became both "an extension of the Brahmin family" and a "prime object of patrician charity."[64] So with surveys of modern Harvard:

> In the days when Boston was the Athens of America, Harvard and Boston were tied very closely, financially, culturally, and socially. The great Boston families — the Lowells, Saltonstalls, Lodges, Forbeses, Wigglesworths, and many others — sent their sons to Harvard and built up its endowments. . . . Older members of the faculty [in 1960] are concerned about the decreasing proportion of students from Boston, for Harvard's relationship with the great families of Boston once gave it financial and intellectual strength.[65]

That the clues have not been followed owes something to the comparatively scanty coverage of the early nineteenth-century university and something to the occasionally myopic angles of vision in urban and cultural historiography. But it also owes something to the fact that while Harvard was clearly the prime object of antebellum charity, the university, unlike (say) the Athenaeum or the Massachusetts General Hospital, was not strictly an antebellum creation. It was rather an inheritance of the colonial age with a complicated governmental structure established by charter in the seventeenth century.

The Harvard charter, for example, provided for two separate governing bodies. One was the Corporation, a seven-man body which met frequently to supervise finances, personnel, and other aspects of university activity and which nominated candidates to fill its own vacancies. The other was the Board of Overseers, a much larger body which met less frequently to ratify Corporation decisions and establish broad guidelines for university operations. The composition of the Overseers varied from time to time — chapter 8 provides a brief sketch of its changing composition — but always the Board included ex officio members of the ministry and the state government whose presence ostensibly guaranteed a broader public function for Harvard and therefore inevitably cast it in times of social conflict into what an antebellum university president called "the very trough of a politico-theological sea."[66]

The university, in addition, was a vastly more complex institution than its antebellum counterparts, involving greater sums of money and larger numbers of people and possessing multiple constituencies deriving both from its public obligations and from the fact that it was a college rather than a library, lecture forum, or hospital. One such constituency was the broader public — the popular "community" of the region — whose interests were manifested at one remove in the Board of Overseers and at another in the state legislature. But there was also a much narrower group of private financial patrons here as in other civic institutions. There was, in addition, a faculty, which was important in campus governance and in the provision of intellectual and other services. And there were, finally, students, whose concentrated weight as long-term voluntary resident always influenced, however indirectly, college policy decisions.

Governmental structure and multiple constituencies thus made the development of Harvard considerably more complicated than that of the Athenaeum or other elements of the cultural complex, which as original elite creations enjoyed an enviable structural simplicity and comparatively exclusive, or at least well-defined, social responsibilities and control mechanisms. In point of fact the story of antebellum Harvard, in a very real sense, consists largely of the struggle to shuck off the public presence and the public responsibility and to conform, like its counterparts, to the interests of a single increasingly homogeneous and modern constituency. That the struggle succeeded only after much time and effort highlights, among other things, the differences between an ancient, quasi-public university and a recent private library or hospital; and also the dilemma, from the standpoint of the evolving elite, of excessive inherited responsibilities.

The following chapters, then, consist of a detailed account of the transformation of antebellum Harvard with two primary objectives in mind: to complete the picture of elite institutional development in antebellum Boston; and to reveal, by way of this case study, the functions of the large cultural institutions of the city in the emergence of its upper class. But the work should shed much incidental light as well on a formative but relatively unexplored stage in the development of what remains even today the most powerful of American universities.

Growth and Governance at Harvard

As with all the components of the cultural constellation, the pattern of transformation at Harvard began with growth. For the first half-century the dimensions are suggested by the data in table 1.[1]

Table 1: Growth of Harvard University 1800–1850

	1800	1850	Percent Increase
Occupied acreage	24	55	125
Total buildings	6	20	217
Endowed professorships	6	21	250
Professional schools	1	4	300
College library volumes	15,000	65,000	333
Total assets	$250,000	$1,250,000	400

The university area expanded considerably, but within the context of much more rapid plant and faculty expansion. In 1800 the ill-organized medical faculty was the sole professional school; by 1850 there were four, including law, divinity, and science, plus an observatory. In 1800 there were perhaps a half-dozen university buildings; by 1850 there were twenty. In 1800 there were six endowed professorships; in 1850, twenty-one. The holdings of the college library (excluding those of the professional schools) increased still more rapidly, reaching 70,000 volumes by 1857. In 1800 total assets were under (probably well under) $250,000; fifty years later they were perhaps five times as large.

This kind of growth was unprecedented in two respects. First, there was its sheer pace, as shown by the figures in table 2 on financial contributions over a 150-year period.[2] By the middle of the nineteenth century, new funds were accruing to Harvard at a rate three times greater than in the early nineteenth century, and twenty times greater than the rate of a century before. And if such growth was unprecedented, it was also unmatched. The

Table 2: Growth of Financial Contributions, Harvard, 1700–1850

	Total Contributions	Quinquennial Average	Percent of 1700–1850 Total
1700–1800	$182,000	$9,100	12
(1801–1825)	(298,000)	(59,600)	(20)
(1826–1850)	(980,000)	(196,000)	(68)
1801–1850	1,298,000	127,800	88

university's total assets in 1850 were five times those of Amherst and Williams combined and three times those of Yale. Its library was three times the size of the combined holdings of Amherst and Williams, three times those of Princeton, Columbia, and Pennsylvania combined, twice those of Yale.[3] The first half of the nineteenth century was therefore Harvard's first great period of growth. By 1850 it was a genuine university, "unequaled in facilities," as a budding scholar put it, by any other institution in America — the "greatest University," said another, "in all creation."[4]

The second novel factor in this growth pattern was the dwindling role played by the state. The medical school expanded partly through a series of legislative grants amounting to $100,000 between 1815 and 1824, and as late as 1820 Harvard spokesmen were arguing for state financial assistance on the grounds that private fortunes were too small and insecure, and the obligations of private persons to the community too tenuous, to sustain an outstanding university.[5] But it was altogether true, as a Corporation spokesman put it in 1856, that it was to "the munificence of private individuals, that the preeminence of this institution over all others in this country . . . is owing."[6] Table 3 shows the development of this trend.[7]

Table 3: Sources of Financial Contributions, Harvard, 1700–1850

	Percent of Contributions from Public Sector	Percent of Contributions from Private Sector
1700–1800	55	45
(1801–1825)	(33)	(67)
(1826–1850)	(0)	(100)
1801–1850	8	92

For the period 1801 to 1850 as a whole, the private contributions amounted to some 92 percent of the total, the only exception being the ten years of state grants ending in 1824. In the final period of very rapid expansion, all funds were from the private sector. In this period, therefore, the funding of Harvard came to resemble — indeed, to be identical with — that of the other major civic institutions of the Boston area for the first time in its entire history.

Who exactly was responsible for the creation of what was, for the time, so mammoth a cultural enterprise? Since approximately 95 percent of the private funds from 1801 to 1850 accrued in the form of grants of $5,000 or more — about $140,000 from eight subscription drives, the rest (some $1,175,000) from individual donations — the constituency whose philanthropy created antebellum Harvard may be reasonably identified through the analysis of these large-scale benefactions alone. (The remainder presumably followed a not dissimilar pattern and in any case represented a comparatively marginal input.) The major pre-1850 subscription drives, then, were as shown in table 4.[8]

Table 4: Major Subscription Drives, Harvard, 1805–1846

	Amount	Number of Contributors	Purpose
1805	$31,333	152	Natural history
1817	30,000	over 200	Divinity school
1826	19,322	215	Divinity school
1829	13,180	52	Divinity school
1838	12,000	42	Scholarships
1841	10,000	"various"	Divinity school
1842	21,000	34	Observatory
1846	5,000	"various"	Observatory

Analysis of the subscription data reveals a number of interesting points. First, the number of subscribers appears to have declined from about 200 to fewer than 50 after 1829. Second, later subscribers were more concentrated in the Boston–North Shore area of Massachusetts — 100 percent by 1826 compared to 90 percent in 1805. Third, large donors were increasingly dominant. In 1805 half the funds came from 20 percent of the subscribers; in 1826, from 10 percent. In the large subscription drives, therefore, the small-scale non-Boston donor gave way to the large-scale Boston donor.

At the same time, moreover, there was a trend away from the subscription to the large individual grant, as indicated in table 5.

Table 5: Subscription and Individual Grants, Harvard, 1700–1850

	Percent of Private Funds Subscribed	Percent of Private Funds Granted Individually
1700–1800	7	93
1801–1825	33	67
1826–1850	12	88

The figures suggest that at the inception of the antebellum growth phase, when the state financial role was diminishing, it was in part the broad-based private subscription drive — an alternative form, in a sense, of collective community support — that replaced it. In fact, the purposes of the subscription drives (five of eight being for divinity or scholarships) have a traditional public-spirited, though now anachronistic, eighteenth-century flavor about them. As the century progressed, however, the base for subscriptions contracted, and the subscriptions themselves faded both absolutely and as a percentage of total funding.

Subscriptions were never irrelevant, to be sure. They accounted for a tenth of private giving even in the second quarter of the century, when state aid had ceased. In the five years immediately after the Civil War they generated almost $100,000 in university benefactions. Moreover, the college library grew partly from the gifts of a thousand individuals over half a century, and these donations may be legitimately considered as a kind of open-ended standing subscription of great worth and significance.[9] To this extent the pattern of funding resembled that of Boston institutions such as the Athenaeum which flourished on relatively small contributions from relatively large numbers of contributors. But these qualifications notwithstanding, it is clear that by mid-century Harvard's money came overwhelmingly in the form of the large individual grant.

It follows from the nature of the benefactions that the precise origins of patronage may be fairly clearly established through examination of the twenty-eight individual grants of $5,000 or more which accrued to Harvard between 1801 and 1850. These were as follows:[10]

Year	Donor	Amount and Purpose
1811	Samuel Dexter	$5,000 for divinity
1814	Samuel Eliot	20,000 for Greek
1815	Samuel Parkman	5,000 for divinity
1815	Abiel Smith	20,000 for Romance languages
1816	Benjamin Thompson	28,000 for applied science
1818	Israel Thorndike	6,500 for library
1821	John McLean	20,552 for history
1822	James Perkins	20,000 for mathematics
1823	Samuel A. Eliot	5,000 for library
1826	Christopher Gore	95,000 unrestricted
1829	Nathan Dane	10,000 for law
1833	Samuel Livermore	6,000 for law
1834	Joshua Fisher	20,000 for natural history
1835	Sarah Jackson	10,000 for divinity
1836	Nathan Dane	5,000 for law
1840	Francis Parkman	5,000 for divinity
1841	Benjamin Bussey	300,000 for law, divinity, and agriculture
1843	David Sears	5,000 for observatory
1844	Israel Munson	15,000 unrestricted
1845	John Parker, Jr.	50,000 for student aid
1845	David Sears	5,000 for observatory
1846	George Parkman	20,000 for medicine
1846	Jonathan Phillips	10,000 for library
1847	Abbott Lawrence	50,000 for scientific school
1847	John C. Warren	10,000 for medicine
1848	Edward B. Phillips	100,000 for observatory
1849	Abbott Lawrence	50,000 for scientific school
1849	Jonathan Phillips	10,000 for library

Perusal of the list reveals several points. First, 69 percent of the grants and 85 percent of the funds accrued after 1825. The grants increased in size, therefore, even more rapidly than in frequency: as with the subscription drives, fewer people supplied a larger share of the funds. Second, although the grants numbered twenty-eight, there were only twenty-one family names on the lists. Drawing the cut-off line at a lower but still sizeable figure (for instance, $3,000) and including individuals who contributed this total in several smaller grants would enlarge the group to some forty individuals and thirty families. Even so, it is apparent that the great expansion resulted mostly from the actions of a small group of families, who largely supplanted the legislature, the small donor, and the community subscription as the source of university wealth. Finally, only about one-fifth of the individual bequests were for divinity or scholarships, the traditional favorites of the community-based subscription drives or the legislative grants of the colonial era. The new patterns of funding thus propelled Harvard ineluctably toward the modern, the private, and the secular.

The collective identity of the group of large-scale donors who created antebellum Harvard may be summarized as follows.[11] First, the residential pattern resembles that of the subscribers. All but one (96 percent) lived in New England; all but three (84 percent) lived in the Boston–North Shore region; all but five (80 percent) lived in the vicinity of Boston. In fact, all those contributing after 1836 lived in Boston. Of the twenty Boston dwellers, at least five had been born elsewhere; but all twenty, migrants included, resided not just in Boston but (for at least most of the year) on Beacon Hill.

Second, the group was wealthy. The average value of the estates left by major donors was $620,000; the median value was $300,000. Both figures represented huge fortunes for pre–Civil War America. All of the twenty-three donors for whom figures are available left estates ranking roughly in the top 2 percent of the Massachusetts population; eighteen of them (86 percent) left estates in the top 0.2 percent. In addition, while about one-half the group descended from eighteenth-century families of comparatively high social status, almost two-thirds actually made their own fortunes. Of these, one made his money almost wholly in the eighteenth century, while five made theirs almost wholly in the nineteenth. Moreover, of the one-third with substantial inherited wealth, only two came from families who had been rich before the Revolution. The pattern thus confirms in a general way the prevalent scholarly impression of the post-Revolutionary, antebellum origins of the American seaboard elites, at least in Boston. But it also lays bare some threads of continuity between old wealth and new.

Third, the occupational pattern of the donors was tilted heavily toward business. Of the twenty-three New England men in the group, sixteen (70 percent) may be classified as businessmen. Nine of these engaged principally in traditional commercial activities; four others accumulated mercantile wealth, then shifted to manufacturing and other industries after 1820; three were predominantly industrialists throughout their careers. Of the eleven who lived beyond 1825, all but four became heavily involved in noncommercial enterprises such as textiles and railroads. The seven professionals of the group — three lawyers, three doctors, and a minister — had business experience and interests or were members of business families, including two with large-scale manufacturing investments. Twelve of the New Englanders (52 percent), nine of the sixteen businessmen (56 percent), and seven of the eleven businessmen from the period after 1825 (64 percent) were directors of the Provident Institution for Savings, the Massachusetts Hospital Life Insurance Company, or the Suffolk Bank.[12]

Fourth, the donors enjoyed a social status appropriate to their wealth, occupation, place of residence, and family connections. Of the twenty Bostonians, for example, 80 percent were shareholders in the Athenaeum, and half served as officers or trustees of either the Athenaeum or the Massachusetts General Hospital. Of the total group, 35 percent had attended Harvard College, and 28 percent were members of the Massachusetts Historical Society.

Finally, the donors conformed politically and religiously to the prevailing elite persuasions. All but two were Unitarians, including a minister and several lay leaders of Unitarian societies. The two exceptions were Episcopalians. All but one were either Federalists or Whigs, including numerous party leaders and officeholders as well as pure financiers such as Israel Thorndike, a principal paymaster of the stellar spokesman of

New England Whiggery, Daniel Webster, who was Thorndike's
Beacon Hill neighbor, it being deemed "a happy circumstance
that the intellect of the community in one of these adjoining
houses should be backed by its purse in the other."[13]

An eminently qualified, though not altogether unbiased, observer commented in 1857 that it was "the cold embrace of commercial conservatism" which had "piled up wealth" on Harvard
in the last half-century. The insight seems thoroughly borne out
by the evidence. The sinews of university expansion did derive
overwhelmingly from the wealthy, enterprising, and politically
conservative (if religiously liberal) families of post-Revolutionary
New England.[14] Questions may remain, of course, as to the
depth and breadth of the commitment of these families to Harvard, even at this strictly financial level. But as to depth, it may
be reiterated that of the total Boston charity funds from 1801 to
1860, approximately 12 percent went to Harvard alone, making
it much the most heavily endowed civic institution in the region
during this period. And it may be further noted that the great
Harvard donors contributed approximately 8 percent of their
estates (some $1.2 million out of $15.5 million) to this single
institution, a figure which compares quite favorably to the total
charitable contributions of wealthy philanthropists in the twentieth century.[15]

The financial support, moreover, was broad. Approximately
80 percent of the Massachusetts millionaires of the antebellum
period contributed $1,000 or more to Harvard, as did 68 percent
of the directors of the largest New England textile firms and 52
percent of the Boston Athenaeum board of trustees. The names
of some 90 percent of the wealthiest 200 Boston families of 1848
appear on the Harvard subscription or individual contributors'
lists, as do those of 85 percent of the antebellum directors of the
three leading Boston financial institutions. Money is not the only
means of supporting an institution, and indeed is not always the
most crucial. It is a vital means, however, particularly in such
take-off eras. At Harvard the picture seems clear enough: as
business families grew richer, settled in Boston, and became
more established, they poured funds into the university at a

remarkable rate. By 1850 the pattern of funding for the ancient regional university fully conformed to that of the Massachusetts General, Athenaeum, and other local institutions of the antebellum decades. The great families built Harvard, so to speak, while building themselves.

The great contributors, however, did not build Harvard alone. Patronage was intimately related to governance and especially to the Harvard Corporation, the primary governing board of the university. While the first large subscription drive occurred in 1805, observers usually located the real inception of the growth phase at about the beginning of President John T. Kirkland's eighteen-year administration in 1810. President Jared Sparks and other members of the Corporation in 1851 stated that the "character and personal influence" of Kirkland accounted for many of the benefactions "so freely made during his official connection with the College."[16] And so with his colleagues and successors: "While much must be attributed to the generous impulses of the givers, much is also due to the disinterested zeal, the direct solicitations and personal influence of the President and Fellows, which stimulated and confirmed those generous impulses, and guided them to the end so happily attained." The contributions were proof of a confidence "not only in the men to whom these munificent gifts were immediately entrusted" but in the organization and stability of the Harvard Corporation "to whose management the donors believed them to be forever consigned."[17]

Financial trust and control were obviously important in the case of unrestricted gifts such as Christopher Gore's or when the Corporation had more limited discretionary powers, as with the James Perkins endowment for an unspecified professorship. They were also important, advised Judge (and Corporation member) Theophilus Parsons in 1812, because the founder or benefactor of a charitable corporation such as Harvard had no power to interfere with its administration beyond the initial contractual agreement unless specified by the charter — an opinion

which might limit the power of the legislature to interfere with
the Corporation but also limited private donors concerned with
the proper usage of their money and hence reliant upon its ad-
ministrators.[18] Administration was important, too, because
financial management determined the scope and tempo of development as well as the adequacy of particular endowments.

Sometimes patron and administrator were virtually the same.
In the case of the early subscriptions for the new divinity school,
the funds were controlled until 1831 by a special "Society for the
Promotion of Theological Education in Harvard University."
The Society's main function was to insulate the university from
imputations of sectarianism, the school being at this juncture
mainly a Unitarian enclave. But the arrangement also served to
place the funds under the control of Society officers such as
Samuel Parkman, Israel Thorndike, Peter Chardon Brooks, and
other representatives of the very group which subscribed
them.[19] Individual donors, in turn, were sometimes members of
the Corporation or otherwise influential in university governance. Thus Gore and Samuel A. Eliot were both donors and
Fellows. John C. Warren gave $10,000 to the medical school at a
time when his influence there was great. When Peter Chardon
Brooks gave $10,000 for a new president's house, his son-in-law,
Edward Everett, was the incumbent president.[20]

On the whole, nonetheless, it was the general character of the
Corporation which was crucial. This was true even in these
exceptional circumstances of overlapping identity, since the
Theological Society funds reverted to the Corporation after a
decade or so and the giant Gore legacy became operative only
after his death. For the rest, the donors had to be persuaded of
the common purpose and community of interest necessary to
their involvement. Thus a contemporary wrote of the Kirkland
years from 1810 to 1827,

> The Eliots, the Gores, the Smiths, the McLeans, the Perkinses,
> the Thorndikes, the Lymans, the Parkmans, the Boylstons, were
> his intimate friends, and were probably induced to make these
> endowments, not merely because he convinced them of the
> necessities of the College, and the importance of increasing its

means of usefulness, but because they cherished a high respect for him personally.[21]

Thorndike expressed these sentiments in a letter accompanying his $6,500 gift to the library, presented "as a mark of the great esteem I feel for those who compose the government of that seminary."[22] Similar considerations operated during the years after 1827.

Friendships were doubtless important in instilling this mutual trust. But even a brief career-line analysis of the thirty-six men elected to the Corporation from 1800 to 1860 (listed here with their years of tenure) suggests that there was a solid social base for such donor confidence in the Corporation:

William T. Andrews, 1853–57	Charles Lowell, 1818
Nathaniel Bowditch, 1826–38	John Lowell, 1810–22
William E. Channing, 1813–26	John Amory Lowell, 1837–77
Benjamin R. Curtis, 1846–51	Harrison G. Otis, 1823–25
John Davis, 1810–27	Theophilus Parsons, 1806–12
Edward Everett, 1846–49	Eliphalet Pearson, 1800–06
John Eliot, 1804–1813	John Phillips, 1812–23
Samuel A. Eliot, 1842–53	Eliphalet Porter, 1818–33
Ebenezer Francis, 1827–30	William Prescott, 1820–26
Christopher Gore, 1812–20	George Putnam, 1853–77
Francis C. Gray, 1826–36	Josiah Quincy, 1829–45
George Hayward, 1852–63	Jared Sparks, 1849–53
Ebenezer R. Hoar, 1857–68	Lemuel Shaw, 1834–61
Charles Jackson, 1825–34	Joseph Story, 1825–45
Jonathan Jackson, 1807–10	Samuel C. Thacher, 1816–18
John T. Kirkland, 1810–28	Samuel Webber, 1806–10
Amos A. Lawrence, 1857–62	James Walker, 1834–60
Charles G. Loring, 1838–57	Thomas W. Ward, 1830–42

The collective portrait of the Corporation Fellows in fact resembles that of the major donors in most respects.[23] They ranked high in social status, for example. Slightly more than 80 percent were shareholders in the Athenaeum; slightly fewer than half were trustees of the Athenaeum or the Massachusetts General Hospital or both. More than half were members of the

Massachusetts Historical Society; 92 percent had graduated from Harvard College. Both of these latter proportions were considerably higher than for the donors, although it might be noted that only 78 percent of those elected after 1825 were Harvard graduates.

In religion, every member elected to the Corporation between 1805 and 1860 was a Unitarian, with the exception of three Episcopalians. Eight were Unitarian ministers, though most of these were elected before 1825; two others filled Unitarian pulpits briefly before moving into other careers.[24] Most were ministers of churches patronized by the elite. Kirkland and Samuel Thacher both served at Boston's New South Church, which was attended by "a large number of men in high position, and leaders of society." William Ellery Channing's Federal Street Church was equally fashionable; Charles Lowell's West Church was in an aristocratic parish with a congregation of the "highest respectability." Both Eliphalet Porter and George Putnam were successively ministers of the Roxbury Church, "large, indeed, rich and with many distinguished men and families on its roll."[25]

These Unitarians, moreover, were notable for their theological advocacy and social conservatism. Thacher as early as 1808 debated with Trinitarian spokesmen and in 1814 gave one of the first expositions of Unitarian doctrine. Channing signaled the formal acceptance of the Unitarian creed in a famous sermon at the ordination of Sparks in 1819. James Walker was known as the "warrior of Unitarianism."[26] Charles Lowell was described as a conservative; aloof from social reform movements; hostile to "zealous religion." Walker was "cautious and reticent" regarding reform and "never failed, either in public or in private, to throw his whole personal influence in favor of law, order, and peace." The views of Putnam, who "questioned liberal . . . missionary responsibilities," were well characterized by an industrialist who wrote Putnam to urge that "you may long continue to hold forth such doctrine, & may *never* so far lose your discretion or judgment, as to fall into the popular . . . *Nothingarianism* that is so prevalent among our brethren at the present day."[27]

Politically, everyone elected from 1800 to 1860 was a conservative Federalist or Whig, with a single Republican exception in the 1850s.[28] Many were in fact party leaders. Of Theophilus Parsons, who was instrumental in electing Kirkland to the presidency, his son recalled:

> It need not be said that he remained always a Federalist, for the Federalist party was the party of conservatism; and therefore he was always, thoroughly and without reserve or qualification, a Federalist. He was of the school of Strong, Lowell, Cabot, Ames, Otis, Pickering, and Prescott; and was, I suppose, (Ames perhaps, not certainly, excepted,) the most determined, resolute, and uncompromising — his opponents said the most violent — of them all.[29]

No fewer than three of these Federalist comrades — John Lowell, Harrison Gray Otis, and William Prescott — were antebellum Corporation Fellows. John Quincy Adams, himself no flaming radical, called this Corporation a *"Caucus Club* . . . bigoted to religious liberality, and illiberal in political principle."[30]

In later years the pattern was much the same. An acquaintance of Whig Corporation Fellows Francis C. Gray and George Hayward wrote that "these gentlemen . . . are thorough conservatives. In English politics they rather leaned to Toryism." To Edward Everett, who volunteered in the 1820s to bear arms against slave insurrection, democracy itself was ultimately a "war of *numbers* against *property*." Charles G. Loring, in whose character mingled both "conservatism and enthusiasm," had party convictions "which, in their essence, did not vary through the changes of the party names from Federalist to Whig to Republican." For Joseph Story the essence of political wisdom was "order and restraint," the "rights of property" and the "stability of our institutions," all sorely threatened by the "spirit of radicalism" and the "frightful dogmas of the Egalitaires."[31]

Samuel A. Eliot (also a financial patron) sympathized with the anti-Garrison mob of 1835 and supported Daniel Webster's position on the Compromise of 1850. So did Benjamin Curtis, who fought against popular legal codification for two decades and in 1851 wanted to indict Free-Soil leaders as treasonous agitators.

Abolitionists were appalled not only by the "scandalous treachery of Webster" over the Fugitive Slave Act but by "the backing he has received" from Harvard. Of the forty-two signers of an "Appeal" in 1860 for the rescission of the Massachusetts personal liberty law, no fewer than five — Curtis, Lemuel Shaw, George Putnam, Jared Sparks, and James Walker — were or had been members of the Corporation.[32]

All the Harvard Fellows were, of course, residents of the Boston area, where they had to live in order to attend Corporation meetings. However, half were also born there, and two-thirds were born either there or in the Salem area. Time reinforced this pattern. Of the twenty-two Fellows elected between 1800 and 1829, ten (45 percent) were born in Boston; of the fourteen elected from 1830 to 1860, nine (64 percent) were born there. Again, while all the Fellows necessarily lived in the vicinity of Boston, those elected after 1830 were more likely to live in Boston proper, especially in the Beacon Hill neighborhood, rather than in Cambridge. By mid-century, then, the Corporation had acquired a decidedly more Boston coloration as to both origin and address.

The Harvard Fellows were also uniformly wealthy, though not quite so wealthy as the donors. The average estate of the thirty-six Corporation members at time of death was $329,000; the median estate was $145,000. Each figure was about half that of the patron group. Three-fourths of the Fellows left estates in the top 1 percent of the Massachusetts population, a very high level indeed, though falling somewhat below the lofty rank of the major contributors. Here, too, however, there was change over time: the Fellows elected after 1830 possessed estates with a median value of $170,000 as compared to $50,000 for their predecessors; and they ranked uniformly in the top 0.5 percent of the population. Both figures indicate sharp movement on the part of an already prosperous Corporation towards an absolutely and relatively higher level of affluence.

Perhaps the greatest difference between patrons and Fellows was in their occupations. Of the thirty-six Corporation members of this period, 22 percent were ministers as compared to only 4 percent for the donor group. It was this high ministerial component which accounted in part for the comparatively high proportion of Harvard degrees and the comparatively low level of wealth among the Fellows. On the other hand, the Corporation group had only 28 percent businessmen as compared to 70 percent for the major donors. Almost half of these, to be sure, were directors of one or more of the three major Boston financial institutions, and at least a fourth had significant industrial and manufacturing interests. In general, however, business prowess was less evident among the Fellows over the period as a whole. Among the other Corporation members were a scholar, a politician, a doctor, and thirteen lawyers, so that the nonclerical professionals on the Corporation were simultaneously more diverse and more heavily represented by the legal profession.[33]

Again, however, one notes two temporal developments. First, ministers declined markedly in importance. Of the twenty-two Fellows elected between 1800 and 1829, eight (36 percent) were ministers; of the fourteen elected from 1830 to 1860, only two (14 percent) were ministers. In the latter period, two members were ex-ministers, and the nonministers were often articulate Unitarians. But the steady secularization of the Corporation is quite clear. In fact, it underlay such complaints as this in 1838: "Why is it that the clergy have, of late years, been excluded from their places in the Corporation of Harvard College? But a short time since, from 1818 to 1828, they had *three* members there out of *seven*. They now have but *one*."[34]

The second occupational shift involved greater representation for businessmen, who comprised 23 percent of the Fellows elected from 1800 to 1830 but 36 percent thereafter. In the latter period, moreover, the lawyers, too, had extensive business interests. Thus Charles G. Loring, whose law practice was based on expertise in marine insurance, realty, bankruptcy, and trusts, was also an officer and investor in a cordage company and a water power company and served for fourteen years as actuary of the Massachusetts Hospital Life Insurance Company; while Benjamin R. Curtis earned over $650,000 in the service of a "wealthy, prosperous, and active" clientele, demonstrated a business acumen smacking of the "workshop, countinghouse, and quarterdeck," and invested in numerous textile, railroad, and other industrial enterprises.[35] The occupational tone of the Corporation by mid-century was therefore much more commercial as well as decidedly more secular.

In status, religion, and politics, then, patrons and Fellows were practically identical, with the main difference probably the larger proportion of Fellows with Harvard degrees and their greater ideological articulateness and aggressiveness. In wealth and occupation the differences were more noticeable, for Corporation members were somewhat less wealthy and business-oriented than donors. Here, however, there was a convergence of position in the latter part of the era, with Fellows becoming richer, more secular, and more commercial and industrial. A similar convergence appeared in origins and residence, with both groups more likely by the period's end to have been born in Boston and also to live there.

After 1840, appropriately, perhaps the single most influential member of the Harvard Corporation was John Amory Lowell, nephew of the founder of the New England factory system and great-nephew of the lawyer who first led the Lowell clan from Essex County to Boston in the Revolutionary era. Indeed, it was Lowell's election in 1837 which has generally signaled to observers the formal ascendance of "State Street" in Cambridge; and while this observation is not quite correct as to timing it is certainly correct as to tendency. By 1835, according to a leading theorist of American development, John Amory Lowell

> had already assumed the direction of the widespread concerns of the Boston associates of the Lowell family connection. Enterprises he directed included the whole gamut of operations from manufacturing textile machinery and steam engines in the Lowell Machine Shops, distributing water power through the Locks and Canals, railroading on the Boston and Lowell Railroad, cotton manufacturing in the Boott, Massachusetts, and other mills, banking in the Suffolk Bank, insurance in the Massachusetts

Mutual and the Massachusetts Hospital Life Insurance Company and other firms. Meanwhile he found time to oversee the affairs of the Boston associates through his son, Augustus, his cousins and other members of the Lowell family group.[36]

These interests by no means exhaust the list of Lowell's business involvements, which reached into shipping, real estate, and miscellaneous manufacturing as well as into the major industries. Nor is there any mention of his steadfast Unitarianism and his role as "éminence grise" of the Massachusetts Whig party. The main point, however, is perfectly clear. One of the region's greatest businessmen — perhaps its single most important industrial developer — was now a key figure at its greatest cultural institution.

But Lowell, as the data indicate, was not alone on the Corporation. He was, indeed, more typical of than exceptional among the mid-century Fellows. By this time there had been a near-perfect fusion of business and cultural interests at Harvard. Its governing board thus assumed the social attributes of its patrons. As Emerson wrote in 1846, "A man of letters — who was purely that, — would . . . be as much out of place there as at the Brokers' Board."[37] The trust between contributor and manager was solidified, in sum, not so much by compatibility and friendship as by a close, growing, and indissoluble conformity of outlook and interest.

The Financial Regime

THE convergence of position and opinion among university patrons and Fellows was so sudden and striking and occurred so early in the development of the institution as to warrant close investigation. For a number of reasons, the radical change in the composition of the Corporation seems worth attending with particular care: for its impact on Harvard, the details of which will emerge more fully later in this book; for what the change reveals about the evolution and consolidation of the Boston elite, and especially its capacity for and modes of absorbing new elements at critical times under crucial circumstances; and more generally, as an attempt to clarify both the relationship of business power and institutional culture and the significance of that relationship for the future development of class and culture. The following discussion, then, is offered in one sense as an analysis of a specific vital episode in the history of a key cultural entity but in a sense, too, as a case study of elite absorption and assimilation. It is an episode important in its own right, to be sure; but it is representative as well.

It will be helpful to begin by pinpointing the years of transition through the data in table 6.[1] The decade of the 1820s was clearly the great period of change: after 1830 the Fellows were consistently much wealthier and more business-oriented than before. But table 7 provides a still sharper focus. While the Corporation Fellows were considerably more affluent by the middle of the decade, they were still all professionals. The businessmen came in a rush after 1825.

As might be expected, elections to the Corporation in the late 1820s elicited much interest and comment in elite circles. Observers realized that a different order was emerging. Some complained about the wholesale displacement of the ministry. Others described the new regime as a "financial" or "business"

Table 6: Wealth and Occupation of Corporation Fellows, 1800–1870

	Ministry	Business	Law	Median Wealth
1800	4	1	2	$ 17,000
1810	3	0	4	12,000
1820	3	0	4	66,000
1830	1	4	2	147,000
1840	1	3	3	150,000
1850	1	2	3	225,000
1860	1	2	2	157,000
1870	1	4	1	400,000

Sources: Quincy, *History of Harvard University*, vol. 2; *Our First Men*; Wilson, *The Aristocracy of Boston*; Forbes and Greene, *The Rich Men of Massachusetts*; Morison, *Harrison Gray Otis*; Shlakman, *Economic History*; Massachusetts probate records.

administration. They referred here to certain reforms — tighter control of finances, better accounting procedures, more aggressive investment policies, closer supervision of faculty and students — which had been discussed in the Board of Overseers and elsewhere during the 1820s and which the so-called "financial administration" labored to impose over the affairs of the university. The desire for stricter administrative and financial arrangements was in fact a major reason for the election of so many new figures to the Corporation in so brief a period.[2]

But the phrase "financial administration" also referred to a new quality in the men who wielded power on the Corporation as of 1830, a quality which seemed to stand in sharp contrast to that of earlier administrations. From 1810 to about 1826 the dominant figure in the university's affairs had been President John T. Kirkland, a former minister and strong Federalist of considerable elegance and good connections. It was under Kirk-

Table 7: Wealth and Occupation of Corporation Fellows, Selected Years

	Ministry	Business	Law	Median Wealth
1821	3	0	4	$ 66,000
1825	3	0	4	114,000
1829	1	4	2	147,000

land that private wealth began to flow in earnest to Harvard, and in some areas of early development — notably in the law and divinity schools and in the life of the college or "academic department" — his leadership was valuable. Yet near the end of his presidency, it was being acknowledged even by admirers that he was excessively lenient and indecisive in regulating the university, "did not know how to take care of money, manage accounts, and keep records," and was basically "unsuitable" as a president.[3]

Actually, a kind of effete indecisiveness was typical of Kirkland at every stage of his life. In 1789 he had written, as a young man, of his career alternatives: "In Divinity I love the peace, innocent studies, and domestic pleasures of the clergyman. . . . In Law I dread the arduous competition for a trifling preeminence, the dry and sometimes low subjects of dispute. . . . I am in a stationary condition at present, and a decisive choice may be suspended awhile." A year later he wrote from the Phillips Academy at Andover, where he was an instructor, that "so gentle and sleepy is the current of my days here, that I do not notice its rapidity." And a short time later: "The vexations of . . . the Academy, are enough to waste my spirits, and unfit me for any but amusing studies, novels, newspapers, and the like. I feel the deepest regret at the irrevocable waste I made of collegiate hours. . . . You know I was ever dreaming of greatness, but never using the means to attain it."[4] In after years Kirkland, true to form, was never a profound scholar or forceful preacher, read desultorily rather than systematically, and gave his sermons casually and with little preparation. Even his conversational wit was delightful only when not "repressed by modesty or indolence."[5]

As president of Harvard, Kirkland's professed objectives were to educate "Christian ministers" and shape the sentiments, tastes, and manners of both his students and the surrounding community, where admirers saw him mainly as a fine cultural "ornament" and "adornment." He was "a man of genius," agreed James Russell Lowell, who then added, "but of genius that evaded utilization, — a great water-power, but without rapids, and flowing with too smooth and gentle a current to be set turning wheels and whirling spindles."[6] Kirkland's steward and chief administrative assistant, by the same token, was Stephen Higginson, a failed businessman whose special interest was "the well-being of the churches and the well-doing of the Cambridge divinity students." Higginson's public image exuded "the court-liness and refinement which belonged to the born aristocracy of an earlier generation" and which Kirkland himself strove to cul-tivate. The administration treasurer was John Davis, a judge of no great business interests or acumen.[7]

These men were all Unitarians and Federalists of adequate social standing and obviously, up to a point, seemed perfectly solid and respectable to the great donors. They also enjoyed the very competent assistance of Boston lawyers such as John Low-ell, who was a Fellow until 1822, and William Prescott, who served until 1825. Still, it is not surprising that in the early 1820s Harvard was plagued with student unrest and faculty dissension or that its accounts and records were in disarray. Men com-plained ominously that the "management of the college" seemed shrouded in "as much mystery as possible."[8]

The traits of John Kirkland's successors seemed markedly, even shockingly, different. Josiah Quincy, who replaced Kirkland as president in 1829, studied law and served as a Federalist con-gressman and mayor of Boston, where his main accomplish-ments were to clear Beacon Hill of its low-income district; to preside over the replacement of the "fierce democracy of town meetings" with a more complex governmental arrangement; and to raise city expenditures for streets, marketplaces, and institu-tions of punitive reform.[9] Rigorous and well-organized in his personal habits, Quincy kept a private journal with a record of hours allotted to various duties, including a stiff regimen of physical exercise which he maintained daily for forty years. Haughty and aristocratic in bearing, a member of William Ellery Channing's Unitarian congregation, possessed of a formidable sense of social gradation, Quincy was yet not above working with "middling" types such as Boston's carpenters and contractors to accomplish his political and administrative objectives, and his right-hand man during his Boston mayoralty in the 1820s was a grasping land speculator and construction boss who, like Quincy, benefited handsomely from city building projects.[10]

If Kirkland, then, had represented the "gentle divine and accomplished scholar," Josiah Quincy was clearly "the great man of business, financier, and disciplinarian, of uncommon physical and intellectual energy."[11] Indeed, Quincy owed his elevation to the Harvard presidency principally to his reputation as "a man of the world, accustomed to business," with great "business capacity" and "business talent"[12] He had been a director of the Provident Institution for Savings, the Massachusetts Hospital Life Insurance Company, and the Massachusetts Fire and Marine Insurance Company. He had also prospered handsomely from Boston real estate transactions, in the process accumulating an estate in the neighborhood of $700,000 by the time of his death in 1864.

Quincy was the first person, in fact, to possess what would later seem "essential to the full usefulness of a Harvard president, a considerable personal fortune."[13] By 1833 a Boston editor was writing that "the business talent of [Quincy] was long known and highly valued in another sphere, and it is quite sufficient to say, that the expectations of those who placed him where he is, have been most amply redeemed." Another observer wrote in 1837 that while Harvard may have had "more learned Presidents than Josiah Quincy, they never [had] a better one nor one so well qualified to manage to the best advantage that noble establishment." Elected as a "stout reformer," he came to be known as "The Great Organizer of the University," with "every department of the institution and every detail in its affairs . . . searched and controlled by his marvellous capacity for labor."[14]

Nathaniel Bowditch, who served on the Corporation from 1826 to 1838, was also a "man of great order and system." A great mathematician whose "habits of accurate calculation and rigid method" made him in succession a navigational expert, an engineering consultant for the early cotton mills, a director of the Commercial Insurance Company, and the first actuary of the

Massachusetts Hospital Life, where he introduced a number of crucial financial and accounting procedures during the 1820s, Bowditch, too, acquired a comfortable, if not enormous, estate. He also drew an annual salary of $6,000 from the Massachusetts Hospital Life, making him the highest-paid business executive in the country at the time.[15] "There are few," said a contemporary, "who have done so much for the community in some of the most intricate branches of business, particularly in those relating to navigation and insurance, or who have given so much thought and attention to business."[16] Indeed, as a historian of American science writes, it was precisely his "success in business" that "enabled Bowditch to complete his greatest scientific contributions" in mathematics.[17]

Bowditch, appropriately enough, disliked the merely "ornamental" with some intensity. Having played the flute as a young man, he abandoned it as "unprofitable" and conducive to bad habits, and advised a friend that music and business were incompatible and that no one had ever succeeded at both. While traveling, he preferred the sight of mills and machines, with their "strong *marks of usefulness*" and "great saving of labour," to mere scenery. At all times he loved "authority," dealt "harshly" with deviations from "the straight line of his directions," and "abhored the capricious exercise of mercy."[18] He was naturally offended by Kirkland's airy indiscipline and affectations of elegance; but he naturally worked exceedingly well with Quincy, who was a veritable alter-ego. As Bowditch told Quincy's daughter in 1827, "There has a great deal been wasted and lost at Cambridge, but there is a noble property left. Mr. Francis and I have put the finances in order, and if you ladies will only let Mr. Quincy go there, the Corporation will do everything for you."[19]

"Mr. Francis" was the Corporation's new treasurer, Ebenezer Francis, a "shrewd and close financier" whose "rare mercantile talents" had long been "concentrated upon the acquisition of great wealth."[20] Francis began his business career in shipping and real estate, where he was so "exceedingly economical" that he "wheedled" writing pens from his clerks and forced them to collect his rents as well as record his ladings. But he was also a founder and officer of the Massachusetts Hospital Life and the Suffolk Bank and a director of the Boston Bank, the Massachusetts Mutual Fire Insurance Company of Boston, the Charles River Bank of Cambridge, and of large textile firms in Massachusetts, New Hampshire, and Maine. So utterly successful was Francis's quest for wealth that he left an estate of some $3.4 million, the largest ever probated in antebellum New England; and so imposing was his business reputation that when Bowditch urged the resignation of Kirkland's steward, Stephen Higginson, it was argued that under Francis even Higginson might do adequate work. Quincy saw Francis's financial reforms as the bedrock of Harvard's future development. As Francis's son-in-law tactfully phrased it, "Few of his contemporaries had a clearer understanding of the working of our institutions."[21]

Another member of this administration was Francis C. Gray, an heir of millionaire shipper William Gray. Gray studied law but, like Quincy, never bothered to practice, spending his time instead in Whig politics, in such organizations as the Historical Society and the Academy of Arts and Sciences, and in becoming an economic writer of some note.[22] But Gray's interests also involved large business ventures, notably the Merchants Bank of Boston, the Western Railroad, a Boston machine shop, a Boston ropeworks, a New Hampshire textile mill, and the New England iron manufacturing firm of his brother, Horace Gray.[23]

The Corporation of 1829 also included two prominent lawyers, Charles Jackson and Joseph Story. Both were jurists and legal scholars who made their living teaching, practicing, and adjudicating the law. Both, however, had significant business interests as well. Jackson was a heavy investor in the Waltham and Lowell textile mills which his brother Patrick Tracy Jackson had helped to organize. He also owned an iron rolling mill in East Boston and, according to his brother James, "kept busy enriching himself and all of us who were concerned with him in his Pennsylvania Iron Works."[24] Jackson seems in fact to have been the first Corporation Fellow with substantial industrial investments outside New England.

Joseph Story's tenure on the Corporation coincided with his

tenure on the United States Supreme Court, which understandably occupied much of his time, and with his law professorship in Cambridge, which occupied still more of it. In his judicial capacity alone Story was of immense practical value to Harvard, as will be seen later. But he was a fitting and active member of this particular Corporation as well. He was, for example, a director of the Salem Savings Bank and an officer of the Merchants Bank of Salem, and his contemporaries considered him an "able financier" whose direction made his commercial bank a "model" for others to emulate.

Indeed, as recent biographical work demonstrates, it was Story's intimate banking interests, among other things, which gave him his exceptional insight into the workings of the emerging capitalist economy. He thus promoted an "industrial development board" for Salem; took the lead in urging the passage of limited liability legislation for Massachusetts corporations; and sought, as a jurist and scholar, to bring "order to the law governing the American economy," now clearly a "mobile, business-oriented economy rather than a static agricultural one."[25] His opinions, accordingly, aimed at encouraging venture capital by securing the rights of property and also at stimulating industrial technology by securing the rights of inventors; and his works proved the "cornerstone" of American commercial and patent law. Story urged the establishment of a chair of commercial law at Harvard and dedicated a renowned work on promissory notes, appropriately enough, to the famous Boston merchant, Thomas Handasyd Perkins. Equally appropriately, he supported the election of "stout Quincy" to the presidency.[26]

These same interests, attitudes, and values appeared throughout the "financial" administration. Thus Charles Sanders, who replaced Higginson as steward, was a former associate of Salem millionaire Dudly Lowell Pickman, who recommended him as "very correct and methodical in his accounts" and exactly suited for the office. Once installed, Sanders initiated "a rigid financial system in the details of college expenditures, similar to that initiated by Mr. Francis in the management of the funds." Meanwhile, he accumulated for himself an estate of some $500,000.[27]

Benjamin Nichols, who worked on the administrative records and financial accounts in the late 1820s, was a director of the Suffolk Bank, the Massachusetts Hospital Life, and the National Insurance Company. Of Nichols, who also held stock in several Massachusetts textile mills, a leading financier said that "he unites the Lawyer, the Investigator, and the Man of business more than almost any one."[28]

Three other men rounded out the regime to perfection. The first was Samuel Hubbard, who served as counsel for the Corporation in this period and was a director of the three great financial institutions of Boston and an officer and stockholder of the largest New Hampshire textile mill. The second was Franklin H. Story, who acted as counsel in the early 1830s. Story was a director of the Globe Bank and the Boston Manufacturers' Mutual Fire Insurance Company and also assistant agent of the American office of Baring's, where by the 1830s he earned the very considerable salary of $5,000 per year.[29]

Finally, Thomas W. Ward, who replaced Ebenezer Francis as treasurer at the end of 1830, was not only head of Baring's American branch but also a director of the Provident Institution for Savings, the Massachusetts Hospital Life, the Boston Marine Insurance Company, the Boston and Worcester Railroad, and a substantial investor in New England textile mills. "A life of constant exertion and activity," Ward wrote to a friend early in his career, renders "business a pleasure to me." So important was his position as Baring's agent in Boston — in which capacity he accumulated some $250,000 in manufacturing stocks alone — that by 1830, when he became Harvard's treasurer, he felt able to say of virtually any fellow industrialist, "If I say I know him to be a man of property his credit is for the time established."[30]

These new Fellows did not hesitate to mold the Harvard Corporation in a different image. Where Kirkland had been tolerant and lackadaisical in his administration, exercising light and flexible control over faculty and students, Quincy and his colleagues worked with considerable success to tighten their control over the faculty, increase the severity and regularity of student discipline, and establish or reorganize the departments, professional schools, library, and observatory on a fresh basis.[31] They also revamped the financial procedures by updating the books, supervising expenditures more closely, and establishing sounder but more vigorous investment policies. Under Bowditch and Francis the university opened accounts with the Massachusetts Hospital Life; under Quincy it made important acquisitions of Boston and Cambridge real estate; under Ward its standing balances went to the Suffolk Bank.[32] The Corporation now pressed its debtors harder, disregarding the plea of one businessman that this would mean "destruction to me as a man of credit and prudence and capacity" and treating others in a hectoring, admonitory manner. In cases where the university was residuary legatee of an estate, as with the McLean and Gore legacies, it sought to influence the trustees' handling of the estate in its own interests.[33]

The sobriquet "financial administration" was well earned, therefore, particularly in contrast to the relaxed and genteel Kirkland years. But the sobriquet, it must be noted, was also part epithet, for there was criticism from within elite circles not only of the aggressive financial policies of the new Corporation but of its abrupt and disrespectful treatment of its predecessors. Thus, when Bowditch demanded Higginson's resignation as steward on grounds of incompetence, he antagonized many important families, including the Lowells and Cabots, who consented to the sacking of their kinsman only with great reluctance and complained about it as late as 1831. Francis's replacement of John Davis provoked a similar response.[34] The forced resignation of Kirkland, long associated with Harvard and recently ill, went down especially badly. "Edward Brooks," commented Charles Francis Adams, "is very much excited about the resignation of Dr. Kirkland which has created much noise everywhere. . . . I centainly think it a shameful business. But some men have no delicacy." John Lowell, who served with Kirkland for twelve years, wrote similarly, "I think, that those, who raised the College, from its state of depression in 1810 . . . have been treated with the most abominable, and outrageous injustice." An anonymous letter to the Boston press criticized the "disgraceful violence" of the new Corporation.[35]

Nor, for that matter, was "financial administration" the only epithet. There was also much "cynical criticism" that the "Salem element" was very strong in this administration. In fact, it was often called the "Salem administration" or "Salem junta," and Bowditch, one of its leading members, the "Salem sailor." As a contemporary wrote:

> Judge Story and Dr. Bowditch, both of them Salem men, were leading members of the corporation; and they had added to the Board as treasurer, Ebenezer Francis, a native of Beverly, hard by Salem, and had employed Benjamin R. Nichols, another Salem man, for a full year, in examining the accounts of preceding years. . . . At the same time, Charles Sanders, a Salem man, was made steward.[36]

Of these five men, moveover, all except Francis had moved to Boston after 1820. In addition, Charles Jackson was born in Newburyport, also "hard by Salem," where he practiced law until 1803, and Thomas Ward had arrived from Salem as late as 1809, as had Franklin Story. Even the new college librarian, Benjamin Peirce, was a Salemite.

The clannishness of the regime made it all the more distinctive. Nichols and Sanders, for example, were in-laws of Peirce; all three were connected to the Pickerings and Pickmans, well-known Salem families. Joseph Story's brother Franklin assisted and exercised a power of attorney for Ward, who was also a close friend and fellow clubman of Francis C. Gray, whose father had originally been a Salem merchant. Bowditch was another of Ward's friends, both in Salem and after their migration to Boston. When Ward was bonded for $100,000 as Harvard treasurer, Bowditch and Gray served as sureties and Franklin Story as a witness; Ward was also a frequent companion of the Quincys at the theatre and elsewhere. One of Bowditch's sons entered Ward's business firm and married a daughter of Nichols; another studied law with Nichols and married a daughter of Ebenezer

Francis. Francis, to complete the circle, married a daughter of Israel Thorndike, a Beverly-born millionaire (and Harvard patron) who had arrived in Boston in 1810.[37]

Like "financial," however, "Salem" had pejorative connotations, as its coupling with words such as "cynicism" and "sailor" would suggest. The epithet implied that the new men were in fact parvenus, at least as compared to the families of somewhat longer standing — Winthrop, Eliot, Adams, Brooks, Lowell, Cabot — who were most prone to use the term. There was, of course, substance to the insinuation. Bowditch was a cooper's son who began his career as a clerk and a ship's hand; Francis's father was an impecunious Continental soldier whose death in 1777 left his son to his own resources.[38]

In the same vein, it was said that these were men "without classical education, or not originally belonging to the Alumni of Harvard." And indeed, of the four non-Harvardians elected to the Corporation during the nineteenth century, three — Bowditch, Francis, and Ward — belonged to this "financial" or "Salem" group. Josiah Quincy, with his indisputable colonial antecedents, surely served to redress the balance. But even Quincy's nomination reportedly "startled" the Board of Overseers in much the way that Charles Eliot's nomination did in 1869, and a third of the Board actually opposed his election.[39]

This new regime thus seemed to many observers simultaneously materialistic, abrasive, clannish, and arriviste — hardly, on the surface, an auspicious reputation on which to build. It is important to note, therefore, that the group was not only elected in spite of this image but drew strong support from an increasing range of elite families. Backing came first, understandably enough, from Essex County, where the new Fellows retained close ties with men who became large donors or were influential on the Board of Overseers, including Pickerings and Pickmans, Saltonstalls and Silsbees, Danes and Peabodys, most of them in the process of moving to Boston, like the new Corporation Fellows.

Additional support came from families such as the Lawrences and Curtises, whose interests and antecedents (commercial-industrial, nouveau-arriviste) were similar to those of the new group. Textile magnate Amos Lawrence thus wrote to Bowditch's sons in later years:

> I hardly feel that I am a competent judge, where any question comes up touching your father's labours & trials in reforming the college, for I was a daily witness of them for *months* & *Years*, & sympathized in all his feelings. He is entitled to the gratitude of the public for these labours, *& will receive* it & be remembered for good, when Dr. K[irkland] will be forgotten.[40]

Further support came from conservative politicians such as Rufus Choate and Daniel Webster, who wrote to Joseph Story in connection with the election of Quincy, "*I am against a clergyman. . . .* He is not to soar up the shrouds, nor to go out in the Boat, but to stand at the helm and look at the needle."[41] Finally, even such erstwhile critics as the Lowells, Cabots, and Brookses came round. Remarks about parvenus and materialism gradually subsided. By 1835 or so support was reasonably solid throughout the elite.[42]

The acceptance of the new Corporation, after so comparatively cool a reception, resulted partly from the gradual accommodation of conflicting personalities, an accommodation made much easier, no doubt, because the new group was as uniformly Federalist (proto-Whig) and Arminian (Unitarian) as the old. But acceptance derived from three more fundamental and interrelated circumstances as well. First, the emergence of the new regime represented the "arrival," both residentially and economically, of an element so cohesive and influential that it could not easily be denied access to positions of appropriate status and power in the elite community. Such accessions to prominence, though perhaps more spectacular in this case because of its abrupt "phalanx" quality, were not atypical in the evolving Proper Boston of the nineteenth century. Service on boards such as the Harvard Corporation was an important step of absorption and consolidation within the elite. The ascension and acceptance of the Salemites, precisely because of their own internal cohesion and influence, their involvement with so large and prestigious an institution, and the unique visibility of the process, was among the most important and interesting consolidating steps of all.

Second, the group represented financial and industrial interests — textile mills and other manufacturing interests, New England railroads and British investment banking, the major Boston financial institutions as well as traditional maritime commerce — which, again, involved a kind of concentrated economic power difficult to deny. In many cases these interests had not existed prior to 1820; certainly they were not so thoroughly represented on the Harvard Corporation before 1825. Nor, it should be noted, was the time lag very great, for these concerns were rapidly becoming primary investment outlets for the elite as a whole, as attested by the concomitant triumph of protectionism in Boston political circles. In this sense, therefore, the Corporation served as a mechanism for the maintenance of a healthy relationship between a central elite cultural institution and the economic forces which were becoming the foundation of elite development. At Princeton, Yale, and the University of Pennsylvania, by contrast, the governing boards remained nonsecular and noncommercial for another half-century.

Finally, and perhaps most crucial, the financial regime introduced to Harvard a cast of mind whose chief characteristics, as perceived by contemporaries and as worked out in practice, were discipline, precision, regularity, utility, and productivity — "bourgeois" characteristics, as it were, which were deemed essential because the university was now larger and more complex and required more effective governance and also because its funds now derived solely from business patrons who exhibited this mentality in their own affairs, prized it for its own sake, and favored its extension, at least at this administrative level, to Harvard. The president of the university, accordingly, was no longer a teacher or preacher or cultural "ornament" as before or as his counterparts at Yale, Princeton, and Pennsylvania would remain till late in the century and beyond.[43] At Harvard, for better or worse, the president was now an administrator, his role

one of "ever-increasing importance" on through the middle decades of the century. So, too, with the heretofore rather casually
considered office of treasurer. By 1840 Thomas W. Ward was
calling its duties "onerous"; by 1860 many believed it to be as
important as the presidency.[44]

Piety, elegance, and learning were by no means disregarded in
mid-century Cambridge; nor would the business-culture connection at Harvard necessarily be the crude type which obtained
between certain late nineteenth-century private universities and
their Robber Baron patrons.[45] In spite of its steady secularization, for example, the Corporation always included a minister,
and, in spite of commercialization, often a scholar of some kind.
As a rule, too, Corporation members probably remained more
highly partisan in religion and politics, or at least more articulate
and voluble, and possibly (not certainly) a shade less acquisitive
at the core of their being. Ralph Waldo Emerson noted of Edward Everett's election to the presidency in 1846, "The satisfaction of men in this appointment is complete. Boston is contented
because he is so creditable, safe, & prudent, and the scholars
because he is a scholar, & understands the business."[46] Thomas
Ward, writing to an English banker in 1850, described John
Amory Lowell in similar terms of balance and proportion: "He is
in the government of Harvard College, has the sole care of the
Lowell Institute, and although a thorough man of business is also
a man of taste and great literary acquirement."[47] Men recognized
the fact that a university was not precisely a textile mill nor a
professor precisely an industrial functionary, and that an effective Fellow required a multiplicity of interests and an appreciation of intellect as well as efficiency. Hence the identity of
patron and governor, however close, would never become absolute.

Nonetheless, since organizational complexity and business patronage were more or less constant at Harvard for the rest of the
century and beyond, the business presence was likewise more or
less constant. This was the underlying meaning of the financial
administration: it was the vehicle whereby the Boston elite, almost in spite of itself, projected business values and practices

onto its central cultural institution. The election of Lowell to the Corporation in 1837 did not therefore signal the ascendance of State Street at Harvard. It simply finalized a development well under way by 1830. Thanks to Quincy, Bowditch, Francis, Story, and Ward, whatever the university's broader social functions might be, administratively and financially it would hereafter reflect the banker's mentality and the rhythms of modern industry. With all qualifications acknowledged, in sum, the consequence of the infusion of private business wealth into Harvard was the "purchase" of its primary governing body.

· 4 ·

The New Faculty
and the Locus of Power

SCHOLARS concerned with curriculum and pedagogy and with
the development of "progressive" or "professional" academic attitudes have probably devoted more time and attention to the
scholarly and instructional interests of Harvard faculty members
in the antebellum years than to any other university topic. The
literature on certain individuals and trends is accordingly rather
extensive.[1] What is lacking is not so much a satisfactory description of internal trends as a satisfactory depiction of the shifts in
the functions, authority, and status of the faculty as a whole.
Clearly the new patterns of funding would affect the teaching
community as they affected the composition and behavior of the
Corporation.

And in fact, as the size, funding, and control of Harvard
changed in these years, so did the university faculty. Harvard
professors experienced a transformation in their situation fully
commensurate with the broader transformation of the institution
as a whole. It was one filled with complexity and seeming
paradox, to be sure, in which the faculty found itself simultaneously more important, less powerful, and more genteel at the
end of the era than at its beginning — in a different relationship,
that is, to the governors of Harvard and to the entrepreneurs,
clans, and cultural enterprises of Boston. Yet for students of the
cultural dimension of nineteenth-century upper-class development, especially in its Boston form, the understanding of the
nature and provenience of this new relationship, however complex, is of the utmost importance.

Perhaps the most immediate visible impact of university development on the faculty was to increase its prominence on the
New England cultural scene. In part, of course, this resulted

from the sheer growth engendered by the pattern of large-scale private benefactions from 1800 to 1850, approximately a third of which went toward the endowment of new faculty chairs. In 1800 there were six endowed professorships; in 1850, twenty-one. By 1860 the total instructional staff numbered thirty-six as compared to only ten in 1800.

Faculty also remained with the university longer, their positions being generally better financed and more prestigious. The twenty-nine professors appointed before 1830 had an average tenure of seventeen years; the thirty-seven appointed after 1830 remained an average of twenty-eight years. The faculty presence thus grew more formidable: many long-term professors tended to bulk large the way few short-termers had not.[2]

Faculty prominence derived from more than mere numbers and staying-power, however. It also derived from a far greater importance in the provision of services to Harvard students and to the broader community. Scholarly writing has understandably emphasized the faculty role as academic mentor in these years, since it was this function which was most closely related to the much-admired internal reform movements. And in spite of other equally significant functions — as socializing agent and role model for the students, as provider of intellectual work for the community — the academic function was clearly vital. The faculty, for example, staffed the new professional schools and observatory and enlarged the college curriculum. The law, medical, divinity, and scientific schools acquired nine professorships from 1800 to 1850. The college proper acquired a dozen others, mostly involving the study of science, society, and literature. The 1820s in particular witnessed a proliferation of new professorships and course offerings. College freshmen and sophomores still concentrated exclusively on rhetoric, mathematics, and the classics, but upperclassmen could choose from such subjects as natural philosophy, chemistry, natural history, anatomy, geology, moral philosophy (including economics), law, and modern languages. The scientific courses were exceptionally innovative and far-sighted. But even traditional subjects such as mathematics and moral philosophy were modernized through the introduction of European works on calculus, government, and political economy.[3]

The principal objectives of such curriculum modernization were to introduce students to subjects with which "every gentleman of liberal accomplishments" should be familiar and to prepare them for careers in business, teaching, government, law, and medicine as well as the ancient standby, the ministry.[4] "Our early colleges," said an instructor in 1816, "were founded for the express purpose of forming ministers, not scholars, and it is unaccountable that the system of education has been persevered in till this time, which never required . . . any critical knowledge."[5] Parents and patrons agreed. One compared a young professional's liberal knowledge to a young merchant's stock of money. Another wrote to his son that "in this age of improvement in every kind of art which can promote intercourse, & excite enterprise etc., mathematical knowledge is useful in almost every pursuit."[6] Even modern languages and the classics came to be justified, like the sciences, partly in terms of commercial and professional success.[7]

This modernizing trend was limited, it must be noted, by the still prevalent idea that students should acquire a common culture based on the ancient wisdom of the classics. After about 1845 there was actually considerable resistance to the further proliferation of new professorships and courses at the expense of the traditional curriculum, valued as it was as a force for standardized discipline and values. Even so, the process continued. New chairs of Latin and Christian morals were created after 1850. So, however, were professorships of geology, astronomy, and music. It was in the 1850s, in fact, that Harvard science, at least in some branches, acquired its modern "experimental" quality and came to exert a major influence in academic life.[8]

Innovations in subject matter and curriculum led in turn to innovations in pedagogy, particularly the lecture and elective systems. The lecture format, which first flourished under President Kirkland, enabled professors to dispense knowledge in subjects with few adequate textbooks and to enliven increasingly abstruse or complex courses with anecdote, example, and illustration. By the mid-1820s the preparation of lectures was considered an important means of intellectual discipline for instructors, and the lectures themselves "ideal vehicles for the propagation of new discoveries and for the discussion and elucidation of questionable theories."[9] The immediate inspiration for young lecturers in the 1820s may have been Germany and Scotland, but the rapid and widespread adoption of lecturing — which by 1860 had displaced recitation as the common mode of instruction in almost all the upper-level college and professional courses — was rooted in the practical considerations attendant upon the enlargement of the faculty and the enrichment of the curriculum.[10]

The elective system, which first flourished under President Quincy, was a mechanism whereby new course offerings could be introduced into the curriculum without undue encroachment upon the traditional studies of the college. By 1835 the idea of electives for upperclassmen was widely accepted. By 1845 it was possible for even a freshman to make limited "elections," as in substituting a modern for a dead language during the second term. (Modern languages comprised perhaps the main pool of elective courses during the 1830s.) At this point the system became slightly mired in the "standardized discipline and culture" concept, with its insistence on thorough grounding in the classics and mathematics, and for the next two decades, course options were mainly the preserve of juniors, seniors, and students in the professional schools. Yet at mid-century an important alumnus still forcefully defended the basic principles of the system:

> We teach the student enough of several important branches to enable him to render himself a thorough proficient, in after life, in the one, or the few, to which he may devote himself. . . . We believe it is better, in our country, at least, than a truly German scholarship in Latin and Greek, and an utter ignorance on other subjects.[11]

By the 1860s, courses in philosophy, history, and the sciences had joined the modern languages as common electives, and sophomores and freshmen had acceded to the privilege of taking them.

Both lectures and electives were expected to improve student academic performance, the one by providing information and inspiring personal models, the other by appealing to individual intellectual tastes. But academic standards, especially in the college, were stiffened in other ways as well. Recitation sections became smaller and more closely supervised, in some cases amounting almost to a tutorial system. New textbooks were introduced, and texts in general were more scrupulously inspected by deans, Corporation Fellows, or both. The traditional oral examinations (usually conducted by Overseer committees) became more systematic and rigorous; in the 1850s some departments introduced written exams. The library was enlarged and made more accessible to students, who also had ready access to the observatory and scientific collections.

In the 1820s the modern language department was divided into classes by proficiency. In the 1830s, President Quincy instituted a Scale of Merit which ranked students by academic performance and survived, despite criticism and shortcomings, into the postwar era.[12] Finally, the academic demands on students' time increased. A member of the class of 1802 wrote to his son, a student in the class of 1844: "When I was a freshman, they did not require of me more than three hours study in a day. I am glad that more is required now, but I hope you will not find them too severe." An 1856 memorial from the parents of Harvard students went so far as to protest that the academic pressure threatened their sons' health![13]

The counterpart to faculty pedagogical importance — the neglected side of the college coin — was that professors were assuming a greater role than before in the socialization of Harvard students, especially the undergraduates. In the middle and late eighteenth century, as reminiscences from that era make clear, contact between instructors and students was minimal, and such as existed left a bitter aftertaste. Parental missives to entering freshmen dwelt almost wholly on the need to read the proper books with the proper diligence, with perhaps a perfunctory

reference to the need to obey one's professors.[14] Relations between faculty and students were not expected to be intimate or
even very important, except occasionally in a strictly academic
sense. The sight of an instructor in social intercourse with a
student was "rare and uncommon" even as late as 1810.[15]
"Obedience" itself was at best sporadic, as witness the recurring
student disturbances and rebellions during the half-century following the Revolution.[16]

Attitudes were changing, however. In 1811 a Boston lawyer
began a letter to his son, then about to enter Harvard, by observing that the moment was "the most anxious, and I may almost
say, the most distressing of my life." He discussed not only the
college curriculum and his son's reading program but the attitudes and habits which he should adopt as a collegian, ad-
monishing him in particular to treat university officers with the
respect due to "representatives of parental authority." President
Kirkland was to be treated "as you have been accustomed to treat
me," and his instructors should receive "all affectionate attention
and respect." By conducting himself in this fashion the boy
would gain the "invaluable friendship" of men of "distinguished
talents, learning and virtue," such as Kirkland.[17] A Boston merchant was soon writing of the obedience and emulation which
"the Talents, genius & learning" of the university staff should
exact from students.[18] A prominent Salem lawyer admonished
his son in 1841 to esteem and submit to the college instructors "at
this most important event in your life."[19]

Kirkland made it a point to increase his contacts with students
and make himself more accessible to them, and he encouraged
his instructors to do likewise. Clearly these efforts met with but
partial success, for as late as the 1820s observers noted an unfortunate distance between students and faculty, highlighted by a
severe student upheaval in 1823.[20] Again, it remained for the
Quincy-Bowditch administration to institute more systematic
measures. One, for example, was the holding of a fortnightly
"soirée" at the president's house where students and faculty
could mingle socially. Another was the presentation of informal
weekly lectures in the college chapel which students and faculty

families could attend together. A third came with a combination
of smaller recitation sections and a Corporation decree that professors should conduct their own recitations wherever possible; a
fourth, with special meetings conducted for undergraduates by
divinity faculty, with the encouragement and blessing of the
Fellows and Overseers.[21]

By the late 1830s the "line of belt ice which parted the students from their teachers" was melting.[22] Taking a cue from
Kirkland and Quincy, many faculty developed "an intimate relation" with their students both inside the College Yard and out:
"The Professors' houses were always open, and . . . the instruction was of a cordial, friendly, courteous, and humane kind."[23]
The language, rhetoric, and history professors seem to have been
quite close to their charges; so, increasingly, were the scientists
and mathematicians.[24] The growth of electives and the introduction of the laboratory system in the sciences tended to establish
"more pleasant and profitable personal relations between
teachers and students."[25] So, occasionally, did that more imper-
sonal pedagogical tool, the lecture. As a member of the class of
1846 recalled:

> A youth who listened to the eloquence of James Walker or heard
> his exposition of the principal systems of ethics or metaphysics;
> or who sat at the feet of Judge Story as he poured forth the lessons
> of jurisprudence in a clear and inexhaustible stream, caught an
> inspiration which transfigured the very soul of the pupil.[26]

A Boston lawyer believed that "our personal association with
the professors was of the greatest service."[27]

In 1871 Henry Adams concluded that the harmonization of
student-faculty relations was the most important single change at
Harvard between 1800 and 1860 — a remarkable statement,
given the checkered relations of the Adamses with Harvard.[28]
But the change which Adams detected was a natural one. It
flowed directly from the new expectations and contacts of the
Kirkland-Quincy years, with the 1830s perhaps marking the real
turning point in faculty-student relations and the real assumption, therefore, of greater faculty responsibility for student

socialization. It was during this decade that professors began to address students respectfully as "mister" and to host the annual "Senior Spread," a dancing-dining party on Class Day during which instructors mixed with students and their families.[29] The last significant large-scale student disorder occurred, appropriately enough, in 1834; comparative peace reigned for more than a century thereafter. In 1851 an alumnus wrote appreciatively that "the relations between the faculty and the students, and those of the members of each of these bodies among themselves, are, to a great extent, similar to those existing among the members of a large family" — sentiments identical to those concerning the Athenaeum.[30]

The faculty's increasing functional importance thus derived in part from its dual service to the student body, instruction and socialization. But it also derived from a third function: the provision of intellectual services to the broader community. The great writers and thinkers of antebellum New England are sometimes thought to have been mainly residents of Concord and Beacon Hill with few, if any, academic attachments, a view with obvious merit as regards transcendental essayists and Romantic historians. "Little thought," writes a historian of higher education, "was given to securing professors of great distinction, to the means by which their scholarly work could be forwarded."[31] Consider, however, the following:[32]

> Men appointed to Harvard professorships in the antebellum era wrote 670 *North American Review* essays from 1815 to 1877, or 24 percent of the total, plus as many more for other leading periodicals;
> they presented 706 lectures at the Lowell Institute from 1839 to 1860, or 47 percent of the total, plus scores of lectures at lyceums and elsewhere;
> they published some 300 scholarly books, almost 20 percent of which ran to ten or more editions;
> they served as editors of at least eighteen New England periodicals, including the *North American* and the *Atlantic Monthly;*

more than half served as officers or trustees of the American Academy of Arts and Sciences, the Society of Natural History, the Horticultural Society, the Mount Auburn Cemetery, or the Massachusetts Historical Society;

almost a third were officers of the Boston Athenaeum, the Massachusetts General Hospital, or both.

As to quality, professors appointed to the antebellum faculty included the men commonly thought to have been America's leading anatomist (Jeffries Wyman), botanist (Asa Gray), surgeon (John C. Warren), mathematician (Benjamin Peirce), and legal scholar (Joseph Story). Among them were also the country's most famous poet (Henry Longfellow), geologist (Louis Agassiz), and literary critic (James R. Lowell); the leading editor of American historical documents (Jared Sparks); the chief historians of Spain and New England (George Ticknor and John G. Palfrey); two prominent Biblical scholars (Joseph Buckminster and Andrews Norton); and two of the foremost early students of German culture (Convers Francis and Charles Beck). In addition, there were the first American teacher of entomology (William Peck), the man who coined the term "technology" (Jacob Bigelow), the originators of astronomical photography (William and George Bond), the first scientist to attempt to classify elements by atomic weight (Josiah Cooke), and organizers of the American Society of Civil Engineers and the Archaeological Institute of America (Henry Eustis and William Goodwin). Six of the antebellum appointees had international reputations, with honorary degrees from European universities and access to European journals; another dozen enjoyed high national acclaim. Many of these reputations have long since faded. It is interesting, however, that the editors of the twentieth-century *Dictionary of American Biography* commissioned essays on no fewer than sixty-one of the group's sixty-six members.[33]

As to timing, Harvard professors made noteworthy contributions to scholarship throughout the era. Before 1820, for example, came Levi Hedge's *Elements of Logick*, which went through thirty-six editions; in the 1830s appeared Joseph Story's monumental *Commentaries* on law; the 1850s saw the publication of Francis Bowen's *Principles of Political Economy* and Benjamin Peirce's *System of Analytic Mechanics*. But there was also change over time, if sheer output is any measure. The thirty-seven professors appointed after 1830 produced 50 percent more scholarly works per man — and more original scholarship, as opposed to edited and translated works — than their twenty-nine predecessors. In addition, more of these works appeared during the author's tenure at Harvard (over three-fourths as against three-fifths) and in more editions. That is, the professors produced less nonacademic "amateur" work and fewer one-edition books of lectures for Harvard students only. Some 20 percent of the works, in fact, went through ten or more editions, compared to 8 percent by professors appointed from 1800 to 1830. Mid-century Harvard professors thus produced more original scholarship and literature for their intellectual and professional peers, but also more works for the general literate public and for use by the nation's college and secondary school teachers.[34]

These findings corroborate recent assertions that the leading antebellum scientists and scholars usually had academic training and connections and that college faculties were becoming more professional.[35] Thus, while 17 percent of the Harvard faculty appointed from 1800 to 1830 attended professional schools and 31 percent studied in Europe, the corresponding figures for the 1831–1860 group were 42 percent and 44 percent, respectively. As a consequence the instructors became rapidly secularized, as President James Walker observed in 1855.

> It is within the memory of some of us when professors and tutors were taken, almost as a matter of course, from among clergymen and students in divinity; now as a general rule, a professor is as much a layman as a lawyer or a physician is.[36]

In this matter, as in numerous others, the professors followed the pattern observable among members of the Corporation.

More to the point, perhaps, and more interesting because less obvious, was the growing variety and complexity of the different faculty functions. Professors were expected to produce — and, as seen, did produce — more original scientific and scholarly research and perform editorial, administrative and other tasks on behalf of culture in the broader community. But at the same time they were expected to provide more novel and more intense instruction to their students, whom they were simultaneously to serve as social mentors and models as well as intellectual and professional ones. The emphasis on teaching undoubtedly diverted the gathering impulse toward research and writing; the stress on socialization doubtless diverted attention from both rigorous teaching and original research. Nonetheless, by mid-century all three functions were quite vital; and together with sheer numbers and longevity, they made the faculty as a whole far more important in the life of both the institution and the society than ever before.

The issue of the proper relationship between thinker and patron, cultural artisan and businessman, intellectual worker and administrator, was much in the Boston air in the years after 1815, when so many cultural as well as economic enterprises either got under way or began to exhibit modern contours. A writer for the *North American Review* reflected that while "middling and ordinary people might read and appreciate," it was actually men of "influence, talents, wealth and learning" who, for all their "selfish purposes" and concern with "transitory pleasures," might enable one to secure a "durable and lofty reputation."[37] Meanwhile, a Harvard instructor was telling the Corporation of the harm to letters and society which could result from the distance between scholars and patrons and that a Harvard professorship, to be precise, was not sufficiently respectable or influential, even though its duties were multiplying.[38] Clearly the issue was a ticklish one, the resolution of which might not be to the satisfaction of all concerned. But equally clearly, the question of institutional authority, and therefore ultimate cultural sovereignty, could not drift indefinitely.

It was almost inevitable that Harvard, with its mushrooming endowments and expanding faculty, would be the scene of the definitive resolution of this issue and that the resolution would in fact occur in the 1820s, when enlarged benefactions were beginning to enhance the faculty's appreciation both of its own worth and of the general tenor of institutional development. In 1824, therefore, faculty representatives directly raised the question of institutional authority in order to flex the muscle of their new status and also, no doubt, to capitalize on what they hoped might be latent community resentment over recent changes in the customary ways of conducting the affairs of the university. In that year Professors Edward Everett and Andrews Norton, addressing the Board of Overseers on behalf of eleven instructors, argued that the nonacademic, nonresident composition of the Corporation contravened the original Harvard charter, wherein "Fellows" signified resident teaching fellows such as those of the English universities. Since Harvard's own faculty consisted of "fellows" in this sense, they of right constituted the true Corporation.[39]

Everett's assertion was a strong one. He argued that the recent ejection of faculty representatives from the Corporation was a virtual usurpation:

> It is only since 1806 that out of a body of instructors more numerous, and I hope not less respectable, than at any former period, the non-resident gentlemen have not found a man worthy to sit by their side. . . . All the confidential and important trusts connected by the charter with the office of residential Fellows have been taken away. By slow degree, they have been deprived of one seat after another in the corporation, till for the last eighteen years, the entire control of the college has been carried from its walls and monopolized by the leading gentlemen of Boston.[40]

The professors insisted that nonresident nonscholars whose livelihood and prestige did not depend on a flourishing university could not direct college affairs so well as professional scholars. Legality and expediency, not to mention justice, thus required that the faculty itself make the key decisions in such areas as appointments, salaries, curriculum, and student behavior.[41]

It was fitting that Norton and Everett should broach the issue, for more than most early instructors they tended to symbolize the new faculty dispensation. They were popular teachers with much scholarly promise whom the parents of Harvard students often pointed out as appropriate role models for their progeny. They were also forceful advocates of the Unitarianism and proto-Whiggery of the 1820s whose marital alliances with the Brookses and Eliots (both patron families) had made them very wealthy and very well connected.[42] What more natural than that they should wish to translate this prominence into real institutional power; should have the temerity to attempt openly to do so; and should lead other faculty members in their wake? In the process they touched unerringly upon institutional metamorphoses — a large faculty, a more complex university, a changing Corporation — of considerable moment, even if they did so partly in their own immediate interests.

Nothing, then, could more strikingly demonstrate the stringent limitations to faculty authority or signify the true locus of institutional control in antebellum Boston than the decisive rejection of this initiative. Both the unanimity of the opposition and the nature of the polemical rejoinder are notable. Joseph Story told Everett that his arguments had "staggered a great many who had no previous doubts," and the Corporation at first refused even to consider the question for fear of somehow legitimizing it.[43] Story's own lengthy and complex pamphlet disputing the faculty's interpretation of the charter was one measure of the concern. John Lowell prepared two critical pamphlets of a more general nature, and George Ticknor (perhaps the most important faculty defector) still another. Francis C. Gray and Charles Jackson also prepared antifaculty arguments for presentation to the Board of Overseers, and even William Ellery Channing, normally not intimately involved in university affairs, was moved to draw up an advisory rebuttal.[44]

The rejoinders emphasized the controversy's legal aspects, which the faculty had perforce stressed and where Mr. Justice Story's work and reputation seemed to secure the Corporation's defenses. But Lowell and Ticknor countered the arguments from expediency as well, thereby broadening the debate and suggesting some of the anxiety surrounding the issue. Lowell, for instance, made three major points. First, he argued that the very size and complexity of the university as of 1824 made a wise division of pedagogical and administrative labor all the more urgent; if the faculty assumed the responsibilities of administration as well as the heavy instructional duties now incumbent on them, the situation would surely deteriorate. Second, the change would damage the university financially: not only would it encourage the kind of irresponsible extravagance recently exposed at Oxford and Cambridge, but it would shake the confidence of potential donors and dry up the private funds, which had flowed in "much larger sums since the non-resident fellows constituted the majority, than before."[45]

Lowell argued, finally, that the expertise of the professors was far less relevant for governing a university than the interests and experience of nonprofessors:

> Precisely in proportion as they shall have devoted their *lives* to the business of education, they must have had fewer opportunities of knowing the world; its wants, and expectations; its opinions and feelings; its business and concerns.[46]

Everett had felt it "too much to argue that the insurance offices must be frequented, the courts of law followed . . . in order to give a man such a knowledge of the world, as would enable him to administer a college."[47] Lowell rejoined that a Corporation "mixing with the world" like the present one, "selected out of various professions, and generally composed of men of eminence," would have more "public confidence," would exercise a more "commanding influence" in government and "private society," and would provide the broader vision and consciousness required of the Harvard Corporation.[48]

Beyond a brief reference to the efficiency of a division of labor, it will be noted that the burden of the argument rests on a positive defense of governance by nonscholars: the university would derive greater organizational skill, financial support, and overall direction from a Corporation of nonresident businessmen and professionals enjoying the confidence of (and exercising influence over) the community at large. To be sure, this train of reasoning was partly a reaction to the sarcasm of Everett, who wrote that when a professor was recommended to sit on the Corporation, the "non-resident gentlemen" instead judged a Boston lawyer "better acquainted with the college affairs, and more conversant with the administration of literary institutions" — a point to which self-justification, if not group loyalty, demanded a strong response.[49]

But the emphasis on, first, organization and financial acumen and, second, greater community representativeness suggests larger concerns at play here. The rejection of faculty claims to de jure authority would establish an important principle at an important time — namely, that the new wielders of economic and social power ought not to forfeit the right to wield cultural and intellectual power as well. In this way, no insular enclave would come to control vital elite social and cultural institutions, whether Harvard, the Athenaeum, the Lowell Institute, or the medical complex. Rejection of the professors' claims would thus reduce the danger of a fissure between the cultural and entrepreneurial branches of the evolving elite at the same time that it promised the continued infusion of cultural ventures with modern organization and commercial values. Indeed, by thus subordinating culture to the activities of accumulation and dominance which sustained it, the decision insured, at least in elite eyes, the very vitality and relevance of culture itself.

The Corporation won its fight in the Board of Overseers, whose members obviously took such arguments very much to heart, and then moved quickly on several fronts to consolidate the victory and prevent a recurrence of this type of controversy.[50] In appointing a Boston lawyer to a vacancy in their ranks in 1825, the Fellows justified their choice to the Overseers on the grounds that the selection should be consonant with current Corporation policy and that faculty pretensions should not even appear to be an influence. At the same time they changed the name of the faculty from "immediate government" to "faculty of the university," thereby removing this slight intimation of governing authority.[51] Immediately after, of course, came the rigorous and domineering Bowditch-Quincy regime with its close supervision of all university affairs. Many of the chief Corporation defenders in its struggle with the faculty — Story, Gray, Jackson — were members of the Quincy administration. In contrast, by 1833 nine of the eleven instructors on the faculty side of the conflict no longer taught at Harvard.[52]

In the mid-1840s, interestingly enough, the same issue arose in different guise and more muted form when several instructors publicly criticized what they saw as Harvard's excessively high tuition fees and wildly proliferating elective system. They criticized these trends on the traditional grounds that they discriminated against poor but deserving students who were interested in pursuing basic scholarship rather than career-oriented studies. But once launched, mere criticism soon escalated into a call for faculty control of university admissions and curriculum, or at least faculty influence in the larger decision-making processes.[53]

This controversy differed from that of the 1820s because it was an argument over specific policies, to change which required control of the Corporation, rather than a general assertion of faculty governing authority. Equally fundamental questions were raised, but for a different, and perhaps even more threatening, purpose, one which, as will be seen, went directly against the very raison d'etre of Boston's new institutional culture. Moreover, the faculty, now numerous and diverse, was much less united than before, and the burden of debate fell mainly to a group of college traditionalists led by Andrew Peabody and Francis Bowen, who found themselves partially at odds with the scientists and the professional school instructors. Their demands, therefore, though articulated forcefully and at some length, never reached the level of the Overseer agenda and were accordingly never seriously considered outside the faculty, which itself dropped the issue not so long after picking it up.

The "worst times of dissent between governors and governed"

were clearly over.[54] By the 1860s the faculty was reduced to skirmishing over the authority of the president to regulate their affairs, including the right to select classroom texts without authorization. No broad claims were made to faculty governing power, either for its own sake or to change policy. The Corporation, tolerant in its impregnability, was moved only to reassert its authority, via the president, to supervise faculty activities as closely as "deemed necessary," and to deny any whisper of financial or other autonomy to the proliferating schools and departments of the university.[55] Thus the situation in 1862, as in 1832, was essentially that of 1842:

> The officers of instruction are entirely in the power of the Trustees of the corporation, and whenever this body is active and chooses to assume its authority, it has entire control over the discipline, the choice of text-books, and the whole place of education. In some cases, the opinion of the instructors respecting a proposed alteration in the studies is never asked; and, if they resist the change, they are turned out.[56]

"Regardless of the sentiment of professors," a historian has written, the Fellows had "law and tradition on their side, as well as the more powerful elements in the community."[57] The statement is incorrect in two respects, since tradition partly supported the faculty and the law was at best unclear. But the point concerning power is dead right. As an observer pithily phrased it, it was the Corporation alone at Harvard "who had the keys and the money and the power."[58]

· 5 ·

The New Faculty and
the Process of Consolidation

THE impression of Corporation — and therefore elite Boston — control over the affairs of the professors of Harvard, though undeniably accurate, must nonetheless be qualified. While the nineteenth-century faculty may have relinquished its formal authority to the representatives of "State Street," there were a number of trends which helped to remove some of the sting of this loss. Sheer institutional growth, for example, made it difficult in practice for the Fellows to supervise all the details of faculty work in every branch of the university, while the genuine appreciation of creative teaching and research — and the increasing expertise required for the mastery of the subject matter of a given course — often made it unwise in practice to attempt to do so. A nonteaching Corporation, moreover, meant in fact a Corporation whose members had wide-ranging outside interests. This was considered a source of great strength, as elite spokesmen asserted. But it was also a source of some distraction. The president, to be sure, was a full-time administrator and Corporation spokesman, and his role was formidable, especially after 1830. But in spite of occasional faculty grumbling, mid-century presidents tended in the nature of things to exercise their hard-won power in the interest of maintaining "a harmony and union between all the varied characters that constitute the faculty and associates of Cambridge."[1]

But there was more to this seeming paradox of the light-handed use of absolute authority than institutional complexity, intellectual expertise, extracurricular diversion, or even the gradual acquiescence of instructors to institutional subjugation, important though these things were. A full understanding requires, in addition, a close look, first, at Corporation hiring and control practices and, second, the manner in which these practices were shaped by the multiple functions which were now expected of antebellum professors. It requires, as well, an appreciation of how the exercise of this particular kind of Corporation power led to a quite remarkable standardization of faculty views and an even more remarkable modification of faculty social standing which, together, were perhaps more relevant than any other factor in reducing the need for close supervision. The consequences were impressive enough for the university alone. They were of immense significance for the evolution of culture and class in Boston.

There is no question that the Corporation deemed its power to appoint faculty members to be as crucial to the proper conduct of the university as its power to allocate resources or establish rules and regulations. When the Corporation submitted a financial endowment for ratification by the Board of Overseers, it usually submitted the name of a particular individual to fill the new chair and then requested ratification of both endowment and individual simultaneously. So valuable was this power to hire that even large bequests, such as one to the medical school in 1855 which was made contingent upon the right of the donor to handpick a new medical faculty, were rejected when they threatened the Corporation hiring power. When the founder of a professorship stipulated an initial appointee, as in law in 1829 or science in 1847, the Corporation's acceptance implied its agreement with the selection.[2] Simply put, as the number of professors and their cultural influence in the community rose, so, naturally, did the significance of the power to appoint them.

The "search process," to use a modern term for an incipient practice, involved a fairly standard set of procedures by the 1830s. When the appointment was to fill a newly established chair, the opinion of the donor was considered. For an existing position the recommendations of the incumbent were generally sought, together with opinions of relevant members of the Boston community and, very occasionally, other members of the Harvard faculty or members of other college faculties or preparatory schools. The individual's prior record at Harvard was a further factor; many prospective instructors had attended Harvard or served there as proctor or tutor. Once a selection had been tentatively made, the president then consulted with the candidate concerning duties and expectations. In 1840 President Quincy thus reminded a junior instructor of the terms of his recent employment:

> I . . . distinctly stated to you that . . . I held it an incumbent duty of every officer of the Institution to abstain from any act tending to bring within its walls discussions upon questions on which the passions and interests of the community are divided, and warmly engaged.[3]

Criteria for faculty selection were varied, but some criteria extended well beyond the boundaries of mere pedagogical or scholarly competence. There was, for example, a fairly clear quest for gentility generated by the socializing function — the need to provide proper role models and authority figures for Harvard students. The record reveals, in fact, a highly discriminating touch here. An applicant for a faculty post in 1839 was derided for his "singular habits and eccentricities."[4] An idiosyncratic candidate for the chair of history in 1850 was dismissed as a "worthless fellow."[5] Two otherwise undistinguished candidates for the professorship of modern languages in the 1850s were recommended and seriously considered as (respectively) "a gentleman in manners and appearance" and a potentially "agreeable addition to our society."[6] Henry Torrey, the comparatively unscholarly man who became professor of history in 1856, was praised as "refined, sensitive, modest, the finished gentleman" — and also a competent teacher.[7] Even the most pedestrian of instructors were, it was agreed, "high-bred gentlemen." The best of them had a "princely" and "autocratic" bearing altogether appropriate to the position.[8]

After the struggles of the 1820s, institutional loyalty became another important criterion. Thus, a libel suit levied in 1828 by Daniel Webster (a Dartmouth graduate) against Theodore Lyman, a prominent Bostonian and Harvard patron, was reputed to have cost Webster an offer of a law professorship in spite of his generally conservative politics and staunch defense of Harvard's interests during the Massachusetts constitutional convention of 1820. Simon Greenleaf, in line for appointment to the law faculty in 1833, wisely and cautiously sought the permission of the Corporation before representing its opponents in a legal action over the university's economic affairs.[9] Chairs of natural history and mathematics were denied to qualified candidates in the 1830s in part because of their past disagreement with Corporation policies.[10] Indeed, the point was driven home so forcefully in these years that it seldom arose thereafter except in connection with men whose positions were reasonably secure or who were circumspect in their criticism. By the 1840s the assertion of institutional loyalty was a self-evident virtue.[11]

Finally, there was a desire for soundness in politics and religion which, though related tangentially to institutional loyalty, derived principally from the faculty's instructional and scholarly functions. The first of these functions shaped the opinions of the students; the second helped shape those of the public. In combination, as the Quincy letter suggests, they made "right thinking" a serious matter in the selection of faculty candidates. Simon Greenleaf, in seeking his law position, assured the Corporation that his arguments in the suit involving Harvard would avoid "everything 'peoplish' or agrarian in character" or tending to the "destruction of vested rights."[12] Candidates with egalitarian political sympathies — Jeffersonian Benjamin Waterhouse, for example, and Jacksonian George Bancroft — were either passed over for important appointments or never seriously considered. In the 1840s Charles Sumner's pacifist and other reform statements caused him to be twice rejected for a law professorship, in spite of his reputation as Joseph Story's protégé. "The conservative Corporation of Harvard College," wrote an observer, "consider Sumner in the Law-school, as unsuitable as a Bull in a china-shop."[13] An outstanding applicant for the vacant chair of history in 1851 was rebuffed for his abolitionist zeal.[14] James Russell Lowell's youthful antislavery proclivities almost cost him the chair of modern languages in the 1850s in spite of his sterling family connections. Only Professor Longfellow's support and Lowell's own assurances to President James Walker enabled Harvard, as a recent scholar has it, "to reclaim him as a professor and tame her wayward son."[15]

Understandably, therefore, most early Harvard faculty members were "pronounced and decided Federalists" who followed "naturally in the train of the president," whether Kirkland or Quincy.[16] The only two early Republicans were either forced out of the faculty or resigned before being forced out. After 1830, in turn, most professors were (in the words of an English observer) "high Whigs, which means Tories."[17] In the mid-1830s four instructors, normally Whiggish in party politics, expressed sympathy with the incipient antislavery movement in Cambridge. Two of these soon found themselves cautioned by President Quincy; another had his appointment terminated at the instigation of an important university patron.[18] Professors during the 1840s gave speeches "of the most ridiculous ultra conservative character," hostile to Jacksonism and "vehemently opposed to the abolitionists."[19] As of 1850 faculty politics constituted a rather "timid conservatism" supporting mainly "the success of Webster [now venerable again] and the great Whig party."[20]

During the 1850s, with the fragmentation of traditional party alignments and sectional perspectives, a group of perhaps eight instructors (of a total of approximately thirty-five) were antislavery in sympathy. Only five of this small band went so far as to support the Free-Soil party, however, and even this entailed some risk: "Fortunately for Longfellow, his connection with the university ceased not long after Sumner's election to the Senate; and the unpleasantness of his position may have been the leading cause of his retirement."[21] Others confined themselves to a moderate brand of Republicanism at a time when even the Harvard Corporation included one Republican. Most members of the antislavery group were in fact cautious by temperament and opposed to unnecessary controversy and "violent denunciation."[22] Several, though moderately progressive on the issue of slavery, were still sufficiently sound on economic and social questions to hold "Socialism in a kind of holy horror."[23] They "shied from indecency in literature" and defined democracy as government by the "cultivated and educated" minority.[24] Overall, only about one-fifth of all the members of the antebellum faculty may be described as even mild political dissidents from the prevailing elite persuasion, and most of these merely adhered to the restrained Republicanism of the late 1850s.

The same pattern held for religion. "Since Unitarianism has become the prevailing creed in Boston," a European explained in 1837, "that sect has predominated also amongst the professors of Cambridge."[25] The Harvard Divinity School was the main center for training future Unitarian ministers, and its faculty naturally included important spokesmen for the denomination, among them Andrews Norton, the "Unitarian Pope," and James Walker, the "Unitarian Warrior."[26] But elsewhere in the university the creed also held sway, spreading influence among the students and polemics abroad. Before about 1840, interestingly enough, these faculty polemics dealt primarily with the "harsh and primitive superstitions" of Orthodox Calvinism. Thereafter, they dealt far more with the anarchistic tendencies lurking on the transcendental fringes of Unitarianism itself. Divinity faculty united with other professors against Emerson's notorious Divinity School address of 1838. More important, Harvard patrons such as the Lawrences began to shift their philanthropy from theology to science in part as a response to the "infidelity, atheism and wild jacobinism" of such Unitarian extremism.[27] "You are entirely right about Cambridge," wrote Samuel Lawrence to his brother in 1844, "and the sooner the authorities see it the better, and a Divorce takes place. The Divinity building would make a good stocking mill with a steam engine, and I know a party who would like it."[28] By the 1850s, in consequence, a few non-Unitarians were evident in the law schools and scientific departments, and Unitarian advocates such as Walker, Francis Bowen, and Andrew Peabody stood grimly and openly opposed to what they considered the excessive "religious liberalism of the time."[29]

Even so, the prevailing tone at antebellum Harvard was

clearly Unitarian, for some 80 percent of the professors appointed in these years could be classified as Unitarians, with the
remainder largely mid-century Calvinists and Episcopalians.
Moreover, the most zealous Unitarians, at least after 1840, were
also reliable conservatives on social and political issues. Not uncharacteristically, the "catastrophist" geological and zoological
theories of Harvard's most famous antebellum scientist, Louis
Agassiz, simultaneously supported racial supremacy, undermined belief in the literal truth of the Bible, and stressed the
heresy latent in developmental conceptions of nature. They thus
provided a deistic but nonscriptural framework for the doctrine
of racial hierarchy which conformed almost completely to the
ideological predilections of the institution's elite sponsors. In
fact, Agassiz conformed still further by inveighing against
socialism and various other philanthropic schemes to uplift the
poor and the black — whom his science had already proclaimed
inferior.[30]

The impact on Cambridge of this type of selectivity according
to gentility, loyalty, and political and religious correctness was
striking. In the early 1800s Harvard instructors had been "little
better than Monks," full of "enmity and suspicion," with the
benevolence and grace of "the crew of a Privateer."[31] By the
1830s dinner with Harvard professors and patrons — "choice
spirits" of a "brilliant and fascinating society" — had become de
rigueur for traveling Europeans, and a mid-century French visitor called Cambridge a "fashionable oasis."[32] A British journalist wrote during the Civil War:

> Of all academical dignitaries whom I have known — and I have
> known a good number — I should say that the Professors of
> Harvard College were, as a body, the pleasantest. They are all
> men of scholarly education, some of them of European repute,
> and yet they are also men of the world.[33]

An Oxford don compared genteel Cambridge to the quieter
phases of "English country society."[34] A Cantabridgian stated
that the Harvardians' "gracious and ready hospitality . . . made
for a rare and delightful social life."[35] Such were the consequences of policy.

Genteel manner involved more than polite manners, however. Gentility, like conservatism, connoted a certain standing in the community, a degree of "opulence and earning capacity," according to a sardonic later authority, which would engender in scholars a "habitual sense of what is good and right in these matters."[36] The authority of the Corporation to hire selectively according to standards based on multiple faculty functions was a definite aid in producing standardized faculty views and behavior, which the latent Corporation authority to supervise and coerce helped in turn to maintain. But a man with sturdy elite ties and substance of his own might be a good deal more likely to think and behave correctly than one who acted from mere intimidation alone.

In 1860 one of Louis Agassiz's students made something like this point in his diary.

> This morning Prof gave us a rather strong lecture on behavior etc. . . . We must give up all our social times & in fact not care for dress or anything; be real diggers. At the same time seek refined & cultivated society. With ragged breeches for instance! Told us, poor as he was, he would not change his position for mere living. I thought of the income he is receiving from his book & school; his 1500 a year as Professor; his wealthy wife; the house in which he lives for nothing; his children already engaged to the wealthiest. O consistency, thou art a jewel![37]

While students often overestimate the status and comforts of their instructors, this particular student struck so close to the mark that his sentiments may be generalized: the gentility and conservatism of an Agassiz flowed rather easily from the wealth and connections of an Agassiz. The last facet in the process of faculty development, therefore, was the creation of such a bond of common interest between elite and professors as would instill reflexive right bearing and belief among all the instructors of Cambridge.

Given this perspective, it is no surprising discovery that the material circumstances of the faculty rose very dramatically over the years. Table 8 measures the rise.

Professors appointed to the Harvard faculty before 1830 were well off, compared to most New Englanders. Perhaps 60 percent

Table 8: Wealth of Harvard Faculty, 1805–1860

	1805–1830	1831–60	Rate of Increase
Faculty w/$100,000	27%	39%	44%
Average faculty wealth	$81,000	$144,000	78%
Faculty w/$50,000	43%	79%	84%
Median faculty wealth	$33,000	$75,000	127%

left estates in the top 2 percent of the Massachusetts population; more than a quarter left substantial wealth at their death. But the group appointed after 1830 was still more prosperous, with two-fifths possessing substantial wealth (sometimes amounting to several hundred thousand dollars) and four-fifths lagging not far behind. The exceptionally high rates of increase in the two bottom categories of table 8 — faculty with $50,000 and median wealth — suggest, moreover, the extent to which affluence was becoming a genuine common denominator among professors. There were no true millionaires in the post-1830 group, and a few of the estates were actually worth under $25,000. Even so, fully three-fourths of the faculty (Louis Agassiz included) by now possessed estates ranking in the top 1.3 percent of the population of the state.

It was this rapid infusion of wealth, as Agassiz's students appreciated, that underpinned the well-known genteel style. As of mid-century most Harvard instructors (save for the few residing in Boston) lived on plots of land ranging from five to fifty acres located within a half-mile of the college yard. The homes of professors appeared on city maps as landmarks and tourist attractions. Old Cambridge, where the faculty resided, was the growing city's richest area and "most desirable part" for residency, with more than half its leading taxpayers connected in some fashion with Harvard.[38] A guide to (of all places) Chicago noted that the "real aristocracy" of that new city lived in a section with homes "like the houses of Cambridge, Massachusetts, surrounded by spacious and beautiful grounds filled with a profusion of stately shade trees."[39] A young Bostonian in Paris observed that a professor who had turned down an offer from the Sorbonne for Harvard "knew which side his bread was buttered on. . . . The professors' houses and apartments [in Paris] are small, old, gloomy, tumble down affairs in comparison with which his present residence is a palace."[40]

There were intense, and at times perhaps excessive, pressures on faculty members to live in a manner appropriate to their means and station. In the mid-1840s, for example, President Edward Everett insisted upon the resignation of Pietro Bachi, an Italian instructor who had gone bankrupt.[41] In the late 1840s John Webster, a professor of chemistry from a prosperous Boston family, "most foolishly built a large and expensive house in Cambridge, expended much upon the land, in books and furniture" in order to maintain a fitting appearance. Unfortunately, Webster found himself borrowing to keep up this mode of living. Eventually, he not only sold his house (at a loss) but died on the gallows for murdering his chief creditor, Samuel Parkman.[42] Bankruptcies and murders were the exception, needless to say. Friends of Harvard professors described them as "bourgeois" in the sense that "they habitually paid their debts and lived within their means" — those means being, of course, ample.[43]

Ample means derived in part from ample salaries. Excluding the medical faculty, which drew its pay partly from student fees, the average instructor's salary over time is shown in table 9.

Table 9: Average Salary of Harvard Instructors, 1825–1865

	Average Salary	Rate of Increase
1825	$1,400	
1845	1,950	39%
1865	2,550	31%

Source: Salary averages derived from the Harvard treasurers' reports for the years cited. The 1845 figure excludes the $4,000 drawn by Joseph Story the year before his death in 1845, an amount far above that paid to other nineteenth-century instructors.

While professors clearly did not become wealthy from their salaries alone in these years, they did make well above the $1,500 which would enable a family in 1850 to "live very nicely" in a "comfortable" house with two servants.[44] It might be noted as well that in the 1820s instructors received more money than Boston bank executives ($1,200) and in the 1840s more than Massachusetts district attorneys or judges of common pleas ($1,550) and almost as much as treasurers of textile firms ($2,300).[45] The fact that Harvard salaries increased as sharply and steadily as they did — as much, perhaps, as those of any salaried group of that era — is probably one reasonable index of the Corporation's intent with regard to enhanced faculty status.

In its concern for loyalty, gentility, and rectitude, the Corporation did more than pay its professors well. It also drew them from a different source. It drew them in the first instance, of course, from the ranks of former Harvard men, believing, as was commonly noted, that instructors should "all be graduates of our own college."[46] Over the whole antebellum period some 85 percent of the faculty appointees held a Harvard bachelor's degree. Even after 1830, when scholarly output was both higher and more crucial, almost 90 percent possessed degrees from the college or professional schools. Non-Harvardians invariably evoked comment, as did even such promising figures as George Ticknor and Henry Longfellow, both from Dartmouth. As was said of an unhappy instructor in the 1850s, "He was not a graduate of Harvard College, which was a misfortune, and he did not get into the Harvard way."[47]

In fact, professors often came from the immediate circle of Corporation members and major university benefactors. Six antebellum instructors were themselves Fellows or patrons; another six were brothers or sons of Fellows or patrons. Six others were brothers-in-law or sons-in-law, and two more nephews, of Fellows or patrons.[48] Elite families with university connections sometimes played a part in the selection of nonrelatives as well. The Lowells, for example, influenced no fewer than five offers from 1805 to 1862; the Eliots, probably as many. Other wealthy men also assisted their favorites, as, of course, did the founders of chairs who stipulated a particular recipient.[49] Elite observers came, understandably, to refer to new faculty in the first person plural possessive — "our Eustis," for instance, for an engineering professor in 1849. An Englishman thus reported in 1853 that professorships were "given away quite as much by interest here as elsewhere."[50]

Not surprisingly, the proportion of Bostonians on the faculty rose from 35 percent for those before 1830 to about 45 percent for those from 1831 to 1860. The number of non–New Englanders such as Louis Agassiz, a Swiss, also increased slightly, as the search for talent widened. However, the proportion of New Englanders from outside the Boston–North Shore area — the less-favored small-town or rural parts of the region, that is — fell from 40 percent of the total for the pre-1830 group to 28 percent thereafter.

Equally significant, the new instructors were more likely to be the sons of prosperous professionals or businessmen. Of the faculty appointed before 1830, about the same numbers were from farming or ministerial families as from legal, medical, or business families. Of those after 1830, almost 60 percent were the sons of lawyers, doctors or businessmen. The rise in "prosperous Boston" antecedents undoubtedly reflected the parallel rise of Boston as a regional metropolis with a flourishing secular elite. The selection of Harvard instructors thus represented, at a somewhat different level, the same forces which produced the new "financial" or "Salem" Corporation or, indeed, the new university patron group. Like the close ties to Fellows, patrons, and elite Boston families, moreover, the process suggests the gradual circumscription of the candidate pool as the Corporation searched for skilled and proper gentlemen.

While some professors derived wealth from inheritance, others made money from business interests of their own. Nine instructors served as directors of banks or insurance companies; four served on the boards of manufacturing, transportation, or land corporations; three served as consultants to industrial firms. One man, science professor Daniel Treadwell, held positions in six enterprises over a thirteen-year period, mostly in manufacturing; another, Sidney Willard, was a leading promoter of Cambridge banks, roads, and land developments. Two professors, Treadwell and his successor Eben Horsford, accepted their appointments only on condition that they be permitted to continue their business pursuits. Many instructors were substantial investors in land or industry. Some were also "shrewd and practical businessmen" in the publishing field and in the preparation of popular editions of their scholarly works.[51]

To be sure, faculty business interests, though sometimes connected to those of wealthy Bostonians, were generally smaller and less strategic. Only two professors were board members of the largest Boston banks; only one was on the board of a leading textile mill. Faculty entrepreneurs tended also to come from the earlier group. While one post-1830 appointee, Horsford, made a fortune in agricultural chemistry and another, Benjamin Peirce, served as an insurance and shipping consultant, nine of the fifteen antebellum faculty directors (including the three directors of major banks and mills) came from the group appointed before 1830.

On the other hand, most members of the faculty after 1830 certainly held stock in important firms. Every member of the law and medical faculties in these years had elite stocks in their portfolios, as did virtually all the college faculty for whom evidence remains. In some cases professors with extensive wealth simply invested in thriving industrial ventures as other wealthy men would. On other occasions rich Bostonians would tender gifts, loans and investment advice to faculty members. Only real estate (comprising 40 percent of faculty estates as compared to 30 percent for other elite Bostonians) competed with corporate securities as investment outlets. In sum, the faculty increasingly tended to generate extra income by writing, by owning land, or by investing in large firms rather than by conducting businesses of their own. They thus became, as befitted men with demanding scholarly and pedagogical concerns, more of a rentier than an entrepreneurial group — though no less rich or reliant on the great Boston business ventures.[52]

Closing the circle, finally, was the propensity, as an observer in the 1830s put it, of "our rich girls to buy themselves a professor."[53] Indeed, faculty marital ties seemed singularly Bostonian in their convolutions. Professors George Ticknor and Andrews Norton both married daughters of Samuel Eliot, a Harvard benefactor and father of a member of the Corporation. Professor John C. Warren, also a major donor, married the daughter of Jonathan Mason, a wealthy Boston lawyer; Professor John Gorham in turn married Warren's sister. Professor Walter Channing, the brother of two faculty members and a Corporation Fellow, married a niece of the famed merchant, Thomas Handasyd Perkins; Professors Cornelius Felton and Louis Agassiz then wed the daughters of Perkins's son-in-law, Thomas G. Cary. Altogether, perhaps a quarter of the antebellum faculty married heiresses. And again, the rate was an accelerating one, for of those appointed after 1830, as many as a third married into wealth. At mid-century a European remarked that, unlike most American businessmen, Boston "bankers and money kings pride themselves in being connected, by family-ties, with the aristocracy of intellect."[54]

It was the new patterns of private funding which underlay the transformation of the faculty. It was the great benefactions for schools and professorships which ultimately made the faculty at once larger, more professional, and more crucial to the university and the community. The faculty in turn filled positions at the Massachusetts General Hospital, the Boston Athenaeum, the *North American Review*, and the Lowell Institute and, in a sense, knit together the cultural labors of the entire constellation of Boston institutions in the same way that patrons and governors knit it together financially and administratively. But simultaneously, the faculty became more important than ever in the socialization of Harvard students. The development underscored the role of culture in the life of the burgeoning elite. It gave Harvard instructors a major part in the provision of this culture both at Harvard and outside it. In fact, so vital was this new faculty, with all its multiplicity of responsibilities and functions, that the Corporation molded it after its own image — hammered it into increasing uniformity of belief and bearing and loftiness of social and financial status, a virtual extension by the 1860s of the elite to which the Fellows themselves belonged.

But the development also underscored the power of the business sector of the elite even within the cultural realm. For after the great struggle of the 1820s the faculty, despite its prominence and wealth, remained organizationally and socially subordinate to the university's governors and benefactors and therefore to the business interests and concerns of the elite. The development infused the Boston elite with a cultural component of great size and stature — an essential precondition to its distinctiveness. But it also ratified the hegemony of the industrial elements within that elite — an essential precondition to its durability.

· 6 ·

Harvard Students
and the Process of Exclusion

AMONG the components of the cultural constellation of elite Boston, there were some institutions — the Massachusetts General Hospital and the Boston Dispensary, for example, and to some extent the Lowell Institute — that catered to a rather broad and inclusive public; and some — the Athenaeum, Mount Auburn Cemetery, the McLean Asylum — that were comparatively exclusive by design or expense or both. The position of Harvard along this spectrum was somewhat ambiguous. Before 1800 its small size necessarily limited the number of boys who could benefit directly from its services. Yet by tradition and the prescriptions of the state constitution, Harvard was to be accessible to the Commonwealth as a whole, its students drawn from various areas and ranks and its graduates catering to the needs of a diverse citizenry roughly in the manner of a modern public university.[1]

The transformation of the antebellum Corporation and instructional staff represented a shift toward the kind of exclusive institutional control which obtained in the other cultural institutions and exerted its own particular sway over elite development. The founding of professional schools and the publishing activities of the faculty, on the other hand, perhaps indicated an expansion of the inclusive public-service orientation, however closely power was held or ideology circumscribed. To this extent the ultimate tendency — whether internal differentiation and consolidation or external influence and indoctrination — of institutional culture generally, and of Harvard University specifically, remains somewhat obscure.

The key to a more thorough understanding of this ultimate tendency would seem to be the identity of the students of the college, or "undergraduate department," whose well-being, for all the proliferation of professional schools and scientific and scholarly research and the great changes in governance and staff, was the chief object of concern throughout the era. Only a third of the major financial contributions went to the professional schools, many of whose faculty also lectured to undergraduates. Moreover, faculty scholarship, though important, was never more important than pedagogy and socialization. As late as 1850, in fact, the Corporation devoted at least 90 percent of its attention to collegiate affairs, and so did the president, who governed the professional schools mainly through deans while directing his own energies toward the Harvard "Yard."[2] Whatever the situation after 1870 under President Eliot, in this period the term "Harvard University" meant principally the college, and a "Harvard student" was principally a collegian, so that to discuss the transformation of the Harvard student body — whether as a test of the true functions of institutional culture or merely to complete the portrait of university change — is to discuss the young men who were seeking their bachelor's degrees in Cambridge.

The first notable feature of the student body is that, unlike the rest of the university, it did not increase very much in size. The average graduating class from 1801 to 1810 was about forty-seven; from 1841 to 1850, about fifty-five. Fifty-four persons received degrees in 1810, sixty-seven in 1850. Classes were somewhat larger in the 1820s and 1850s than before, but this resulted mainly from the influx of Southern students, who comprised perhaps 20 percent of the graduates of the mid-1850s. With their departure upon the outbreak of war, class sizes reverted to their earlier levels for another decade. But as noted earlier, the total assets of the university grew quite rapidly over the first half of the century. Given the stability of student body size, this meant that by 1850 each student was "capitalized," so to speak, at about $23,000 — more than four times as much as before 1810.

But in composition, if not size, the student body underwent a variety of very striking changes. For example, as table 10 shows, there were more students from Boston and fewer from Essex County and especially small-town or rural New England.

Table 10: Geographical Distribution of Harvard Graduates, 1787–1859

	From Boston*	From Essex County (percent)	From Elsewhere in New England
1789–1824	29	10	55
1827–1859	41	6	37

*Boston, Cambridge, Charlestown, Roxbury, and Brookline.

Source: Computed from student residence lists in the printed and manuscript catalogues of the Harvard University Archives. Data for 1789–1824 come from catalogues at roughly three-year intervals; data for 1827–1859 come from catalogues at three-year intervals after 1826.

By 1831 the inhabitants of western Massachusetts were calling Harvard "the college of Boston and Salem, and not of the Commonwealth," and a graduate of 1839 recalled that "the college of that time was equipped mostly by men of eastern Massachusetts, and was for students from eastern Massachusetts."[3] A student of the late 1840s wrote, "We were largely Bostonians. . . . We were a group, cohesive, self-sufficient."[4] An account of the college in the 1850s mentioned its "crowds" of students from "Boston and Brookline and Roxbury."[5]

It was simultaneously suggested, moreover, that the proportion of students from prosperous backgrounds was growing. In the 1820s residents of western Massachusetts referred to Harvard's "Unitarian aristocracy," and for radicals of the 1830s the university was the most notorious of "our aristocratic, incorporate colleges."[6] By the 1840s such remarks were much more common. One observer noticed the increasing numbers of students from "rich and fashionable families."[7] Another believed that "as the poorer class of students . . . have ceased to enter [Harvard's] classes, these are filled in a larger proportion by the sons of wealthy persons."[8] Faculty spokesmen ascribed the shift in the curriculum towards "mercantile and active" subjects partly to the matriculation of "new persons from an influential, wealthy and populous class whose patronage Harvard needs."[9]

A mid-century critic charged that now most Harvard students were indeed "the sons of rich men."[10]

These remarks on the growing wealth of Harvard students have considerable surface plausibility. The remarks themselves are fairly numerous and fairly consistent; more Boston-area students would mean more students from the principal seat of elite residence; the pattern would parallel that discernable among donors, governors, and professors. But in addition, impressionistic information concerning the social backgrounds of the students, their changing standard of living while at Harvard, and their careers after graduation points to the same conclusion.

As regards social background there are several suggestive measures. For example, the names of three dozen families generally associated with nineteenth-century Proper Boston appear three times as often in the graduate lists between 1801 and 1850 as in those for the preceding ninety years, when roughly the same number of students took degrees.[11] A few elite names are, of course, as common before 1800 as after, and a great many more are too common to allow for meaningful comparison. Given the constancy in average number of antebellum graduates, however, the count is indicative of a rising elite concentration — so much so that a local belle could write in 1844: "By living in Cambridge a few years you *get the run of the families* and then recognize each new set of youths *by their resemblance to their older brothers!*"[12]

In addition, insofar as a business occupation connoted wealth, as it generally did, it is notable that the proportion of Harvard students whose fathers were businessmen rose from approximately one-quarter before 1825 to approximately one-half by the 1860s — surely a telling increase. (Along these lines, it is perhaps worth making the noncomparative observation that of the twenty-two antebellum millionaires of Boston who had sons, all but five sent them to Harvard.)[13] Finally, an investigation of the size of the estates of the fathers of Harvard's first scholars from 1801 to 1860 yields the figures shown in table 11, based on nineteen of twenty-six New Englanders for the early period and eighteen of twenty-six for the later.

Table 11: Wealth Distribution of First Scholars, Harvard, 1801–1860, as Measured by Value of Fathers' Estates

	Under $10,000	$10–50,000	$50–100,000	Over $100,000
1801–1830	58%	26%	5%	11%
1831–1860	26	20	6	48

Source: First scholars: annual graduation lists, *Harvard Quinquennial Catalogue.* Fathers' names: classbooks and biographical files of the Harvard University Archives. Estate data: county courthouses in Rhode Island, Massachusetts, New Hampshire, and Maine.

The sample is scanty but illuminating. As table 11 shows, over half the fathers of the early group were in straitened circumstances; almost half the fathers of the later group were very rich.

Change was discernible in the undergraduate standard of living as well. As early as 1813 a Southerner complained of "the extravagance of the students" at Cambridge.[14] Six years later a committee of Overseers agreed that "the increase in the private expenses of the Students is a subject deserving of the most careful consideration. . . . There is a perpetual inclination to indulge in expensive pleasures, & in useless & unnecessary extravagances of dress."[15] The long administrations of Kirkland and Quincy may well have encouraged this tendency.

The real root of the "problem" was probably less the administration than the students themselves, who brought family tastes and family resources with them: "Father wants cheap living; Son has his way; and has his way, because it is not fashionable to live cheap."[16] A report in the 1850s summed up: "A carpet in a college room . . . was 50 years ago, an unknown luxury; and 25 years ago, the want of one would not have been noticeable. Now all the rooms are carpeted; and a similar change has taken place in furniture, dress, and the supplies of the table."[17] By now students stabled their own horses for pleasure riding; paid an attendant to draw their steaming tubs; and sported canes, shooting-jackets, English walking-coats, and other fashionable attire from "favorite university tailors."[18]

The pattern of student social contacts changed in a similarly suggestive fashion. Before 1800 students lived in the same "almost monastic" seclusion as their instructors.[19] Among Cambridge families "social intercourse with the young, and especially with students, was not much cultivated; and invitations to parties in Boston rarely extended to college circles."[20] A student of this period recalled that he was acquainted with only twenty or so of his college fellows, and with almost no one outside the college.[21] By the 1820s, however, students were beginning to appear as guests in the "better" homes in the area, usually with the encouragement of Kirkland and especially Quincy, who not only promoted student-faculty interaction but exhibited "a strong general sense of the importance to young men . . . of mingling in the society of ladies, and of their elders and superiors, as a part of education."[22] Parents came to expect and arrange for such contacts. In the 1830s Harvardians (or at least upperclassmen) commonly attended the "Boston Assemblies" in the ballrooms of Monsieur Papanti, the fashionable dancing master.[23] In 1840 a Salem lawyer informed his son, a new Harvard student, that he would be "well provided with visiting places. I have many friends who will be glad to see you, and who have very pleasant families."[24] By mid-century students regularly rode the new horsecars to the entertainments of their Boston families, friends, and acquaintances.[25]

Finally, career patterns corroborate the overall impression, as in the data on the proportion of Harvard graduates in the different fields shown in table 12. The figures indicate a secular trend in the future professions of Harvard students, with the ministry dropping from second to last place as a career preference and from one-fourth to one-tenth in its share of graduates. The range of careers widened somewhat, with the category "other" advancing from last to third place and including more teachers, journalists, and architects, and fewer farmers. But the "business"

Table 12: Occupational Distribution of Harvard Graduates, 1798–1860

	Law	Ministry	Business (percent)	Medicine	Other
1798–1830	33	24	17	13	13
1835–1860	33	9	24	15	19

Source: Computed from manuscript and printed classbooks, HUA, and Willard, *Memories of Youth and Manhood*, 2:62–63; James C. White, "An Undergraduate Diary II," HCM (June 1913), p. 650; Thomas Cushing, "Undergraduate Life Sixty Years Ago," Ibid., 1 (July 1893): 553. For 1798–1830, seven classes were examined at roughly four-year intervals; for 1835–1860, seven classes at four-year intervals. For the earlier period, approximately 60% of the graduates could be traced; for the latter period, approximately 75%.

field increased its share most of all, rising from third to second in preference and from one-sixth to one-fourth in proportion. Thus, while law and medicine held firm over the era, the ministry, and to a lesser extent farming, lost ground to more modern careers, especially business.[26] At colleges such as Amherst, Williams, and Yale, meanwhile, almost 90 percent of the graduates continued to become lawyers or ministers until late in the nineteenth century.

Harvard students not only pursued business and other modern secular careers with greater frequency. They were also, as a rule, resounding successes in their chosen professions, in the sense of attaining both key professional positions and great wealth:

Harvard graduates in medicine comprised a third of the physicians in Boston as of mid-century as well as 68 percent of the officers of the Massachusetts Medical Society and 95 percent of the Massachusetts General Hospital doctors through 1851.

Harvard graduates in law comprised half the Boston attorneys in 1850 and also contributed some sixty judges to federal and higher state courts.

Harvard graduates in business sometimes became small proprietors and sometimes industrial chemists, mill managers, railroad superintendents, or municipal engineers. Increasingly, however, they ran important financial and industrial enterprises. They thus comprised some 38 percent of the directors of leading textile mills before 1845; but 43 percent by 1870. They comprised 25 percent of the directors of the major Boston financial institutions from 1815 to 1830; but 33 percent from 1831 to 1860.

Harvard graduates in 1833 comprised 23 percent of the Bostonians with a city tax assessment of $250,000 or more. In 1848, however, they comprised 33 percent of such Bostonians; and by 1850, 42 percent.[27]

The career trajectories and attainments of Harvard graduates conform closely, of course, to those of the university's patrons, Fellows, and faculty, who also came increasingly from Boston business families, pursued increasingly secular and business-oriented careers, lived in increasingly affluent styles, and possessed increasingly large estates. The epithet "Unitarian aristocracy" underscored the conformity: as of mid-century perhaps three-fourths of the student body was Unitarian, with Episcopalians a distant second. So, apparently, with politics: in 1860, graduating seniors preferred the Republican ticket over the Democratic by a seven to one margin, with Constitutional Unionism running second.[28]

Not all wealthy families sent their sons to Harvard, and some who did sent only those who seemed unusually studious or especially inclined to medicine or the law.[29] The Harvard experience was not a prerequisite even for future directors of large-scale enterprises. Still, it seems clear that a Harvard education was becoming a common step in the preparation of elite progeny for life, as important in its way as capital resources. A shipper and railroad promoter thus advised a friend in 1848 to "salt down 25 to 50,000 $ in a safe place for the children — so that come what may their college education and a fair start in life will be made sure."[30] An investment banker recalled that after he had graduated from Harvard in 1846, taken a degree at the law school in 1848, and passed the bar examination a year later, his father invited him to join his brokerage firm "to see what trade, commerce, banking, insurance, &c., were . . . and also to know the business community." He never returned to the law. "I sometimes suspect that my father always had this plan in view for me, when my college and legal studies should end."[31]

All the evidence, then, points to the four decades from 1815 to 1855 as the era when parents, in Henry Adams's words, began "sending their children to Harvard College for the sake of its social advantages."[32] It was the confluence of patrons, Fellows, faculty and students after 1830, moreover, that made Harvard a "social extension" of the elite family and Boston society a "leech" on Harvard students. In fact, it was probably less a leech than a magnet which simply drew its sons, like so many iron filings, home for the weekend. But in any case it was over these decades that the university's facilities and benefits, like its governing board and instructional staff, became the near-monopolistic preserve of the Boston elite. Interestingly enough, the last Harvard president without a sizeable estate was Thomas Hill, a minister and mathematician whose tenure from 1862 to 1869 was considered ineffectual in large part because he could not relate to the "polished Boston society" of his students and their families.[33] Hill's eminent successor, not coincidentally, was the very paragon of Brahminism, Charles W. Eliot.

As already suggested, there was some criticism of Harvard's "aristocratic" exclusiveness, particularly after 1820 when the pattern became more visible and pronounced. Finding themselves thus on the defensive, university officers sought to explain the development mainly by reference to the religious bigotry which led Orthodox Congregationalists to keep their sons away from Harvard. They stressed, too, the establishment of other colleges in which young men now matriculated — Williams, Bowdoin, Amherst, and Brown as well as Yale. But while these explanations were valid to a point, neither really satisfied the critics, who were also, it will be recalled, busily criticizing the exclusiveness and elitism of other components of the new cultural constellation of the metropolis and would soon, in fact, push their attacks on Harvard itself to the brink of political and institutional war.

With regard to the matter of exclusiveness and Harvard officials' defense of it, the critics argued that Harvard's liberal ambience in fact reflected the growing preponderance of Boston's Unitarian elite at the college; and that although many boys did attend other "seminaries," they often did so because they could not gain admission to Harvard, whose facilities and advantages were far superior to those of any of its competitors, Yale included. Critics chose rather to stress two other factors which seemed a good deal more relevant. The first was rising costs; the second, rising admission requirements. Together, they appeared more than adequate to explain the new tendencies in Cambridge.

As to the cost of a Harvard education, a variety of literary and other evidence confirms that expenses were indeed moving steadily upward. As early as 1831 critics complained that "the expenses of an education at Cambridge are greater than are necessary," and in 1845 a Democrat charged:

> The expenses of tuition have been increased at least 50 per cent beyond what they formerly were; and for some of the classes 33 and a third per cent beyond what they were when I was a student [in 1817]. Yet the College has all the time been growing more opulent. The charge for tuition is greater in Cambridge than at those institutions where there are no endowments.[34]

The point was well taken. Not only did tuition proper rise from $20 in 1807 to $75 in 1845 to $104 in 1860 — as compared to, say, Yale, where tuition rose from $24 to $39 over the same period — but overall expenses, to which critics generally referred, also increased.[35] University officials placed the minimum cost of a year as a Harvard undergraduate at $176 in 1825, $185 in 1835, and $249 in 1860, a rate of increase not altogether immodest but still much higher than the rate of inflation.[36]

Actually, the minimum costs were probably substantially higher than this. In 1837, for example, a youth wrote to industrialist Amos Lawrence:

> The expense of an education at Cambridge is much greater than is generally supposed; and far exceeds your estimate. Those who are concerned in the government of the University, have ever

represented the *necessary* expenses as less than they really are. Mother has made many inquiries of students, and has taken great care to obtain correct information. But few indigent students have gone . . . to Cambridge, most of them being obliged to enter at some college where they can live more cheaply.[37]

In 1854 a student from New York wrote that tuition aside, "travelling expenses, furnishing the room, etc., though all extravagance was avoided, have required more than we anticipated."[38] "The expense of education at Harvard College," observed a knowledgeable Englishman in 1861, "is not much lower than at [Oxford and Cambridge]. The actual authorized expenditure in accordance with the rules is only 50£ per annum, i.e. 249 dollars; but this does not, by any means, include everything."[39] Though impossible to estimate precisely, the true minimum cost of a year at Harvard may have risen from about $150 in the early 1800s to about $400 by the outbreak of the war.

"The cause of education, of good morals, of sound learning," wrote a critic in 1848, "demand that the expenses . . . should be greatly reduced and brought as low as possible."[40] But in consequence of the rising real costs, even the "well-born" in practice sometimes had difficulty entering Harvard. Poor relations begged funds from their affluent cousins; sons of men in sudden financial straits turned elsewhere or simply did not enter college.[41] In *The Barclays of Boston*, a society novel written by Mrs. Harrison Gray Otis in the mid-1850s, the son of the heroine, Emma Sanderson, was "filled with an ardent desire to go to Cambridge." Unhappily, the widowed Emma was "unable to meet the expenses attendant on a college life."[42]

Basically, of course, expense was as much a question of living standards as of survival, and as we have seen, the standard of living had been rising at Harvard since the turn of the century. Average expenses were, in fact, significantly higher than the minimum estimates and rose equally, if not more, rapidly.[43] Table 13 provides a rough approximation of the increase of average total costs as compared to other types of cost.

Significantly, the average did not rise so precipitously simply because of the inordinate extravagance of a few students, al-

Table 13. Cost of Undergraduate Education, Harvard, 1810–1860

	1810	1835	1860
Tuition	$20	$55	$104
Official minimum costs	n.a.	185	249
Real minimum costs (est.)	150	300	400
Average costs	225	400	700

Source: See notes 35–43.

though expenditures of $2,000 a year were not uncommon by the 1860s. Rather, it rose because a far greater proportion of the students — certainly a considerable majority — spent relatively large sums. The average was more than a mere average. It was also a standard.

By 1840 this newly-fashionable lifestyle was changing the composition of the student body in the same way as minimum costs. "The habits of economy," wrote a critic in 1845, "are affected by the character of the collective body of the pupils. As expenses increase, the sons of the less affluent begin to remain away, and the absence of their influence aggravates the tendency to expensive gratifications."[44] A faculty member noted at the same time that a "standard of expense, in regard to dress, pocket-money, furniture, etc., has been established which renders it almost a hopeless matter for a young man of slender means to obtain an education there."[45] For as an Overseer committee observed a few years later:

> Parents will not, as a general thing, expose their sons to the severe test of sending them to a place where they may possibly meet expenses which are absolutely necessary, but where they will be unable to conform to the common mode of living of the community with which they associate. Such a trial is beyond the strength of most young men of the age at which they usually enter college.[46]

On top of all this, very little scholarship aid was available except of the kind privately extended by the wealthy to impecunious supplicants or kinsmen. Only two of the thirty-four large-scale private bequests to Harvard from 1800 to 1850 were for undergraduate assistance, and the first of these did not accrue

until 1839. Some scholarships did exist, including a few surviving fellowships for boys from designated towns — Henry
Thoreau got one from Concord — and a small grant from the
state. Yet in 1831 only 34 Harvard students received aid as
opposed, for example, to 144 at Yale in that year or to 50 percent
of all Harvard students in the early eighteenth century. In 1851
President Jared Sparks told an inquirer that a good student
might, at best, receive $50 a year outright and an equal sum on
loan. After 1826, moreover, the university reduced the length of
its winter vacation, making it more difficult for needy students
to earn money teaching school.[47]

During the 1850s several aid funds were established in response to political pressure and faculty grumbling over the
caliber of academic performance. By the 1860s Harvard offered
some thirty scholarships worth from $100 to $300 a year, plus
grants and loans of $20 to $80 a year for about fifty students.
Perhaps 20 percent of the students received aid by 1870, although almost never enough to cover all their expenses.[48] But
the fact remained that an exceptionally high proportion of those
who attended antebellum Harvard paid their own way. That
they paid ever more dearly helps to explain the increasing monopolization of the college by the Boston elite.

Expenses were not the only problem, however, for in the eyes of
the critics the college admissions requirements were rising so
rapidly as to have a deleterious effect as well. And again the
contention seems to have had merit. Certainly the requirements
were steadily increasing. In 1818 President Kirkland wrote that
improved schools were producing students who were better prepared in mathematics and the classics. As of 1826 a boy versed in
the fundamentals of English and arithmetic needed perhaps a
year's extra labor in the classics in order to pass the still casual
admission examination. In the early 1830s, however, candidates
began to fail the examination in significant numbers; others were
accepted "conditionally." By the 1840s Harvard's admission requirements were much the highest in New England, necessitat-

ing from two-and-a-half to four years of preparation. In 1845 the
list of classical readings was longer than in 1835; by 1855 it
contained samplings of geography and history. In 1850 the qual-
ifying examination was eight hours long. By 1865 the requirements, though still in the main traditional, were also still much
the stiffest in New England. The examination now took three
days to administer, and "no one could be certain of getting
through."[49]

These higher requirements were undoubtedly one factor in
raising the average age of entering Harvard students from
roughly fifteen and a half in 1810 to seventeen and a half in
1850.[50] But they also seemed to affect the social composition of
the student body, so that an observer in 1845 questioned the
notion "that higher qualifications should be the requirement of
admission." Such requirements could "easily be made a part of
instruction in the excellent public school in Boston and in some
few Academies and private schools." They could not, however,
be made "general" and would therefore "shut the doors of Harvard College still more effectually against almost all but the sons
of residents in Boston and a few favored places."[51]

Since the American upper-class preparatory school system is
usually thought of as a late–nineteenth century phenomenon, it
is interesting to note that antebellum New Englanders believed
they could discern the rudiments, at least, of such a system
around them, particularly in connection with Harvard. An undergraduate of the mid-1830s observed that the stricter requirements favored boys from "the Public Latin Schools of Boston
and Salem, the academies of Exeter and Andover, and the famous Round-Hill School at Northampton."[52] A rural student
who entered in the 1840s recalled: "A lad thus partially trained
must enter college badly handicapped in a company of
classmates thoroughly drilled in such schools as the Boston
Latin, Andover, Exeter and the large private fitting schools of
cities."[53] A writer from the 1850s remarked on "the clannish
body from the great schools, — Exeter, Andover, Dixwell's,
Boston and Roxbury Latin."[54]

The surviving evidence seems to support observers who saw a

drift towards the Boston area in the preparation of Harvard students (table 14).[55]

Table 14: Educational Preparation of Harvard Undergraduates, 1801–1870

	1801–1820	1846–1870
	(percent)	
Rural academies	35	30
Private boarding schools	20	2
Private tutors	20	16
Public schools	15	31
Private day schools	10	21

Source: Classbooks and annals of the Harvard classes of 1811, 1814, 1817, 1822, 1830, 1835, 1841, 1844, 1852, 1856, 1857, and 1860. Supplementary sources are listed in note 55. Only about 40% of the earlier classes could be traced, and only about 60% of the latter.

The rural academies, private boarding schools, and private tutors that had provided two-thirds of the early Harvard students were in fact located predominantly in the New England hinterlands, where the local minister, preparing boys individually or in groups in order to supplement his income or as a favor to the inhabitants of the town, was generally in charge. By mid-century these types of arrangement had lost ground to the day schools and public high schools, both located mainly at this time in the Boston or North Shore areas. The academies now consisted chiefly of two institutions, Phillips Exeter and Phillips Andover; the private boarding schools now survived almost solely in a new guise, the Episcopal boarding school. Even the tutors, who still prepared a sizeable proportion of all Harvardians, included large numbers of live-in companions of Boston families.

Analysis of the dozen institutions sending fifty or more boys to Harvard from 1801 to 1870 sharpens the impression (table 15).[56] Of these institutions, six — the Boston Latin and Cambridge High Schools, the Dixwell and Noble Schools in Boston, the Wells School in Cambridge, the Ingraham School in Brookline — were in or near Boston. One — the Salem Latin (later High) School — was in the North Shore area; two

Table 15: Schools Preparing Students for Harvard, 1801–1870

	Active Years	Number of Students Sent to Harvard (approx.)
Boston Latin School	1801–70	750
Phillips Exeter Academy	1801–70	550
Phillips Andover Academy	1801–70	250
Cambridge High School	1820–70	100
Salem High School	1820–70	75
Dixwell School	1851–70	75
Round Hill School	1823–34	50
Wells School	1824–35	50
Milton Academy	1807–60	50
Lawrence Academy	1801–70	50
Ingraham School	1820–50	50
Noble School	1860–70	50

Source: Computed from sources listed in note 56.

others — the Phillips Academy in Andover and the Milton Academy — were within thirty miles of Boston. Together, these nine institutions accounted for some two-fifths of the Harvard freshmen from New England before 1870. (Two of the important "feeder" schools — Round Hill of Northampton and the Lawrence Academy — were in small-town Massachusetts; the last — Phillips Exeter — was in rural New Hampshire.) By the 1850s just two Boston schools — Dixwell's and the Boston Latin — contributed approximately one-fourth of the incoming Harvard classes.

The cost of this preparatory education varied so widely from one decade or type of school to the next that generalizations are difficult. Public schools such as the Boston Latin were tuition-free, as was the private Roxbury Latin School, which supplied perhaps twenty-five boys to Harvard in this era. Among the private boarding schools, costs ranged from $300 charged by Round Hill to perhaps half that for the Wells School to some $50 a year or less for the ministerial schools; in 1865 the new Episcopal schools such as St. Paul's and St. Mark's charged $500. The cheapest of the private Boston day schools cost $80 for the "classical track" in 1835 and $100 in 1855; Dixwell's probably charged around $250 in 1855. Among the academies the two

Phillips schools, which assessed a boarder something like $60 as of 1820, were often cheaper in the early years than other academies, which generally required $80 to $100 a year. But by the 1850s both Exeter and Andover charged a minimum of about $150. A ministerial tutor in 1810 might charge little or nothing; a Boston tutor by 1850 sometimes asked as much as $500.[57]

For all the variety, however, the broad trend is clear: preparatory schools steadily evolved in this period from the transient, the amateur, and the modest to the permanent, the professional, and the luxurious — and from the relatively cheap to the relatively expensive. The public high schools, to be sure, constituted a countervailing current of sorts. But in the mid-nineteenth century these schools, although free, served mainly the progeny of local elites.[58] Thus the Boston Latin was a "select school, principally . . . for the rich and exclusive," and its graduates seemed, like those from Exeter and Dixwell's, "to touch the appreciation of the Harvard examining board a little more deftly than applicants from any other place."[59] In any event the best high schools, especially those with adequate Latin departments, were in or near Boston, like most of their private counterparts.

As table 16 makes clear, it was actually the combination of expense and location that was crucial.

Table 16: Educational Preparation of Harvard Undergraduates, 1801–1865, by Cost and Location

Harvard students from	1801–15	1820–45 (percent)	1850–65
Boston area schools	40	55	65
Schools charging $150 per year or more	0	10	45
Schools from Boston area or charging $150 per year or both	40	60	75

Observers were right, then, in protesting that the stiffer Harvard admission requirements favored Boston-area students. They were right, too, in suggesting that cost was a factor, particularly since the years needed to prepare for the examination were steadily increasing. Ultimately, just three schools — the Boston

Latin, Dixwell's, and Exeter — were supplying 40 percent of all Harvard freshmen. One of these took only Boston boys; the other two, only prosperous ones.

Did Harvard deliberately adopt policies, as critics sometimes insinuated, which excluded the provincial and the poor? Was there the same kind of "covert elitism" here that scholars have found in politics?[60] While the question touches upon difficult matters of intent and motivation which are treated in chapter 7 as well, it may be noted that over the years the administration spent its high tuition fees and lavish endowment funds for such things as the improvement of plant and better salaries for more instructors. It raised entrance requirements, moreover, to improve the quality of incoming students. High tuition and high requirements thus had the seemingly unexceptionable aim of enhancing the quality of student life and instruction. In practice, however, these trends tended by their very nature to improve the situation of a small number of students who came, as critics and defenders alike acknowledged, increasingly from the Boston elite.

The fact that costs and requirements began to rise just as Boston lawyers and businessmen gained administrative power at Harvard doubtless made the situation seem even more vaguely collusive. University patrons and officials, for example, endowed or supervised many parts of the preparatory network — the Boston Latin, Cambridge High, Exeter, Dixwell's, Roxbury Latin, Milton, Lawrence, Round Hill, and Wells, among others. Having made arrangements for their own sons and those of other members of the elite, they could presumably raise requirements with relative personal impunity and then later shape school offerings to match new university requirements, which they also determined. As to costs, wealthy alumni held several meetings in the 1830s precisely over whether to raise large sums of scholarship money in order to diminish the expense of a Harvard education. In every case they rejected the proposal by margins of five to one or more.[61]

The high schools and remaining academies and ministerial

tutors still produced a small stream of deserving but often impecunious boys, some of whom subsequently benefited from scholarship assistance at Cambridge. Yet for the 70 percent who were neither public school graduates nor charity students, the cost of a Harvard degree — three years of preparation and four of residence — was about $2,000, a handsome sum for the time. Charles Francis Adams had remarked as early as 1823 that while men were *"born* free and equal," it was "nonsense to say that they are so educated." By 1846 Theodore Parker was quite bitter about it:

> The poor man's son, however well-born, struggling for a superior education, obtains his culture at a monstrous cost; with the sacrifice of pleasure, comfort, the joys of youth, often of eyesight and health . . . The rich man's son needs not that terrible trial. He learns from his circumstances, not his soul. The air about him contains a diffused element of thought. He learns without knowing it. . . . All the outward means of educating, refining, elevating a child, are to be had for money, and money alone.[62]

In 1867 James Cabot could say with droll understatement, "To be the son of rich parents considerably increases the chance of being sent to Harvard,"[63] for by then the university was essentially what George Santayana called it, "The seminary and academy for the inner circle of Bostonians."[64]

Preparation, expense, and style constituted a three-tiered exclusionary system which encroached steadily after 1800 on the traditional accessibility of the most prominent of the antebellum cultural institutions. The elite thus came to monopolize Harvard University as it monopolized the Boston Athenaeum — at the level of use as well as funding, administration, and control. The process of monopolizing the student body was part and parcel of the process of growth: the more exclusively elite the student body, the more deserving the university of elite largesse; the richer the university, the more attractive to rich parents; and so forth. Similarly with the concern for adequate professors and a competent and representative governing board: gentility required gentility, and the Corporation had to manage the sons as well as the dollars of the elite.

It would not do to insist too strenuously upon the absolute exclusiveness of mid-century Harvard. Boys still came from the hinterlands with slender funds and scant pedigree, as the figures on family residence and wealth show. There was undoubtedly a liberal measure of cooptation operating in Cambridge at the collegiate level just as there was at the level of the Corporation and faculty, where new elements, both financial and cultural, were absorbed into the elite mainstream by virtue of their institutional presence and activities. Thus, Francis E. Parker, the son of a rural minister, graduated as first scholar in the class of 1841, became a millionaire Boston lawyer, and served on many institutional boards, including those of Harvard and the Athenaeum. Francis J. Child, to cite another instance, was the son of a poor tradesman but obtained private help, took first honors in 1846, and went on to become a famous and well-connected member of the Harvard faculty.[65] Absorption and cooptation were as crucial to the formation and persistence of the Boston upper class as of any other, and one of its great strengths lay precisely in the absorptive capacity of its institutional framework.

This said, however, the exclusionary trend remains the indubitably salient feature of university development in this era.[66] Moreover, for all its broader community services, the social functions of elite culture seem increasingly to have been internal and exclusive in, as it were, the Athenaeum manner. It involved the shaping of a restricted upper-class constituency on the one hand and the denial of traditional access and heterogeneity on the other. That the development occurred at Harvard in the face of such long traditions, clear constitutional obligation, and intense criticism bespeaks, among other things, the sheer intensity of the instinct for institutional creation and control within the emergent elite.

Harvard Students and the Class Ideal

THE transformation of the Harvard student body bore directly on the origins of many of the university policies and trends already discussed. The numerous efforts to bring students closer to professors were prompted and facilitated in part by the fact that students and professors came increasingly from the same social circles. The proliferation of courses and teaching techniques similarly derived partly from the desire of elite parents to secure an advantageous education for their sons. The subtle (and at times less than subtle) constraints on faculty expression reflected a concern with the uniformity and soundness of elite principles. The restriction of admissions showed a concern with the engrossment of cultural opportunities; and the control of the Corporation by secular nonresidents, an equal concern with a style of management attuned to a changing university constituency.

The presence of the new student body seems, moreover, to have led to the emergence of a distinctive mode of behavior and expression. Produced partly by spontaneous elite tastes and aspirations and partly by deliberate policy, this style consisted of numerous elements — a blend of beauty and refinement, vigor and discipline, separateness and unity — which, taken together, were exceptional as to both time and place. Commentaries on various manifestations of this style are not rare, particularly from the pens of the many authorities on "genteel" life and letters.[1] Some fresh description of its development and chief features may nonetheless be warranted if only for the purposes of highlighting neglected aspects of the style, pointing up the degree to which it constituted a response to both negative and positive reference groups, and underscoring its institutional dimensions, notably those bearing on the evolution of Harvard. Description should also serve the social historian on two further matters of some urgency: first, for its clarification of the actual long-term social functions of the exclusive, internally oriented cultural institutions of antebellum Boston; and second, as an indicator of the degree of purposeful action involved in the unfolding of these institutions and functions — the degree, in other words, to which the elite march to class stature was willful rather than willy-nilly.

Perhaps the most noticeable single aspect of the new Harvard style was the quest for refinement, a reflection of the preoccupation of the university community with cultivation and polish. "The manners, polish & neatness of the Gentleman," wrote a Harvard mother in 1821, "are acquisitions, I highly prize, as I have no doubt you do, because you must see what a passport they are, to win the favor of all classes wherever you go."[2] A father advised his son in 1829, "You may depend upon it, manners are highly important in your intercourse with the world."[3] By the 1830s a student's "polished manner" was his pride, and those desiring to live like "gentlemen" grew to value form almost as much as substance.[4] In 1846 President Edward Everett thought it appropriate to applaud, among other things, the "elevated tone" of Harvard manners and conduct.[5]

The quest for refinement was a leitmotif of the antebellum years. President Quincy, with his belief in the importance of "society" for young men, inaugurated a fortnightly "levée" at the president's house where students could mix with faculty and with Boston "ladies and gentlemen." These decorous "entertainments" with their music and refreshments provided up to the eve of the war a setting for "a company of young people rarely excelled in ease and refinement, beauty and wit."[6] Quincy also upgraded and renovated the "commons" dining service with imported china and silver embossed with the college arms, raising funds for the purpose from "liberal Boston gentlemen." These arrangements, too, continued until mid-century, when the more affluent students began to board (with Corporation permission) at private tables or clubrooms in Cambridge, leaving the declining "commons" to a remnant of impecunious students.[7]

Quincy and other sponsors of student social events valued

them for, among other things, the presence of "young ladies" — a "cultivated and refined female society [which would] improve the manners, enlarge the ideas, and elevate the morals of the students," who might otherwise be as segregated from feminine gentility as were the students of other American colleges.[8] A love of "good female society," wrote a Harvard parent, was a fine "corrective to many dangerous associations and tendencies."[9]

Also important, interestingly enough, was the presence of wine, a reasonable familiarity with which was considered gentlemanly. In the late 1840s President Edward Everett, under the influence of the temperance movement, banned alcohol from university events. He wrote, however, that "nothing that I did caused greater offence, or shook my influence more in the Corporation," and the ban did not survive long or extend far.

> Class Day — I got up and went to breakfast at 7 o'clock — Fixed up my room & loafed generally till 10 when I breakfasted again at Lyon's oyster saloon. . . . Ate and drank at all the "spreads". . . . In the evening Nick, Billy Milton & I had a supper at Parker's. I ate and drank so much that I had to relieve myself by inserting my fingers in my throat till my stomach came up.[10]

As students became older and more affluent, drinking — though not perhaps on this herculean scale — became de rigueur once more.

Student dress, like student dining arrangements, went through two phases. The first followed upon a regulation promulgated in the 1820s requiring all undergraduates to wear a "black-mixed" suit (coat, pantaloons, waistcoat, tie, hat, shoes, and buttons of prescribed color) purchasable for about $15 to $25. Designed to standardize and elevate student attire and to differentiate Harvard students from non-Harvardians, the regulation remained in effect until the 1840s, when it finally fell victim to the greater dictates of elite fashion. By mid-century the typical Harvard man sported a top hat and cane as well as elegant boots, coat, and gloves, with a merely suitable wardrobe costing perhaps $150 a year. The highest praise President Quincy found himself able to bestow on the graduating class of 1845 was to call it "the best-dressed" he had ever seen.[11]

Habits of grooming and hygiene also changed, though probably less drastically than dress. In this period, for example, came a new university bathhouse on the Charles River and also more servant-drawn tubs in the dormitory rooms, so that students were able to bathe more frequently than in the previous century, no doubt in order to meet the expectations of their new "society" circles and perhaps also to differentiate themselves more sharply from the as yet literally unwashed masses gathering everywhere around them.[12] With the Quincy regime of the 1830s, moreover, came a brusque disapproval, for students, of the "silly" beards and "mustachios" which were increasingly adorning the era's "agitators." Facial hair could bar "any young man from employment on State Street" and was thus singularly inappropriate for Harvard men — a judgment lasting until the war experience transformed such fashions.[13]

Speech and expression received particular attention. Before 1810 John Quincy Adams labored as professor of rhetoric to eliminate "rustic" idioms and pronunciation from the Harvard scene. President Kirkland encouraged the use of "polished language, and courtly address."[14] In 1811 graduates began to deliver English as well as Latin orations; in 1818 the faculty first awarded prizes in elocution; English declamations and forensics appeared in the early 1820s.[15] By now a recognizable "College pronunciation" was taking shape, facilitated no doubt by the growing homogenization of the student body but encouraged by special lectures on proper enunciation and delivery.[16]

Edward Channing, a professor of rhetoric after 1819, was probably the individual who most influenced student speech. Channing abhorred the "slang" and "tawdry expression" of American speech and the "false excitement" of American oratory, with its "vulgarisms, coarseness, slang words and phrases, [and] colloquialisms that would not pass current among people of refined taste." Channing insisted rather on what he termed a "purity and simplicity in the English style" that by mid-century was thought to "characterize in a remarkable degree the speaking

and writing of those who have been educated at Harvard."[17] To
the influence of Channing and such colleagues as Edward
Everett and Cornelius Felton has been imputed the development
of a "classic New England diction — the measured, dignified
speech, careful enunciation, precise choice of words, and well-
modulated voice" long associated with the Brahmin upper
class.[18]

Nathaniel Bowditch's gruff disdain notwithstanding, refinement for Harvardians meant not just elegance and cultivation
but an appreciation of the natural beauty of landscape. Between
1815 and 1820 the Corporation spent substantial sums on trees,
shrubs, flowers, and lawns in Cambridge, implementing what
amounted to the first significant university landscaping effort.
More trees were planted in the 1830s.[19] After 1835 Harvard also
owned a plot in the Mount Auburn Cemetery for the use of
members of its staff without plots of their own there. Indeed, the
ties between the two institutions were extraordinarily close.
Mount Auburn's beauty, tranquillity, and nearness to the college made it a favorite, and a warmly approved, resort for the
walkers and wooers of the university community. From its
grounds, to the great satisfaction of cemetery directors such as
Professors Joseph Story and Jacob Bigelow, one could see the
spires of Harvard buildings above the trees and thus combine
love of nature with institutional reverence.[20] Nature's balm and
the beauty of the sepulture soon made Mount Auburn a "fashionable promenade" for Bostonians who invariably linked it to its
neighbor. As a financier wrote to a Salem friend in 1848:

> I always persuaded myself that when H. is old enough for Col-
> lege you will take a place here and besides a little patch of Mt.
> Auburn for yourself and your's in the neighborhood of our's. . . .
> The thought of an everlasting home for one's dust in a beautiful
> spot near to one's friends . . . presents the dark future with rather
> a pleasing aspect.[21]

Significantly, a member of the class of 1814, listing major
changes which had occurred between then and 1861, balanced
the disappearance of "charity scholars" against the addition of

"quadrangle trees," the "fence around the Yard," and the Mount Auburn Cemetery.[22]

But the love for landscape was to be accompanied by a comparable love for books. This was a wholly logical development, given the "extravagant bibliomania" which prevailed in early nineteenth-century New England, where, as in England, the library was an important token of cultural attainment and family stability for professionals, scholars, politicians, and businessmen alike. Among the Harvard Fellows, for example, Christopher Gore's luxurious country seat contained a large double-storied library as one of its principal rooms. Charles Lowell and his nephew, John Lowell, Jr., both acquired fine libraries soon after their initial career successes. The library of Nathaniel Bowditch was the centerpiece of his Otis Place dwelling. At Bowditch's death in 1838 his sons hoped that "the house and library might remain just as . . . now . . . to remind us of times past." When Samuel A. Eliot lost money in the panic of 1857, friends were "especially distressed at the thought that Mr. Eliot would be compelled to lose his library" and raised a fund to save it for him. Professor Oliver Wendell Holmes stated, finally, that "above all things" the genteel man "should have tumbled about in a library" as a child: "He is at home wherever he smells the invigorating fragrance of Russian leather. No self-made man feels so." Encouraged by a thousand missives to read deeply and sample the wares of both Athenaeum and Harvard, the good student thus sought a bookish as well as a pastoral polish.[23]

The quest for refinement and beauty always had boundaries conforming to the prevailing patterns of nineteenth-century sexual assertiveness and competitive fitness. Just as young men should not drink repeatedly to excess, so they should not become "gloved and lisping dandies" or possess the "perfumed curls," the "slender waists," and the "tiny legs" of "D'Israeli" and the Young Englanders. If they could not be exactly "robust as a farmer's son," neither should they be "whey-faced and feeble, effeminate and fearful."[24]

One antidote to these extremes lay, of course, in physical exercise and sporting events, which were first systematically encouraged and popularized in the antebellum era. President Kirkland hired a fencing instructor in the 1820s and urged student attendance at the "salle d'armes," while other university officers introduced regular instruction in gymnastics. By 1840 many students rode for exercise, either hiring horses from local stables or stabling their own mounts there. By 1850 cricket, baseball, and a crude version of rugby were familiar Cambridge pastimes.[25] During the 1850s the Corporation built a new gymnasium and also welcomed the adoption of crew as a suitably vigorous and masculine student activity. Even this rudimentary athletic program, to be sure, exhibited a touch of refinement, with cricket, rugby, and crew favored partly for their English origins and crew, riding, and fencing requiring a level of expenditure and spare time well beyond the means of most New Englanders. But the new sports were considered an essential complement to the overall regimen of refinement. Mid-century crew members were "not over-mindful if their collars flared a bit in front, and disclosed their well-tanned, muscular throats."[26]

Another antidote to lassitude and indulgence was a new system of student discipline designed to inculcate "a sense of honor and self-respect, which should make severity of discipline unnecessary."[27] The first important change in this area came in the 1820s, appropriately enough, when the ancient but crude system of fines, which even students considered a painless, pointless mulct with little deterrent or punishment value, was replaced with a more complex system of private communications ranging, in point of severity, from preliminary caution to warning to admonition to parental notification. A second change then came with the Corporation's threat in the 1830s to meet student disruption with civil lawsuits rather than wholesale banishment, or "rustication," a procedure long criticized for removing students from the Harvard environment and thereby defeating its own purpose.[28] Both steps were entirely congenial to the "financial" administration and its patrons.

The university thus discarded fines as nugatory and banishments as counterproductive, and replaced them with more flexible but also more severe procedures for eliciting, or compelling, individual responsibility and self-control among students. The procedures also promoted greater family participation in the process of college governance, as they were doubtless intended to do, and in fact parents, rising to the occasion, increasingly urged their sons to "feel the responsibility of your position, and the discipline it requires."[29] Mass student disorders did in fact largely cease during the 1830s, as has been noted. While the main reason for this was no doubt structural, reflecting both the greater intellectual and social opportunities and demands of the era and also the changing composition of faculty and student body, the new disciplinary measures were presumably a factor as well.[30] The emphasis on self-control in any case accorded quite well with the cult of the temperate in the pursuit of refinement and vigor.

The final elements in the new Harvard style involved the sequestration of the students on the one hand and the forging of a greater unity among them on the other. The process of sequestration began in 1811 when the Kirkland administration erected Holworthy Hall, the first college edifice which did not open onto the Cambridge Common and the first to anticipate the formation of a quadrangular college "yard." President Quincy later enclosed — in fact, created — "The Yard" with a belt of trees and "expensive fences." The fences were augmented in the 1840s, and succeeding administrations continued to discuss ways to fully circumscribe the campus until President Eliot finally accomplished it once and for all with brick walls and iron gates after 1870.[31]

Kirkland, meanwhile, had established a separate college church where members of the university community alone were permitted to worship and where they were in fact expected to worship. Indeed, antebellum administrations did not welcome student requests to attend nonuniversity services, especially if the ministers espoused radical doctrines or had lower-class con-

gregations, as was increasingly the case in Cambridge. The use
of the college library was similarly curtailed, with access becoming freer for students but rare for unaffiliated Harvard graduates
and rarer still for nongraduates.[32]

Lastly, Quincy and Joseph Story labored successfully to close
the nearby Cambridge Common to the local stock drovers who
had traditionally used it, and to bar the "by no means quiet and
orderly" local Negroes from the premises during Commencement Day weekend — Quincy's actions here resembling his
early efforts to clear the Beacon Hill slopes of "disreputable"
elements.[33]

Together with this trend toward separateness went an equally
strong trend toward unity. Particularly after 1820 the sense of
closeness, "the strong, centralized feeling, as of many members
of one body," was evoked by graduates, who remembered the
"college atmosphere and the close contact with a generation of
generous young fellows" teaching each other "what was not
learned from books."[34] In 1849 a faculty member described the
typical Harvardian as

> one of a great family, who have gone forth from her instruction,
> and borne manfully the honorable burdens of life. He is bound to
> them and to her by a thousand ties, which nothing in after-years
> can break. He and they may be rivals in business, struggling hand
> in hand in the competition for wealth; but, when they meet . . .
> they are indeed on common ground, with common tastes, feel-
> ings, and hopes.[35]

President Jared Sparks that same year expounded the goal of
considering students not as individuals or groups but "collec-
tively" in circumstances where "friendships are formed, ties are
cemented" that would "endure and rise above the vicissitudes of
life and defy the power of change."[36]

The extent of genuine student togetherness ought not to be
overstated. Students obviously formed groups and sets based on
previous friendships, prep school attachments, residency, or
congeniality, and at times these developed into full-fledged
cliques, so that during the 1850s, for example, students or-

ganized new social clubs for the first time in a quarter-century. In 1857 the faculty, perhaps fearing such divisions and concerned with proper discipline, barred fraternities.[37]

Yet even where they existed, the voluntary associations were steadily diluted by the common experiences of classroom and recreation and seem not to have created real schism or weakened basic loyalties to the university or the student body as a whole. One basis for the development of early Harvard music, for instance, was "the natural desire on the part of students to sing and play *together*."[38] The retention of Latin and mathematics in the curriculum helped to preserve what men such as Sparks and Everett so valued, a "common intellectual culture." The regulations and, later, the habits of student dress and speech served to homogenize as well as to differentiate and refine. Sports such as crew fostered a "team-spirit," an intense feeling of "comradeship and reliance upon each other" that was to hold Harvardians together through life.[39]

The university's officers endeavored in various ways to extend this sense of collective loyalty to the larger elite as well. In 1810 President Kirkland delivered an inaugural address in English for the first time in order to facilitate public comprehension and involvement. In 1828 a number of supporters erected a monument to the college's seventeenth-century namesake, John Harvard, in tribute to an institution "safe, from the vicissitudes to which all else is subject" — or so it was hoped. The bicentennial celebration of 1836 witnessed a massive outpouring of organized sentiment and solidarity, including the composition of "Fair Harvard," which eventually became the school song.[40] The first published histories of the college — by Benjamin Peirce in 1833, Josiah Quincy in 1840, and Samuel A. Eliot in 1848 — now appeared, together with unusually long essays on these books, short histories in themselves, in the *North American Review* and other periodicals. The aims of the works were straightforward enough: Peirce's, for example, to touch "every son of Harvard University" with an appreciation of it as a "component member of the admirable fabric of our New England institutions"; Quincy's, to pay homage to the "merits, sufferings, and sacrifices of the founders, patrons, and officers of the university" in a work of "enlarged form and permanent character."[41]

The campaign for elite involvement was a great success, though the success clearly stemmed in part from the growing elite funding, control, and monopolization of the college. Between 1800 and 1850 Commencement became an even more important annual festival than it had been in colonial times, a day when banks closed and even non-Harvardians made their appearance in Cambridge. "Class Day" and the yearly reunion began in the 1820s; the first printed classbook appeared in 1822.[42] The occasions of commencement and reunion elicited especially deep emotion. In 1844 William H. Prescott recorded in his journal:

> Attended Commencement of Cambridge last Wednesday — when Will took his degree. . . . It is just 30 years since I quitted Alma Mater, and at the same period of life as his. May his destiny be as fortunate as mine. It is worth remembering that Will occupied the same room in old Hollis, which I occupied 30 years ago, and which his grandfather occupied about 30 years before me; three William Prescotts in three generations — and what is remarkable all alive to meet together in the same scenes of boyish recollections, — & did meet there on his having a part at Exhibition.[43]

Leverett Saltonstall wrote to his son, now at Harvard, that he loved to attend Commencement to see "friends whose connection is strengthened by an association for many years" in the "place of my Father's education."[44] Amos A. Lawrence stated in 1860, "My heart is with [Harvard]; whether right or wrong I shall stand by her; no differences of opinion, political or religious, can weaken the ties which bind me to her."[45]

The evolution of style thus came full circle. Students encountered Boston society in search of refinement: society itself became a part of the Harvard community. The preoccupation with style, it should be stressed, was never to become a substitute for intellectual diligence, at least not until very late in the nineteenth century. As already recounted, the academic work load increased steadily and markedly throughout the era, and parents as well as university officers fully appreciated its preparatory and disciplinary value. Moreover, the Corporation had long since committed itself to a regimen of efficiency in the conduct of university affairs, and its members were known upon occasion to inveigh, like Nathaniel Bowditch, against the dysfunctionalism of grace and polish even while tacitly encouraging them. Style was only an adjunct to learning and efficiency, as everyone presumably understood. It was an adjunct, however, of such extraordinary importance and with such an accelerating momentum of its own that the elite itself may have experienced occasional difficulty in maintaining the balanced perspective which proper style was supposed to supply.

The new student style consisted of a reasonably identifiable blend of tastes and accomplishments: an appreciation of cleanliness, grooming, and fashion; a facility with conversation, alcohol, and ladies; an acceptance of the virtues of nature as well as of books; a commingling of sophisticated excess with responsible self-control and worldly grace with physical vigor. This was almost precisely the bundle of stylistic attributes that would define the late nineteenth-century Brahmin aristocracy, and to a lesser degree the Victorian upper class generally, at least in its own eyes and often in those of its antagonists. It is intriguing, therefore, to see it develop almost programmatically in these early decades and interesting to speculate as to its provenience.

To some extent the quest for style clearly meant in reality a quest for distinctiveness. It represented the effort of one social group to distinguish itself from other groups. The very striving for "gentlemanly" qualities connoted a rejection of those without such qualities: the unwashed and the hirsute; the witless and the unfashionable; the unlettered and the inarticulate; the insensitive and the undisciplined; the irreverent, the emotional, the idiosyncratic. Hence the references of Channing, Quincy and others to the "vulgar," the "coarse," the "tawdry," and the "disorderly" and the continual acerbic disparagement of the "disreputable," "undesirable," or "contemptible."

It is possible, in fact, to estimate the identity of these negative groups with some modicum of precision. For example, John Lowell, an influential member of the Corporation from 1810 to 1822, wrote of the New England countryside in this arresting fashion:

> In our *country taverns*, you see the likenesses in terra cotta of the king and queen of France, held up to the admiration of the gazing clowns. We have all of us seen good paintings enough to despise *them*.[46]

The key to the passage is, of course, the floating antecedent of *"them,"* which may stand for the symbols of France — read "despotic corruption"; or for terra cotta figurines — read "plebeian vulgarity"; or for the gazing country clowns themselves — which, in view of Lowell's conservatism, might read "agrarian republicans" as well as "gawking dullards." The animadversions against "rustic" and "colloquial" speech patterns were aimed at rural elements, as was the campaign against the stock drovers in the 1830s. Given the decline of villagers among Harvard's patrons, governors, faculty, and students, the presence of such an attitude is hardly a surprise. It should be remembered, however, that the land itself was now a source of beauty and refinement, and bucolic horsemanship or rural boarding schools were tinged with gentility. The persistence of the rustic image as bad example and unfortunate influence; the tone of lofty disdain which accompanied it; the determination to erase any pastoral impropriety: all suggest that the aspersions being cast were, in fact, aimed at the rural poor, who thus began to serve as a negative elite reference group from a very early date.

But the literature also reveals a growing repetition of adjectives such as "drunken," "unkempt," and "vicious" (as in vice-ridden) which, while perhaps generally applicable, seem to be more urban than rural in connotation, to be rooted rather in the rapid growth of the metropolitan area and its unruly and impecunious population.[47] It was between 1810 and 1825, for example, when Cambridge was acquiring its first lower-class Baptist, Methodist, and Universalist congregations, that President Kirkland established a separate college church. In the 1830s appeared the first really severe town-gown conflicts, when armed Harvard students battled the area's lesser inhabitants, upon whom they were "wont to look with contempt" from behind their new buildings, fences, and trees.[48] Also in the 1830s came President Quincy's purge of Negro merchandisers from the Cambridge Common and his strictures against "bearded agitators" and their "democratic principles."

Faculty members sometimes dealt with the poor on a basis of charity rather than disdain, involving themselves in philanthropic ministrations to the "black and white" needy of the North End, as did Andrews Norton and Henry Ware, Jr., of the divinity school, or in medical care, as did the medical school instructors. Around the Yard meanwhile gathered sundry lower-class types — "old clothes" men, biscuit pedlars, Cambridge "urchins," "malodorous goodies" to tend student chambers, expressmen to transport student laundry — whom the students patronized with varying degrees of tolerant condescension and bemusement.[49]

During the 1840s, nonetheless, relations deteriorated. John C. Warren, professor of anatomy and large-scale university donor, warned increasingly against the "senseless cruelty of the masses," with their debased politics and corrupted morality.[50] Joseph Story and Henry Longfellow felt themselves beset in Cambridge by "suspicious individuals" and "incendiaries."[51] By 1850 Harvard parents were urging more stringent measures to segregate students from "townies"; by 1860 student altercations with "drunken Irish" and "niggers" were frequent.[52] The lower-class rural type thus gained an urban, and at times racial, counterpart. Together, these elements formed an ever more objectionable reference group, separation and differentiation from which became simultaneously more urgent for the preservation of elite esteem and safety and more crucial for the achievement of elite identity.

Important as these negative references were, there was considerably more to the evolution of the style than differentiation. There was also a positive side reflecting positive aspirations. It is clear, for instance, that Harvard graduates expected their education to provide them with "added capacities for pushing their way in the world" and with places to "effectually secure their own well-being."[53] A parent reminded his son in 1840, "You have [at Harvard], & it is a great satisfaction to me to furnish you with, the greatest advantages which our country affords."[54] A Boston lawyer, making a twenty-fifth anniversary survey of the class of 1811, did so unabashedly in terms of material success: "will be opulent," "will be rich," "a wealthy Merchant," "a rich man," "a thriving merchant," "rich," "prospering," and so forth.[55] The idea that "success in the world" tended to follow Harvard men was widespread and, as previously observed, well taken, especially since students increasingly possessed both financial and intellectual capital when they got to Cambridge.[56]

But the attractions of the Harvard experience involved considerations beyond sheer accumulation. While the survey of the class of 1811 dotes on prosperity, it also pays tribute to status — to the "respectable," the "eminent," the "learned," the "ornamental," the "celebrated," and the "reputable," whether genuinely wealthy or not.[57] The students themselves, doubtless reflecting the wishes of their families as well as their own desires, expressed comparable extramaterial values. A graduate of 1830 aspired to "a virtuous character, a high professional reputation, a handsome and independent property, and the pleasures of social life."[58] A senior some years later hoped to be "a merchant, not a plodding, narrow-minded one pent up in a city, with my mind always in my counting-room, but at the same time a literary man in some measure" with standing "among my fellow-men."[59] In 1850 an English traveler generalized from the Harvard-trained manager of a Manchester cotton mill:

Mr. E—— is one of an agreeable class of men in New England, who, like him, finish their education — spend a year or two in Europe in travelling — come home — marry — settle — and become first-rate men of business, uniting the energy of the trader with the polished manners of the gentleman.[60]

A novelist of the 1860s wrote that a member of Harvard College would not only "secure for himself the sure means of future preferment and honor" but see "society of the highest fashion and fortune open [its] doors to welcome him."[61]

University officers, too, took the broad view. Professor John Gorham Palfrey argued that Harvard offered its sons not only success but "intellectual and social enjoyment" and a "power of action" which would enable them to promote the interests of themselves and others.[62] President Quincy saw the university as a "nursery" of "well-taught, well-conducted, well-bred gentlemen, fit to take their share, gracefully and honorably, in public and private life."[63] Indeed, as Professor Francis Bowen attested, Harvardians were men "whose social position and early advantages have given them an influence, the magnitude and permanency of which the possessors themselves are hardly conscious."[64] Outside observers concurred. A journalist described the university as receiving annually "a herd of raw, half informed, half instructed boys" and returning "well informed, well bred men, useful members of society, if not, indeed, its leaders" — a view again rendered plausible by actual career trajectories.[65]

This elite anticipation of wealth, status, polish, and power fed naturally upon the desire of well-situated people to share in life's good things, and to do so in such a way as to exclude the undesirable and unworthy. But a larger ideal was also at work — namely, "the English tradition that a university student should be both a gentleman and a scholar."[66] In one sense this comes as no surprise. European travelers often described Boston as the most "English" of American cities and its higher circles as the most Anglophile of American elites. Also, the English example was plainly evident elsewhere in the cultural constellation: at the Athenaeum, for instance, which was modeled after "gentlemen's libraries" such as the Liverpool Athenaeum and the London Institution; and at the Lowell Institute, modeled partly after the University of London.[67] In another sense, however, the statement requires elaboration, for the immediate inspiration for such well-known innovations as the lecture system and the introduction of new subjects came from Scotland and especially Germany, where a number of prominent Harvard professors undertook advanced studies. Indeed, many held the English universities in comparatively low scholarly esteem in the early years of the nineteenth century, so that they would seem to have been poor stuff for a role model. Moreover, some Massachusetts men considered England to be a competitor in culture as well as commerce, and at times a rather brutal and haughty one at that.[68]

Yet there is no questioning the English orientation of the elite Bostonians, who were tied to the "mother country" by language, tradition and commerce, as were all the American seaboard elites, but also by a common manufacturing interest, a special relationship to the investment bankers of London, and an attachment to the Unitarianism then predominant in the British provincial capitals.[69] Nowhere, moreover, was the preoccupation with England more intense or pervasive than among those who were concerned with Harvard. Thus John Lowell, who called his Jamaica Plain estate "Bromley Vale" after an English country seat and was considered, even by Englishmen, to be pro-British to the point of treason, toured the British Isles frequently in the early decades of the century, noting with envy the "durability of the establishments" and the "solid excellences of character" that he discovered there.[70] Lowell's admiration of English "establishments" and "excellences," and his pleasure at being near them, shone clearly in a letter from London in 1817:

> I met on Saturday Geo. Lee, a Great banker, a prompt, able intelligent man, whom I *exactly suited*. . . . You must understand that he is a man of £250,000 who lives in the country on a great landed estate but who is so looked up to in this business, that nothing is done without him. . . . Now here is a true British banker; Frank, intelligent, prompt, confiding in others as he expects others to confide in him. . . . This is the English fashion.[71]

The Lowells, perhaps the single most influential family at

antebellum Harvard, were remarkably English-oriented, from Francis Cabot, who studied English power looms in 1810, to John Jr., who "moved in the highest London circles" and observed Lancashire manufacturing in the 1830s, to James Russell, friend of English scholars, eventual ambassador to England, and one of the preeminent Anglophiles of his generation.[72] But such sentiments were not exceptional in the Harvard sphere. Joseph Story, a member of the Corporation from 1825 to 1845 and a champion of English conservatism and close correspondent of English jurists, became so enamored of Britain as to commit large chunks of the street map of London to memory.[73] Charles G. Loring, a Corporation Fellow from 1838 to 1857, wrote from England in 1853 that he did not know "what people under the Sun ever had higher claims to national superiority, than [the English] now possess." Loring was himself described by a British traveler as

> the model English gentleman reproduced in all his ease and luxury, surrounded by the comforts of an elegant house, a large circle of friends and visitors, carriages and horses for the pretty drives in the neighborhood, yachts and sailing boats for the bay. . . . [J]ust the sort of genuine squire of Old England. . . .[74]

So with other elite families. Samuel A. Eliot, who was the son of a major university benefactor, the father of a university president, and himself a large-scale donor and Harvard treasurer, wrote from England in 1823 that "a well educated Englishman of good manners . . . is just the finest specimen of human nature I know." He praised the 1830 Reform Bill for extending full power to the "enlightened, educated, wealthy, and prosperous classes" of the nation.[75] Thomas Handasyd Perkins, the brother of a Harvard patron, was in England in 1826 to study an art show in connection with the opening of the Athenaeum gallery, and again in 1830 to observe first-hand the initial experiments with the steam locomotive. Thomas's son was later a partner in Barings and Company of London.[76] Edward Brooks, son of another large-scale donor, toured England in the 1820s, commending inter alia the organization of the great public schools and the role of the two universities in producing graduates of such impressive character and accomplishments.[77] Brooks's brother-in-law Edward Everett, served (like James Russell Lowell) as ambassador to England before becoming president of Harvard, as did the founder of the new Harvard scientific school, Abbott Lawrence, whose "free intercourse with the most distinguished statesmen of the land" was the high point of his career.[78] For as Abbott's brother Amos advised his own son (later a Harvard treasurer) in 1840, "*England*, is worth to you all the rest of *Europe*, for your purposes, and you are to take a look that you will desire to remember all your life."[79]

The identity of the "English gentleman" naturally varied with time and vantage point, as indeed it was varying in nineteenth-century England itself. Occasionally the phrase implied a title, as when the *North American Review* titillated its readers with a list of English aristocrats and their estimated wealth in 1816.[80] In the 1830s Samuel Cabot, who underwrote the salary of his brother-in-law, Professor Charles Follen, for five years, enjoyed the sight of aristocratic lavishness at Bath and other resorts, while George Ticknor, the young Charles Sumner, and other traveling Harvardians frequented the London salon of Lord and Lady Holland.[81] Professor Andrew Peabody applauded the "gentlemanly . . . courteous . . . high-bred men" whom he encountered in the House of Lords.[82]

A British traveler noted, therefore, the typical Boston merchant's assumption that the "natural aristocracy of England, her philosophers and poets," were "identical with, or originated by, her conventional aristocracy."[83] But the reference to "English gentlemen" was a reference to members of the higher bourgeoisie as well: to self-made provincial businessmen such as Liverpool's William Roscoe, after whom several Bostonians named their sons; to the "commercial and manufacturing classes" who increasingly controlled "the property of the nation" and found political representation in such Boston favorites as Prime Minister Henry Brougham and James Mackintosh, the Whig historian;

to the great London bankers and merchants such as Lowell's
George Lee, or Alexander Baring, whose firm had three Bostonians as partners, or Arthur Kinnaird of the Bank of England,
"tall and dark, with a keen eye and pleasant, business-like smile"
and a friend of various Proper Bostonians.[84]

Whether beourgeois or titled, a "gentleman" had certain important attributes. One, obviously, was wealth. "There is nothing," wrote George Lyman from England in 1820, "which cannot be found here, but you must have the money. . . . With it
one can command every comfort with the greatest ease." Indeed,
an "English gentleman of fortune, no matter whether noble,"
was the "most fortunate of men, and his station the most enviable."[85] In the 1860s Edward Everett's son William, recently a
student at Cambridge University, confirmed what the *North
American Review* had insinuated in 1816 — that English nobles
were "important, not from their rank, but their wealth."[86]

Another attribute was cultivation — a "quiet finish and
thoroughbred quality of mind," as a Bostonian phrased it, and a
"good tone . . . and . . . easy, gentlemanly manners."[87] James
Russell Lowell thus wrote in 1846,

> The great power of the English aristocracy lies in their polish that
> impresses the great middle class who have a sort of dim concep-
> tion of its value. A man gains in *power* as he gains in ease. It is a
> great advantage to him to be cultivated in all parts of his nature.[88]

A third attribute, most significantly, was education. Harvard
benefactor Francis Parkman saw England's leaders as enjoying
the advantages of "wealth," "early and intimate friendships with
the great," and a "generous system of education."[89] Theodore
Lyman believed that the "careful education" of the aristocracy
had prevented revolution in England; Charles Sumner, that the
"vast circle which constitutes English society" was "better educated" as well as more refined and "civilized" than at home.[90]
Education sometimes came from the "celebrated English
schools" — Eton, Harrow, and Rugby in particular — which
Bostonians scrutinized as early as 1800 and later used as models
for their own prep schools.[91]

Usually, however, "education" meant Oxford and Cambridge. Here, as Edward Everett explained in 1818, all Americans stood in awe before the associations of tradition and achievement, and were moved by the black-gowned students beneath the trees and the "calm seclusion — court within court — of the quadrangle."[92] George Ticknor was struck in 1835 by the "magnificent" approach to Oxford, the "magnificence" of its colleges, and the "magnificent" situation of Buckland, Burton, and other resident scholars.[93] "Your own imagination," wrote Sumner from Oxford in 1838, "will supply you with the natural emotions incident to this place."[94]

The sentiments of the era thus foreshadowed Charles Eliot Norton's later view of Oxbridge as "the England of one's fancy and one's heart."[95] But as suggested by the general remarks on education, the key factor here was less the powerful impression made by the universities themselves than the shrewd appraisal of their social functions. Edward Everett, like Theodore Lyman, saw Oxbridge as having traditionally molded "family factions" into a "fraternity" capable of insuring social stability.[96] Boston visitors in the 1830s agreed that the students "all seemed . . . of gentle blood," sons of the rich and powerful.[97] Even more, the universities produced "great men" who shaped the nation's politics, culture and economy.[98] As Professor Francis Bowen wrote:

> How much . . . of the present aspect of English literature, of the conservative tone of British politics, of the actual direction of the wealth and power of the mother country, is to be ascribed to the influences at work within the walls of the two great universities of England, and to the nature of the education which is there given. We do not refer merely to the number of authors, politicians, and public men, who were educated at Oxford and Cambridge. It is rather the great body of the English gentry, the wealthy, influential, and intelligent classes, who really hold the reins of power in the country.[99]

When Professor John G. Palfrey asserted that residence at an English university was "to be coveted" above all other situations, the statement thus connoted at once the appreciation of physical place, the acknowledgment of personal elegance, and the recognition of class power.[100]

It may be true that the English universities influenced the structure and practices of Harvard less in this period than either continental models or local impulse. It is equally true, however, that they were powerful magnets for elite Bostonians, who found in them an important foundation for the compelling English equivalent of their upper-class aspirations. Oxford, as an Englishman wrote to a New England friend in 1847, might have "some interest for you — Our University has not perhaps a very large influence in the World of letters & learning, but it has even now I think a good deal to do with the thinkings & doings of our Upper Classes."[101]

To some extent the English example engendered mere envy and the desire for institutional (and personal) approbation — an instinct for ingratiation. A member of the influential Lyman family thus informed a Harvard instructor in 1817:

> I had an opportunity of spending four days in rooms in one of the Cambridge colleges, and of living among the fellows, whom I found truly hospitable ones, and who (it is a matter which ought to be poured into your *Cambridge professorial ear*) drank, in the public hall on Commencement Day, "Cambridge University in New England."[102]

President Quincy cherished a Cambridge professor's expression in 1843 of "affection" and "admiration" for Cambridge's "sister" institution.[103] Elite families appreciated the remark of a Briton in the 1860s that Harvard's leaders possessed "the idea . . . that they were at least following, if not improving upon, the system of University life in old England."[104] Three-fourths of the honorary degrees awarded to non-Americans by Harvard before 1860 went to Englishmen with Oxbridge connections, many given with considerations such as the following in mind:

> I understand Lord Elgin is to be here again this summer, & as another English nobleman is to be here about Commencement time, Lord Ellsmere, . . . it has occurred to me that it would be

proper for us to give both of them a degree. Lord Elgin is one of the most eloquent men of the day, & they are both very important & weighty men.[105]

Elgin and Ellsmere, both Oxford men, received honorary degrees.

But the Harvardians sought to emulate as well as to ingratiate, largely by way of insinuating an English tone and style into the Harvard setting. The dominant buildings of the era — from Charles Bulfinch's University Hall in 1815 to Gore Hall, modeled after King's College Chapel, to the High Gothic Memorial Hall of the immediate postwar years — bore the English impress, as did the campus domicile plan, constantly questioned and debated but as constantly triumphant over European alternatives.[106] Students first began taking all meals in the "commons" hall in open imitation of Oxbridge; their favorite song (rendered daily by first-term freshmen) was set to the tune of a similar Oxford song.[107] Musical pursuits, quietly encouraged after 1815, assumed a fashionable English shape, as did, of course, athletics, speech patterns, and literary taste.[108] Some instructors argued for a classical curriculum because this was the English tradition; others showed a lingering pride in teaching Latin by English rather than European rules of pronunciation.[109] There was an English gardener at antebellum Harvard and also an English gymnastics teacher. President Everett advised a group of sniffly students that "in England, gentlemen never blow their noses."[110]

The English image doubtless reinforced the style of antebellum Harvard even where it did not directly inspire it. Refinement and beauty were elements of the Oxbridge scene which the Anglophile patrons, governors, and staff of Harvard would inevitably have attempted to duplicate in essence if not in detail. And so, too, were exclusiveness and unity. One Bostonian asserted in 1837 that the graduates of Oxford and Cambridge achieved greatness precisely from being placed so early "in the midst of a society, consisting of the flower of British youth, in rank, wealth, and talent."[111] Another agreed in 1844 that Eng-

lish students made "continued advancement among themselves,
both in knowledge and virtue, by mutual excitement, mutual
instruction, and mutual influence."[112] This perception
sanctioned, even where it did not originally underlie, the
exclusionary and restrictive policies of the era, leading men to
justify them on the grounds that the object of liberal education,
"necessarily an expensive accomplishment," was to give the
"best possible education to a few."[113] No doubt it also justified,
and possibly suggested, the promotion of unity among students,
instructors, benefactors, parents, and the broader Boston elite.

Ultimately, however, the crucial point in the perception of
England as a positive referent was neither ingratiation nor
mimicry, for these were at most mere indications of attachment.
The real factor was comparability of social function: the extent
to which Harvard would produce "heroes and statesmen" as
Oxford and Cambridge produced "the great men to whom English liberty and English literature owe their support," or the
degree to which a projected multivolume "memorial of Harvard
Graduates" would become "what Anthony Wood's Athenae
Oxonienses has been and is in England" — a register of wealth,
prestige, and power.[114]

Oxbridge was surely a more plausible model because it now
enjoyed the patronage of urban manufacturers, merchants,
bankers, politicians, and intellectuals as well as of the gentry and
aristocracy, and its socializing function with regard to standardization of accent and attainment of a common culture was
therefore in some ways more important to England than ever.[115]
In any event it is not at all surprising to discover antebellum
Bostonians first asking their British guests what techniques they
used to keep their "young men of family and fortune" in the
university and then quarreling with the Corporation because
Harvard "was not equal to English universities."[116] They quar-
reled for the same reason that they inquired — because they saw
upper-class status within their grasp.

It may even be argued that the impetus for proper university
socialization was singularly acute in elite New England because,
while British students were in most cases aware from the start of

their social position and prerogative, this sort of consciousness
often had to be instilled among the new families of Boston,
where there were few traditions of corporate group power and
still fewer prescriptions of rank — where families were not only
parvenus but enmeshed in a comparatively mobile society without adequate distinctions of title or rank. Moreover, the absence
as yet of a sufficiently developed system of elite boarding schools
and the relatively tender age of incoming Harvard students made
a university in New England a somewhat more critical socializing institution than it would be in mid-century Britain, where
youth usually had a prior institutional experience to condition
them.[117] The comment of a Harvard parent in 1849 that the
"true education" of Oxbridge consisted of "the life led there" by
the students, while accurate in itself, was also a projection of the
situation as it was coming to prevail at Harvard.[118] In 1862,
finally, an Englishman acknowledged, in what must have
seemed warm praise indeed, that Harvard "is to Massachusetts,
and I may almost say, is to all the northern States, what Cambridge and Oxford are to England. It is the . . . University which
gives the highest education to be attained by the highest classes
in that country."[119]

In conjunction, then, with the growing elite monopolization of
the university's facilities went a bundle of measures designed to
engender elegance, self-discipline, and solidarity and to channel
student contacts away from the masses and toward the broader
elite community. Together, they remolded the forms of campus
life as surely as the exclusionary mechanisms transformed the
composition of the student body. The quest for fashion, for
quality, and for homogeneity which led to and sanctioned the
policies that discriminated against the poor and the ill-prepared
also encouraged the new forms and styles of university existence.
Policy in both spheres, moreover, was consistently informed by
a concept of the social function of a university derived from
English institutional models wherein New Englanders perceived
their own desires for permanent status and power. The English
ideal, at once guideline and rationale, reinforced the predilection
for exclusiveness and the function of socialization as well as

many of the embellishments surrounding them. It lent, in other words, a comprehensive significance to what might otherwise have remained discrete and ad hoc developments: the social function of institutional culture was not only internal but oriented to the goal of class distinction and consciousness.

· 8 ·

Mid-century Crisis
and the Shock of Recognition

MANY studies of the elite and upper class, sometimes even very good studies, have a tendency to see their subjects in a kind of social isolation — accumulating, coalescing, consolidating, and persisting in a virtual vacuum, at least for a time. And for the most part this study is no exception. The great tasks of the Bostonians were precisely to accumulate, coalesce, and consolidate, and the evidence bearing upon the functions of the great civic institutions indicates a clear internal concern of this type. An elite becomes an upper class, however, not only through internal development but through the attainment of class consciousness in the face of nonelite challenge for control over valuable resources. In Boston there had already been signs of gathering tension stemming from nonelite fear of, and anger over, the exclusiveness and elitism of the institutional complex; the evolution of nonelite negative referents as a source of conduct and value; and the nature of the funding and governance of what were putative public enterprises. Such tension, from a class perspective, was not only inevitable but essential.

As we saw in chapter 1, the cultural institutions of antebellum Boston acquired an unavoidable "political" coloration by virtue of their sheer size and the importance of maintaining private control in the face of mounting public criticism. As a rule, the more accessible the institution — the more evident its role in shaping popular attitudes and opinions — the more crucial the maintenance of close elite control, as with the Massachusetts General Hospital and the Lowell Institute. But even the exclusive institutions, such as the Athenaeum and the Mount Auburn Cemetery, became objects of a degree of political contention, particularly in the years after 1850.

Harvard, obviously, was to be no exception to this pattern of politicization. Indeed, two factors virtually guaranteed that the university would be engulfed in controversy. First, Harvard possessed a charter from the Massachusetts government; drew some financial support from the legislature, at least before 1825; and was supervised, more or less, by a Board of Overseers comprised in part of members of the legislature or their representatives. Harvard was therefore a "state" university and hence a natural object of political concern. Second, it was much the largest, most prestigious, and most tradition-laden of the New England cultural institutions as well as the one which had in fact experienced the most drastic changes in scope and purpose. The public thus had expectations and interests with regard to its ancient "seminary" which it was bound to express.

Certainly, this combination of formal state connection and established public concern was sufficient to make the university feel to its officers like a "glass hive" open to the closest popular scrutiny and to plunge it into a "politico-theological sea" which seemed rougher even than the seas encountered by the hospital, lecture forum, or library (though they all proved ultimately to be part of the same ocean).[1] Moreover, the encumbrances of law, structure, and tradition made adjustments more delicate and difficult for Harvard than for its newer sister institutions. That such adjustments nonetheless occurred speaks not just of the roughness of the sea and the need for a safe harbor but of the growing importance of Harvard as a component of the antebellum cultural constellation and the life of the Boston elite. The adjustments that were eventually made represented the final phase in the consolidation of the power of the Corporation vis-a-vis other centers of university authority — here exemplified mainly by the Board of Overseers — and in the establishment of elite institutional hegemony vis-a-vis the rest of society — here exemplified mainly by the state legislature. Consideration of the adjustments and the way they came about touches, too, upon the recurring questions of elite intent and, even more, of the timing of elite emergence. For it was in this politico-institutional "combat zone" that the issues of class domination and conflict found their strongest overt expression, and it was the resolution of these issues of class — the "adjustments" in the structure and governance of the university — that helped to produce a well-grounded and distinctive urban upper class.

To treat this crisis adequately requires both a brief survey of the university's position within the politics of the time and a rather close narrative of the maneuvers of the 1850s. As early as 1780 members of the local conventions called to ratify the proposed state constitution had voiced apprehension over possible "aristocratic" tendencies at Harvard, removed as it was by the terms of its seventeenth-century charter from direct control by the government and the people. Over the next twenty years the legislature, partly from budgetary exigencies but partly, perhaps, in response to such anxieties, reduced its financial aid to the institution.[2] As yet there was no attempt to change the composition of the Board of Overseers, which at this time consisted of the college president; plus the governor, lieutenant governor, councillors, and senators of Massachusetts; plus the Congregational ministers of Cambridge, Watertown, Charlestown, Boston, Roxbury, and Dorchester. Nor was there any attempt to modify the role of the Overseers in university governance, limited at this point largely to ratifying Corporation appointments and expenditures, neither of which, given the institution's small size, demanded much time or attention.

But circumstances soon changed. The state's Jeffersonian Republicans, incensed over the election of a pair of notorious Arminians as Harvard president and professor of divinity, respectively, and by the efforts of Federalists to inject a "spirit of party" like a "poisonous weed" into Harvard, began to attack the university's sectarianism; to urge that the Overseers "do their duty" in reducing the "bad . . . violent and erroneous politics" of the Corporation; and to threaten to charter a rival medical school upon gaining power.[3] The still-dominant Federalists responded in 1810 with a legislative measure to change the composition of the Overseers by replacing the council and senate with fifteen laymen and the Congregational ministers of the six towns with fifteen Congregational ministers to be chosen by the current Overseers. This change, when it took effect, so insulated the Board from popular influence, and so thoroughly locked Federalist Congregationalism into position, that when the Jeffersonians (in Josiah Quincy's words) "obtained dominant influence in all the branches of the state government" in 1812, they immediately repealed it. The Federalists upon returning to power in 1814 sought to reinstitute their changes, but this time in more circumspect fashion. The fifteen ministers and fifteen laymen rejoined the Board, thus securing the Federalist position; but so did the state council and senate, thus mollifying the moderate Republicans. In providing Harvard with a ten-year $100,000 grant, moreover, the legislature carefully stipulated that most of this money should go toward the erection of new facilities for the medical school.[4]

These early clashes were predominantly tactical party measures, drawing their steam from Orthodox disgruntlement and the status resentments of the Republican leadership. As party competition faded after 1815, so, then, did Harvard as a hot political issue. The Board of Overseers, with its new thirty-man contingent and a Boston-oriented, neo-Federalist senatorial element, settled again into a passive and broadly loyal posture regarding the actions of the Corporation. The Board was no mere rubber stamp, to be sure, and still possessed what President Kirkland called an "esprit de corps" of its own. In the 1820s it listened attentively to the complaints of faculty insurgents; harbored numerous dissenters to the secular and mercantile drift of the Bowditch-Quincy administration; insisted that the Corporation adhere to proper notification and other procedures; and generally conducted itself with a somewhat old-fashioned sense of responsibility. Corporation attempts to bend the rules of procedure, for example, even over matters of slight import, met with what President Quincy termed "*a warmth of opposition* far beyond anything naturally to be expected."[5] Still, the Board was reliable: listening to faculty complaints but then rejecting them, resisting the Quincy regime but then supporting it, debating in secret when open debate might harm the university's reputation.[6] Though the Overseers might accommodate reluctantly, accommodate nonetheless they did.

Criticism of the drift of things in Cambridge thus found little outlet in the legislature or Board of Overseers after 1815. But the criticism itself did not cease so much as move underground, forming a muffled but insistent backdrop to developments at Harvard for the next three decades. Trinitarians, for example, continued to raise the cry of "heresy" and the accusation of "sectarianism."[7] Non-Congregationalists at the Massachusetts constitutional convention of 1820 opposed the way Harvard bestowed "honors and privileges . . . repugnant to . . . the [Massachusetts] Declaration of Rights" on Congregational ministers.[8] Meanwhile, as has been noted, westerners criticized Harvard's excessively "eastern" bias, and working-class spokesmen abhorred its excessively "aristocratic" flavor. These themes converged, in a sense, when hard-pressed western Calvinists, after rebuffs from Harvard, demanded a state-supported college of their own in Amherst. The "Unitarian aristocracy" in the legislature granted them a charter but no money, opposing this kind of aid so strongly, in fact, that they ended the annual subsidy to Harvard (now with its own resources) mainly to avoid helping Amherst. As a Boston senator informed a leading manufacturer, "We had just refused your particular friends of Amherst in a most discourteous manner, and to have given to Harvard would have raised a hornets nest."[9]

To these arguments were increasingly conjoined the now familiar objections to Harvard's cost (too expensive), its life-style (too elegant), and its number of students (too few); plus the broader point, raised at the 1820 convention in the wake of the New Hampshire legislature's challenge to Dartmouth, that there should be no such "powerful institution" as Harvard, "built up by the State" yet "independent of the State" — that "placing powerful institutions, even partly the property of the State, out of the control of the State . . . ought to be solemnly prohibited" and that the Overseers, therefore, "ought to be under the control of the Legislature" and the Corporation, by implication, subordinate to the Overseers.[10] Attacks thus persisted for many years, understandably, and even grew, so much so that in the very midst of the bicentennial celebration of 1836, just as the new Boston elite was demonstrating its new ardor for Harvard, an observer could remark with perfect justification that the university had "entirely lost her hold upon the feeling of the State" and was doing "worse than nothing in the way to regain it."[11]

In the early 1840s, finally, several "Calvinists" and "political demagogues" became permanent Overseers, including George Bancroft, a Harvard graduate but now a left-wing Democrat whose scathing minority report of 1843 pulled together and documented virtually every significant charge of the last twenty-five years.[12] No longer was the front wholly united or the criticism entirely underground. "The college is now in a critical situation," wrote Joseph Story, with critics "again pressing forward to achieve . . . the mastery and rule of the University."[13] George Ticknor and Edward Everett spoke simultaneously and ominously of "the united attacks of the Orthodox and the radicals."[14]

The dam burst with the mid-century collapse of the Whig party and the successive rise to prominence of the Democratic–Free-Soil coalition, the Know-Nothing insurgency, and the early Republican party. While each of these movements had numerous very urgent interests — slavery, Catholicism, taxation, and the rights of labor, to name a few — which reached well beyond the cultural sphere, it is notable that Harvard, too, was a constant matter of concern. In 1850, for example, leaders of the Free-Soil–Free Democrats in the legislature produced and adopted a report critical of Harvard's exclusiveness, the lack of representation for "all the State's sects and parties" on its governing bodies, and the comparative neglect of utilitarian and vocational education.[15] The charges were sweeping and the tone strident, as in Representative Henry Wilson's arraignment of

a certain class of individuals, who seem to think that they own the institution, president, corporators, overseers, and all, — a class

of individuals who assume it to be their mission to keep Harvard
College from the influences of the outside barbarians.[16]

Seeking drastic and immediate remedies, Wilson and his cohorts
submitted a bill which would have increased the number of
Fellows on the Corporation to fifteen, all directly elected by the
legislature, and failed to pass it only after the strenuous political
labors of well-situated Harvard loyalists.[17]

The contentious mood of the legislators was further revealed
in 1851 when the Overseers rejected the Corporation's nomination of Francis Bowen, tutor at Harvard and editor of the *North
American Review*, as professor of history because of his ideological
conservatism, in particular his expressed aversion to national
liberation movements in Europe and abolitionism in America.[18]
Again the attacks were sharp. Henry Wilson declared that
Bowen "and the class of which he is the head, have converted the
Review into a narrow, intolerant, bigoted organ of that conservatism which shrinks from every thing progressive."[19] The rejection passed, but narrowly, mainly because while the ex officio
political members of the Board voted thirty-eight to one against
Bowen, the permanent lay-ministerial group sustained him by
twenty-nine to one.[20] The coalition thereupon introduced and
passed a bill providing that *all* Overseers be elected by joint
meeting of the two houses of the legislature. The measure was no
root-and-branch affair: it left the Corporation intact, and it
meant that the entire Board would at least be elected indirectly.
A few Corporation Fellows hoped, accordingly, that with changing political fortunes the arrangement might actually be a
stabilizing one.[21] But the measure did sweep away the soothing
cushion of ministers and laymen and produce a Board which was
responsible solely to the legislature, thus bringing the university
in fact to a "critical pass" amidst a "vortex of political excitements."[22]

The coalition leaders pressed their attack further at the constitutional convention of 1853, arguing that Harvard should not
be "a select school for the education of classes or cliques . . . a
sectarian, a narrow, or an exclusive institution" with lavish en-

dowments but few students and a Corporation dominated by "one sect" and "one party."[23] Wilson and others again assaulted that "class of men in, and about the city of Boston, who seem to think that they were born to guard, guide, govern, direct and control, Harvard College."[24] Speaking for the "people of the Commonwealth," the "people themselves," for the "power of the people," they demanded a "popularized" university educating "men of all classes," and they urged specifically that the state's "visitatorial" right be affirmed, including the right to dismiss Fellows, who for that matter should always be elected by the legislature anyway.[25]

The proposed constitution which emerged from the convention met defeat at the hands of a Whig-Catholic coalition — not least because of its Harvard provisions — and university officers heaved sighs of relief. But even so, there still remained the politicized Board of Overseers, which at the end of 1853 vetoed a Corporation proposal for a new professorship of law out of fear that the professor might be Edward Loring, a cousin of Corporation member Charles G. Loring who abhorred abolitionists and admired the Fugitive Slave Law.[26]

The beleaguered university understandably sought accommodations wherever feasible. To the chair of history was appointed Henry Torrey, a deep-dyed conservative but a less outspoken and hence more innocuous man; and to the law professorship Emory Washburn, another conservative but one from Worcester and hence much more politically palatable in the anti-Boston climate of the decade.[27] The rise of the Know-Nothings and then of the early Republicans ensured continued strife, however, in part because of the substantial continuity of insurgent leadership and interests in the 1850s and in part because the Know-Nothings in particular were, at least in Massachusetts, even more radical than the Free-Soil–Democrats or Republicans, sufficiently so, indeed, to be charged with a "low, obscene, feculent" behavior redolent of "Jack Cadism."[28] And still the Overseers continued to snipe at Corporation decisions, opposing warmly but vainly the "back-door" appointment of Bowen to a chair of moral philosophy and the appointment of Frederic Dan Huntington as professor of Christian morals, the concern here being that such a position would necessarily tend to the sectarian and that Huntington himself had exhibited the same "high church" proclivities that Oxford's John Henry Newman had before defecting to the Roman Church.[29] In 1855, after Edward Loring had upheld the Fugitive Slave Law as United States Commissioner in the Anthony Burns case, the Overseers rejected his appointment as a law lecturer by a decisive twenty-to-ten margin.[30]

In 1855 an Overseer committee on the new professorship of Christian morals narrowly ratified the nomination of Huntington to fill it, but at the same time called the Corporation practice of nominating candidates for new chairs "unwise" and a potential source of Corporation-Overseer conflict, as was the Corporation's "too exclusive" management of funds and appropriation of salaries generally.[31] Thus began a series of committee reports over the next seven years on the powers, duties, and responsibilities of the Fellows and Overseers, the relation of Corporation and Overseers, the rules and procedures of Corporation and Overseers, the organization of the Overseers, and similar contentious topics. The reports, signed by no fewer than twenty-six different men, did the following: — complained of the Corporation's secretiveness and the difficulty of seeing its records; — called for more extensive and frequent Overseer meetings, at which the Board would approve all donations and all major expenditures; — insisted that the Overseers as well as the Corporation could limit the terms of university officers or remove them altogether; — rejected the Corporation's presumptuousness in making decisions without consultation; — recommended a system of university governance by a joint Corporation-Overseer committee in order to keep the Board from becoming a "mere cipher."[32] The reports were thus clear manifestations of the continuing popular antagonism to Harvard in these years, whose chief thrust was to undo the policies of conservatism and exclusiveness developed so laboriously by the Boston elite over the past thirty-five years, and to dilute, if not eliminate, the close control the elite had come to exercise, via the Corporation, over its handiwork.

These measures were not all put into practice by any means.

The popular movements whose attitudes they represented had many other concerns, and the university and its supporters were not without resources of their own. That they were broached at all, however, and especially so insistently and repeatedly, suggests that the 1850s were a time of turmoil at Harvard no less than at the Athenaeum or the Mount Auburn Cemetery or the Lowell Institute or elsewhere in the cultural constellation. Here, in fact, the turmoil was exceptionally severe, the product of a backlash generated by Harvard's systematic exclusion of dissident and/or lower-class groups and its persistent disregard for their interests and values in the face of age-old tradition and constitutional responsibility. The opposition of these groups grew fiercest, moreover, just as the elite party machinery for controlling or deflecting it was growing weakest. The insurgents thus had both the grounds for complaint and the means for complaining, and their presence among the Overseers was a constant trial and a recurring danger for the men of Harvard. For there, as a European shrewdly observed, the insurgents represented "the jealous eye of society watching over a benefit it owns and which it does not want to give up."[33]

Harvard's spokesmen and supporters argued forcefully and at great length against the efforts of their antagonists to enlarge the Corporation or Board of Overseers, to make them more representative of the general public, to increase the Board's adminstrative authority, or indeed to take any steps that might lead to a "precarious dependence" on legislative discretion or "subservience" to the popular will.[34] In the early years — in the constitutional convention of 1820, for example — the main focus was on preserving the self-perpetuating thirty-man buffer of laymen and ministers in the interests of the stability and good name of the institution, now fast becoming "the ornament of the land." Changes to the contrary would "subvert" not only the Overseers, who would be forever traduced as "corrupt," but the Corporation, which had ever striven (it was said) for efficiency and justice.[35] Institutions and donors alike, in sum, required a certain broad protection from heedless state intervention. "We should be careful," admonished Josiah Quincy, "not to indulge our own views and biases to the prejudice of vested rights."[36]

By mid-century — certainly by the constitutional convention of 1853 — the danger was not so much the reorganization of the Overseers, which, to the Corporation's chagrin, had already taken place. The threats now came, in the university's eyes, from the "radical error . . . that the Board of Overseers was intended to be an integral part of the Corporation" and, even more, the possibility of direct legislative control, the empowering, in other words, of the government "to take [Harvard] under its entire and absolute control, and bring the election of its professors and fellows, and the direct management of its affairs, into the arena of politics and legislation."[37] As to direct intervention, it was patently foolish to seek more "able and devoted" men than were now on the Corporation, or to attempt, even with an enlarged Corporation, to represent the twenty or more sects and parties of Massachusetts.[38] In any case, a state "cannot manage" a college "so easily or so well as a corporation of private individuals," and Harvard itself "never began to grow . . . towards the great institution that it now is" while the government was constantly "interfering" with it.[39] As for Overseer parity with the Corporation, the very suggestion threatened the "position and character" built up by "private liberality" since the 1820s and in fact constituted a "crisis in the history of the College as deeply affecting its future welfare as any that has ever occurred in it."[40]

Two arguments loomed especially large for the university's spokesmen. The first dealt with money. In the eighteenth century, as we have seen, the government had contributed over half the funds accruing to Harvard, and even in the first quarter of the nineteenth century, when the pace of contributions was beginning to accelerate, approximately one-third of the total still came from the state. The Corporation valued these funds partly as a token of public esteem and partly as a means to deflect public wrath over, say, the lack of accessible medical facilities. In 1820 Harvardians argued, somewhat disingenuously, that the legislators had little need to alter the Board of Overseers since they could impose "such conditions to their financial grants as they should see fit."[41] The growing elite monopolization of Harvard, however, made the legislature more reluctant to give money for fear of promoting (or seeming to promote) aristocracy and made the university more reluctant to seek it for fear of actually experiencing democracy. A Corporation memorandum of 1840 noted, in fact, that dependence upon "public grants" was bound to be "a source of embarrassment, & a real injury to the College in one of its most vital interests."[42] President Quincy's history of the college repeatedly emphasized, by way of illustration, how most, if not all, of Harvard's early troubles had stemmed from its pecuniary dependence on the colonial legislature.[43]

By mid-century, not only had the flow of state funds long since ceased, but private funds were accruing at a tremendous rate. In 1820 university men could argue that private sources were becoming more important than public; by the 1850s they pointed out that private donors had given ten times as much as the state, as Samuel A. Eliot demonstrated conclusively in his history of the college.[44] It was clearly not "the government of Massachusetts" which had "raised up Harvard College to be the noble institution it is," but rather "the munificence of private individuals."[45] The terms of the argument were thus reversed. Even in 1820 the stream of private largesse seemed to entitle "the donors to a little voice in the management of the concerns of the College" — a voice which they certainly gained during the Bowditch-Quincy years. By 1850, according to this logic, they deserved a much greater voice: the "rights of the Corporation" were not larger than they ought to be "for the safe preservation of these funds."[46]

But the Corporation also made two additional arguments with regard to finance. One was that political intervention in Harvard's affairs could alienate potential contributors and hence damage the institution.[47] As a case in point, the published will of John Eliot Thayer, a Boston banker who died in 1855, gave $50,000 to Harvard, *provided* that the legislature did not alter the university structure "without the unanimous consent of every member of the present corporation or their successors."

(Thayer's advisors, interestingly enough, included three members of the Harvard Corporation plus the son of a fourth.)[48] The threat of state intervention similarly cost the university $100,000 from its former treasurer, Ebenezer Francis, and a Corporation spokesman suggested that the total cost in lost donations might reach a million dollars.[49]

The second financial point was less a warning than a naked threat:

> A question may be raised whether the heirs of the donors of funds now held by the College may not be entitled to litigate for the sake of reclaiming them — if existing rights of the Corporation are disturbed by the State. Those funds were given under the pledged faith that they wld. be transmitted thro just such a body of Trustees — a homogeneous, self-electing body — not subject to popular caprice, party favoritism, or political intervention.[50]

While Harvard would doubtless have appreciated large legislative grants without strings, such as the one Louis Agassiz wangled in 1858 for a museum of natural history, the crucial point was this: the private funding of the university had advanced so far by midcentury that the Corporation, far from succumbing to legislative pressures, could itself threaten the stagnation, or even the actual dismemberment, of the institution in the event of excessive state intervention. Obviously the point was better left unfulfilled, but it was a truly formidable weapon to brandish.

The other major anti-intervention argument employed by Harvardians was legalistic rather than financial, resting on the supposed autonomy which the institution derived from its seventeenth-century charter and on the presumed right of the Corporation, by virtue of this charter, to a veto power over legislative efforts to change the structure of the university. Hence Josiah Quincy's reference during the constitutional convention of 1820 to Harvard's "vested rights," and the assertions of other Bostonians that "the University had its rights defined in its charter, and . . . was independent of the Legislature," which had "no right to make any change in the charter, without the consent of the corporation."[51] Hence, too, the rebuttal of all claims to legislative sovereignty from the 1820s to the 1850s, when spokesmen insisted that Harvard, like Dartmouth, was "exempted from all legislative interference. They are not under the control of the State, and are beyond all interference on the part of the government of the State."[52] Samuel A. Eliot, Harvard officer and patron, thus exclaimed (in tones which doubtless seemed less melodramatic then than now) that to modify the Overseers and elect the Corporation meant nothing less than "to decapitate the College, to abrogate its charter . . . — an act of a more arbitrary character than Charles II was guilty of" in seizing the charter of Massachusetts Bay![53]

Harvard officers had always insisted on the sanctity of their charter and the veto power of their Corporation, though never, of course, so vociferously as when these seemed to be jeopardized. The grounds became more solid when Massachusetts Chief Justice Theophilus Parsons, a wealthy Federalist and an influential member of the Corporation, issued an advisory opinion in 1813 upholding the university's point of view.[54] They became more solid still after the Supreme Court's decision in 1819 on Dartmouth College, where the New Hampshire legislature had intervened to change the trustees and policies of the college. The New Hampshire high court had upheld the authority of the state over corporations with public purposes, such as colleges, whether they had received private donations or not. But the Dartmouth decision, which was largely, as historians now know, the handiwork of Justice Joseph Story, ruled that institutions not actually owned by the state were private regardless of any public functions, thus remedying the "dangerous and false presumption" that government could revoke or control a grant "even of its own funds, when given to a private person or a corporation for special uses."[55]

Story apparently considered *Dartmouth College* to be the most important of the great decisions of the Marshall court during his tenure, and he cared greatly about its impact on the nation as a whole, reinforcing as it did the contract clause and the doctrine of implied limitations.[56] But the immediate context suggests that educational institutions generally, and Harvard specifically, were foremost in his mind. In 1818, for example, he conferred with leaders of the important New England colleges, including President Kirkland and other members of the Harvard Corporation, who quickly arranged for his election to the Board of Overseers.[57] During the court session he consulted with Daniel Webster, advocate for the Dartmouth trustees, and expressed sympathy with Webster's remarks that Harvard, having "more friends" today but perhaps "more enemies" tomorrow, possessed "no surer title" than Dartmouth.[58]

Early 1820, moreover, found Story speaking at greater length about Harvard than about any other issue at the Massachusetts constitutional convention, where he urged a provision recognizing the "rights and privileges of Harvard" against legislative "meddling." Six years later he was a Corporation Fellow.[59] Whatever its broader implications, Story's declaration in *Dartmouth* that the state could not "revoke or alter the charter [of an incorporated institution], or change its administration, without the consent of the corporation" was an attempt to place his own university "beyond the control of the people."[60] The invocation of the principles of *Dartmouth* by pro-Harvard pamphleteers and politicians, even after Story's death in 1845, eloquently bespoke their gratitude.

Still, it is interesting that charter rights and the implicit judicial resort were, like the financial arguments, more declaimed than acted upon. Faced, for example, with the Jeffersonian interventions of 1812, the Corporation, though hardly accepting them, still felt it "inexpedient to press the point."[61] Parsons's opinion of 1813 was thus an informal one only; and even Story, "presiding genius" of the *Dartmouth* case, sought to buttress his position with a state constitutional amendment. The Corporation, while abhorring the direct election of all Overseers, accepted this arrangement in 1851 rather than precipitate a flare-up still more injurious. Not once was there a serious move toward the courts, even though Massachusetts Chief Justice Lemuel Shaw was a staunch Corporation member.

The difficulty, of course, was that in times of intense political stress, the university had no wish to press a case which it could conceivably lose (particularly after the passing, first, of Story's great ally, John Marshall, and then of Story himself) any more than it really wished to see the withdrawal of past and present benefactions. They were points to be flourished if necessary, avoided if possible. But such avoidance, in the last analysis, required political leadership, action, and methods, of which argumentation, however formidable, was only a part. Story, appropriately enough, called in his dying year for an administration of "energy, decision, and character, to sustain the college against these reiterated attacks" and urged a "combined action of all its friends" in support.[62]

The need for leadership was eminently clear, the "blunt, stout" Quincy having long since established the standard of resistance which his friend Story was evoking. Jared Sparks, under whose presidency the first fierce assaults of the 1850s occurred, quickly moved to orchestrate the efforts of numerous Harvard stalwarts in defeating the proposal to enlarge and elect the Corporation. In doing so, Sparks relied mainly on Boston Whigs, but he judiciously called as well on the "personal services" of conservative Democrats and non-Bostonians with antislavery credentials.[63] Of the latter, the most notable was probably Samuel Hoar, a "well-to-do" and "naturally conservative" Concord Unitarian and Whig who had served as a legal consultant to the Lowell and Lawrence millowners. Hoar represented Harvard before the legislature in 1851, where his known aversion to slavery doubtless mollified Free-Soil critics, so much so that President James Walker would later say that while other men "served the College," Samuel Hoar "saved it."[64] After Sparks's death in 1853, Walker himself continued the campaign, making sure the Harvard position was duly expressed within the legislature and duly publicized outside it, urging the redoubtable John Amory Lowell to remain on the Corporation in 1856 despite ill health because "we are at a critical pass, and I hope to have the the benefit of your moderation and firmness in helping us to get safely through it."[65]

In fact, during these "critical" years Harvard pursued a consistent two-pronged strategy of placating opponents and organizing supporters. The Corporation's nomination of Henry Torrey instead of Francis Bowen and of Emory Washburn instead of Edward Loring for faculty posts represented a measure of placation, or at any rate discretion, as did the establishment of scholarship funds and additional curriculum changes during the 1850s. About this time, too, Harvard managed to reduce its opposition to and disdain for would-be competitors, applying jointly for state funds with Williams and Amherst, for example, encouraging state assistance for business and technical education, opening its library to the faculty of recently chartered Tufts College. With alternatives available, sectarians and utilitarians might make less insistent demands on Cambridge, whose superiority was in any event now clearly beyond challenge.

To further pacify the Orthodox, as an observer noted skeptically, the Corporation sought to obscure the quarter-century identification of college and divinity school:

> The *on dit* is that the Divinity School is to be separated from the College. I have no faith in throwing such tubs to such whales. The whale who is spouting over and over again a frothy stream of talk about the sectarianism of the college does not wish to hold his peace, and will not be tempted to.[66]

But the move was deemed tactically essential. As President Sparks advised a supporter, "To keep the public mind quiet, we should be very cautious in applying college funds to the schools."[67] The grant to Agassiz's museum went, appropriately enough, to a group of special trustees rather than to the Corporation, which gained authority over the funds only much later.

Two Corporation appointments, both made in 1857 at the peak of the Overseers' committee activities, again suggest the concern with image and appeasement. The first was Ebenezer Rockwood Hoar, son of Samuel. Born and raised in Concord, Hoar was associated with the early Free-Soil movement, joined the Republicans shortly after their appearance in Massachusetts, and might, therefore, have sympathized with the university's

radical non-Boston opponents. His brother George, moreover,
was a Worcester lawyer with his own Republican affinities. But
actually Hoar was a rather conservative Conscience Whig in the
vein of Professor John G. Palfrey. Like Palfrey, he had opposed
the revised constitution of 1853 for its "excessively democratic"
provisions, and Henry Wilson, among others, attempted to
expel him from Free-Soil ranks. He was also a Unitarian and
Harvard graduate grown prosperous by inheritance and as legal
trustee to elite families; his brother's law partner was Professor
Emory Washburn, another "compromise" appointment.[68]

The election of Amos A. Lawrence as treasurer is perhaps less
notable since Lawrence's elite status — a second-generation Boston millionaire and a Harvard graduate from a prominent patron
family — was incontestable. Still, it is worth observing that
Lawrence was an Episcopalian, not a Unitarian; that he helped
bankroll the Kansas adventures of the New England Emigrant
Aid Society; and that he worked closely with the conservative
wing of the Massachusetts Know-Nothings in the late 1850s.[69]
Both appointments deviated modestly from the university norm,
strengthening the Corporation's politico-religious flank without
impairing its integrity or shifting its allegiances.

On all matters the president, with his Fellows, being "little
inclined" to provoke "an occasion for . . . censure on my own
authority or on that of the Corporation" and aware, as always, of
"the delicacy with which any right or custom of the Overseers
must be treated," tried to handle the Board with appropriate
discretion. Even minor changes, "if made," should "seem" to
ensue from "the actions of the Overseers themselves."[70] Yet the
officers conducted their affairs very closely, especially during
this acrimonious era, as when they allowed Overseers to inspect
college records only with Corporation approval and only "under
the eye" of a university employee.[71] Under these touchy circumstances, the appearance of administrative loyalty became as
important as its substance, as important, indeed, as it had long
since become for faculty members. One nervous individual, fearing that "his fidelity will be doubted," sought to assure John
Amory Lowell that he had not personally authorized a recent

Overseer inspection, had only been present "out of prudence," and should bear no responsibility for the consequences.[72]

Yet the fact remained that if these measures to preserve autonomy did not succeed, or if they merely purchased time before the next assault, there was in actuality very little room left in which to maneuver. The public had expectations of Harvard which, given its new elitist orientation, could never be met; the university, at the same time, was uniquely vulnerable to its own newly politicized Board of Overseers. The Corporation thus intoned in 1856:

> The time . . . may arrive, when it might be hazardous to the best interests of the College, if not to the purposes of its foundations, to have this unlimited power placed in the hands of any public body, the most influential members of which are in great part appointed at political elections or by those deriving authority under them.[73]

Clearly, new arrangements were needed to secure the university "on a more stable and permanent basis." And precisely such arrangements were in fact broached at the constitutional convention of 1853. The plan, proposed by prominent Bostonians, was twofold: to cut Harvard "adrift, just sever . . . all connection with [the] State, and let the college stand . . . upon her own foundation"; and second, to elect the Overseers by and from the alumni of "Harvard herself" — meaning, as of mid-century, the Boston elite itself. There was resistance (and eventual defeat) because, in the words of Henry Wilson and his allies, this would remove the university "out of the class of public institutions" and make it private, hence uncontrollable and inaccessible.[74] Yet so natural was this resolution of the dilemma — to place the institution outside the political arena and in the hands of a loyal coterie — that the plan, not surprisingly, gained in momentum over time.

The plan entailed two related but distinct tasks: the organization of the alumni and the severance of legislative ties. The first of these was the simpler, since Harvard graduates had already begun to coalesce, thanks to Corporation guidance and their own increasing homogeneity. The process accelerated between 1840 and 1844, however, when the growth of external antagonism seemed to demand more energetic efforts. The result was the Harvard Alumni Association, brainchild of Story, Quincy, and perhaps a dozen other officers and supporters.[75] The broad objectives were to promote "mutual friendship and union" by embracing "all the Alumni, without discrimination"; to foster a "spirit of kindness and respect for the College" among "her children"; and to strengthen the university in its relations with the public and especially with (in Story's opinion) "the miserable politicians of the day."[76] There were also two other objectives: one, to enhance Commencement Day as an imposing community event; and two, to "do away with the exclusiveness of," if not to "swallow up," the longer-established Phi Beta Kappa society.[77] The latter objective — to replace an older, smaller, academically-based association with a more all-encompassing, experientially based, socially powerful one with no scholarly emphasis — was indicative of prevailing thinking, a further example of the changing nature of the institution and its constituency.

The alumni drive started well, then idled momentarily in the late 1840s before picking up speed again during the travail of the 1850s, when another group of advocates led by Everett, Sparks, John Amory Lowell, and Amos A. Lawrence finally made the Alumni Association the formidable entity initially envisaged.[78] The Association held annual dinners throughout the 1850s, raised funds for university projects, encouraged library and scholarship contributions. By 1860 it was a powerful "link between the body of the Alumni and the College" and a standing "representative" of the university to the public.[79]

Equally important to the success of the plan for alumni control was the "wheel within a wheel" organized in 1855 by a group of 150 alumni at Boston's fashionable Tremont House — namely, a "Club of the Graduates of Harvard College." The "Harvard Club," as it was soon called, met regularly within two months of its founding to plan a clubhouse and consider such matters as how to deal with the "bores" (via a membership committee) and the "clergy" and "country graduates" (via a membership fee).[80] The forty or so earliest Harvard Club promoters included a handful of patrons, Fellows, and faculty and several sons of patrons, Fellows, and faculty, thus ensuring considerable continuity of institutional leadership and responsibility; they were also, almost to a man, Boston residents of great actual or potential wealth, thus ensuring ample ties to the broader elite.

Two other characteristics of these Harvard Club men are of interest as well. First, the group was quite young, almost half having graduated in the ten years prior to the club's founding. Second, well over half had graduated between 1840 and 1844 or between 1849 and 1853 — precisely the points of accelerating popular animosity and political and religious attack.[81] The clubmen, who inevitably became the vital center of alumni opinion and influence, were finished products, in a sense, of the new Harvard, intensely devoted to the university and to one another and singularly conscious of the value and fragility of the private institutional prerogative. Hence there arose within the steadily cohering body of the alumni an inner circle far different from the ancient Phi Beta Kappa, one more attuned to the modern Harvard and more eager to help secure it definitively from Wilson's "barbarians" and Prescott's "many-headed."

There remained now to implement the second part of the plan — to remove the university from the reach of "ordinary political strife & change," of "unwise or hasty interference on the part of the Legislature," and to entrust it to those "whose culture & professions give them most ability & most leisure," friends of the college "interested in its prosperity & reputation."[82] This initiative, too, had long been launched, of course, only to falter against the will of the legislature, where "repeated efforts to get that body to loosen its hold caused many of its members to value the prerogative very highly."[83] Not until Republican solidarity and the excitements of war had reduced suspicions and until the appearance of other colleges (Tufts and Holy Cross in the 1850s, Massachusetts Agricultural College, Massachusetts Institute of Technology, Boston University and Boston College in the 1860s)

had diffused reformist pressures did the hour seem propitious for
a final break. In April, 1864, finally, a group of Harvard loyalists
did act decisively to "forward the movement," "bring every
influence to bear," and establish a legislative committee on "dis-
solving the connection of Harvard College with the Commonwealth."[84]

The leadership of this drive was formidable: past, present, and
future presidents of Harvard; several members, past and present, of the Corporation; a number of prominent faculty members; "excellent allies in the Legislature," including the heads of
the relevant senate and house committees; able publicists; elite
Bostonians with deep pockets. [85] Even at that, however, much
caution and some guile were needed. For example, the university's representative at the committee hearings was none other
than Ebenezer R. Hoar, the Concord Republican and Corporation Fellow whose father had performed similar services in 1851.
Assisting him were several Harvard politicos from the embattled
classes of the early 1840s and 1850s (most important was committee chairman Darwin E. Ware, a cousin of the Cambridge
Wares and a thriving Boston lawyer) and several non-Harvard
graduates whose presence cast the matter in a less partisan
light.[86] Indeed, Hoar advised President Thomas Hill that it was
not "prudent or expedient that the Corporation should appear as
an applicant for the change" or even as an "active promoter of it,"
since the chief obstacle would be "jealousy on the part of the
legislature."[87] Boston sympathizers suggested that the president
had best "not refer to any outside friends of the College" and
thus "screen them . . . from all suspicion of agency," and Ware
contacted many legislators privately before deciding that a resolution for severance could be "safely introduced."[88] Nor was the
caution ill-conceived, for more than a year was required to pass a
bill transferring the election of all Overseers to the alumni of the
college "voting at Cambridge on Commencement Day." Even
then, the margin of victory was but a single vote in the senate,
and in the house the "slenderest majority."[89]

A brief glance at the changing composition of the Overseers, as shown in table 17, vividly reveals both the consequences of the Act of 1865 and why it was deemed so essential.[90]

Table 17: Characteristics of the Harvard Board of Overseers, 1828–1870

Overseers elected between:	Wealth		
	Estates $25,000+	Estates $50,000+	Estates $100,000+
		(percent)	
1828–51	85	63	41
1852–58	58	45	28
1866–70	89	82	68

	Residence and Ideology	
	Religious and/or political dissidents	Non-Boston/non– North Shore Residents
	(percent)	
1828–51	15	12
1852–58	35	38
1866–70	0	14

	Education and Status	
	Harvard graduates	Also members of Corporation
	(percent)	
1828–51	95	9
1852–58	48	0
1866–70	82	21

The data indicate very clearly that the intense strife between Corporation and Overseers during the 1850s was related to the fact that the Board of Overseers contained so large a proportion of members from a nonelite socioeconomic stratum, a reflection of corresponding changes in the legislature. Thus, fewer than a third of the mid-century Overseers possessed sizeable estates, and two-fifths verged on the impecunious. More than a third belonged to opposition political or religious groups, and even more resided outside the Boston–North Shore area. Fewer than half were Harvard men; and not a single Overseer elected in the 1850s was ever a member of the Corporation. The figures for every category represented a sharp decline from those of the previous two decades, when the self-perpetuating segment of the Overseers was altogether rich and reliable.

After 1866 the picture shifted drastically. The new group

contained not one single ideological dissident, and only a small handful without Harvard College degree or from outside the Boston-Salem area.[91] In each category the figures either approached or improved upon those from 1828 to 1851. In terms of wealth the curve sloped upward still more steeply, with estates of $100,000 or more showing the sharpest rise of all over both previous groups. Indeed, the disparity in wealth was even greater than this, for fully 57 percent of the members of the final group were worth $250,000 or more when they died. Six of them were millionaires.

Small wonder, then, that so many of these latter-day Overseers were tapped for service on the Corporation: the two bodies, in terms of social characteristics, were identical. The cultivated and leisurely "friends of the college" entrusted with its safekeeping turned out, not very surprisingly, to be little more than the Harvard Club of Boston, the core of the urban elite. And since there were now no ex officio politicians on the Board to balance, harass, or otherwise destabilize the new group, a situation rather different from the early period and quite different indeed from the 1850s, the time of entrustment might safely be assumed to be forever. The circle of patrons, governors, faculty, students, and guardians was at last — and in the nick of time — complete.

This fine solidarity was the product of a rather complex dialectical process. First came an array of policies — the largesse of an economic elite and the assumption of control of the Corporation by members of this elite, the monopolizing of university facilities by elite progeny and the development of distinctive living arrangements and curriculum, the acquisition of a subordinate but elite-oriented faculty — designed to create a self-conscious metropolitan upper class after the English model with appropriate national modifications. The very success of these policies, however, antagonized radical, rural, middle- and lower-class groups who were at odds with the new elite and who attempted to radicalize and democratize the university through legislative action. Faced with this hostility, the university's leaders took obvious, if difficult, steps to crystallize the loyalties of its patrons and to transfer responsibility for university supervision out of the legislature and into the hands of this loyal element.[92]

The culmination of this complex chain of developments was the Act of 1865, which thus possessed a dual significance. First, the Act preserved the composition and authority of the Corporation and hence guaranteed the continued primacy of elite interests and objectives at Harvard, as they were being guaranteed rather more easily elsewhere in the cultural constellation. Second, the battle of Harvard, like the lesser struggles at the library, the cemetery, the hospital, and the lecture forum, further awakened the elite to the nature of its institutional obligations and to its exposed position under democratic conditions and hence intensified its consciousness of itself as a genuine upper class — as, in fact, what the world would perceive as a Brahmin aristocracy.

The Brahmin Aristocracy

IN spite of its colonial establishment and community traditions, the story of antebellum Harvard conforms very closely to the broad pattern of institutional development in Boston. The initial phase of university expansion before 1830 reflected the growing concentration of wealthy families in and around Boston and their desire to patronize the major extant civic institution of the area at the same time that they founded a spate of new institutions to accompany it. The phase of accelerated funding and administrative rationalization after 1830 reflected the rising tempo of economic accumulation and the shift within the patron community from traditional commercial to modern financial and industrial enterprise. At Harvard, as at the Athenaeum, the Lowell Institute, and the Massachusetts General Hospital, the funds for growth came largely after 1815, followed soon after by administrative systemization. The funds derived principally from families who had become wealthy since the Revolution. Their civic ventures, like their banks, mills, and railroads, were at once cause and effect of the basic processes of residential and economic concentration — both the urbanization and the stratification — that were the salient characteristics of the New England of this era.

Harvard's growth served, in turn, to unify an institutional world which was already comparatively cohesive by virtue of interlocking functions, facilities, and personnel. Half the Harvard Corporation members were trustees of the Athenaeum, the Massachusetts General Hospital, or both. Harvard professors staffed the hospital and its satellite institutions; edited and wrote for the *North American Review* and other periodicals; organized the Mount Auburn Cemetery; directed the Massachusetts Historical Society; and served on the staffs or boards of the societies of horticulture, natural history, and arts and sciences. The trustee of the Lowell Institute served simultaneously on the Corporation and drew his lecturers partly from the Harvard faculty, whose members, when not lecturing themselves, proffered advice as to the selection of nonuniversity speakers.

Harvard's relationship to the world of business, if not so central as in culture, was nonetheless close. It was a closeness which derived in part from the university's size, adoption of the business community's methods of operation, and reliance on elite financial institutions for administrative and investment services. Primarily, however, it derived from the interests of the professors and Corporation members, who after 1830 were heavily involved in the management and promotion of the chief economic enterprises of the region: its largest textile mills; several of its railroads; the three great financial institutions of Boston plus a dozen lesser banks and insurance companies and the major English investment house; and a wide range of other manufacturing, maritime, and real estate ventures. By mid-century both faculty and Fellows had reached unprecedented heights of prosperity and possessed business connections and concerns which were as fundamental and extensive, generally speaking, as their ties to culture.

The institutional diagram presented in chapter 1 may therefore be extended roughly as follows, with the solidity of the line indicating the closeness of the relationship:

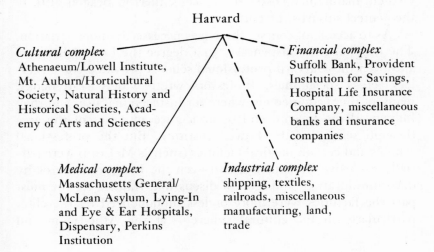

Harvard

Cultural complex
Athenaeum/Lowell Institute,
Mt. Auburn/Horticultural
Society, Natural History and
Historical Societies, Academy of Arts and Sciences

Financial complex
Suffolk Bank, Provident
Institution for Savings,
Hospital Life Insurance
Company, miscellaneous
banks and insurance
companies

Medical complex
Massachusetts General/
McLean Asylum, Lying-In
and Eye & Ear Hospitals,
Dispensary, Perkins
Institution

Industrial complex
shipping, textiles,
railroads, miscellaneous
manufacturing, land,
trade

In this way Harvard linked the civic institutions more tightly to one another and to the economic complex, forging in the process virtually a single institutional whole. Hence institutional culture was not so much the counterpart of institutional business as part and parcel of it.

Certainly the new Boston elite dominated the university as it dominated all the components of the cultural complex which its money created. Before 1830 the Harvard Fellows, like the Athenaeum and Massachusetts General trustees, were high-status ministers and other professionals with a literary bent and sense of service. Thereafter, they came increasingly from the business community and ranked consistently in the top 1 percent of the Massachusetts population by wealth. With few exceptions they were Unitarians in religion; with still fewer exceptions, Federalists, Whigs, or conservative Republicans in politics. Harvard professors, like Massachusetts General doctors, ranked in the top 5 percent of the population by wealth; were markedly richer at the end of the period than at the beginning; were commonly related by kinship or economic interest to the patron families; and were generally liberal in religion and conservative in politics. More Fellows and faculty were born in Boston. More of them maintained costly residences either on Beacon Hill, in the genteel suburbs, or both.

As to access, of course, there was necessarily more variation. The hospitals, the dispensary, to a degree the Lowell Institute and even the Harvard professional schools provided some services across social lines. Professors wrote widely read books, many of them adopted elsewhere for instructional use, and they influenced the lyceum and other lecture activities of the area through service at the Lowell Institute. But the professional schools and certain medical facilities (such as McLean) were partially exclusive by expense, and even the Institute lectures by decorum, location, and level of discussion. Indeed, for the most part the facilities were more or less monopolized by the elite, particularly in the cultural sphere — at the Athenaeum and

Mount Auburn by expense and location, at the Academy of Arts and Sciences by membership committees, at Harvard by expense and, increasingly, admission requirements. (Rising admission requirements in turn had a certain exclusionary effect on the system of secondary education in the region.)

Harvard, then, was almost wholly an elite institution after 1830 and, as such, facilitated elite evolution in ways that paralleled and complemented those of its institutional counterparts. Like the Athenaeum, for instance, the university contributed to the group consolidation so crucial to a collection of essentially arriviste families with disparate antecedents and diverse interests. This consolidation occurred on two levels. First, the common experience of acquiring a bachelor's degree helped to socialize the young into a "larger family" — a common mid-century metaphor for the constituencies of both library and college, although the length and intensity of a stint at Harvard was hardly to be matched elsewhere in the elite universe. Second, the common experience of governing the college and its sister institutions aided in the acculturation and absorption of parvenu elements, who had to deal respectfully and responsibly with large-scale collective assets in return for the benefits and satisfactions of influence and acceptance.

Thus, the emergence of the institutional constellation helped the elite to overcome the potential disruptions of excessive egoism and family loyalty. For this burgeoning elite, at least, the key institution of early nineteenth-century urban society was by no means the family, as much modern scholarship would suggest, but rather the civic institutions which facilitated the transcendence of family — notably the great cultural establishments and, in particular, Harvard University.

Given this position, it was logical that Harvard, like other institutions, should play a major part in the provision of a set of appropriate values for its youthful population. The university facilitated, for example, the acquisition of a uniformly genteel style, inculcating an appreciation for landscape and literature in the manner of Mount Auburn and the Athenaeum, but also a disposition to class segregation and a regard for controlled social grace, a sophistication tempered by mental and physical discipline. It also provided suitable education, of course, ensuring sufficient intellectual grounding for professional training and career success as well as an easy familiarity with books and world literature and a due awareness of modern science and legal, political, and economic thought. The actual instruction, however, was always tinged with ideology, with a subdued religiosity tending to deism, with a Whiggish politics stressing obligation to society, skepticism of democracy, and, above all, stability. Finally, Harvard inculcated the value of responsibility — to oneself and one's family, understandably, but increasingly to one's peers (classmates, mentors, social acquaintances) and institution (Alma Mater). The focus of responsibility thus shifted from village, region or sect, as in agrarian society, and from self or nuclear family, as in petit bourgeois society, to clan, peerage, and institution, as befitted an evolving upper class. The provision of values thereby performed the same consolidating role as common experience.

Here, too, was satisfactorily resolved the vexing question of the proper relation between business and culture. In the early years of the century Harvard, like the Athenaeum, tended to draw strong support from professional men and other literati, partly but by no means entirely from Boston, men who looked to institutional culture to moderate and refine the seemingly fragmenting, materialistic tendencies of commerce and to sustain the traditions of clerical and other cultural service in the region. But business patronage, responding in part to the calls of the cultivated for assistance, soon flowed very heavily. And with it, as seen, came business control. Sporadic, belated efforts to redress the lost ministerial and scholarly balance failed, leaving nonresidential, secular, commercial interests dominant for the remainder of the century and defining, as it were, the elite center of gravity. Significant pecuniary-nonpecuniary conflict could not, and did not, emerge thereafter because the business hand, quite simply, was too solidly in control to permit it. To speak with any accuracy of the Boston upper class or Brahmin aristocracy, then, is to speak in the first instance of business prowess and industrial wealth and only then of the strict men of letters who always, whatever their connections and wealth, exercised less real authority than their commercial cousins.

In fact, however, the business community wielded its administrative authority but rarely. Patron families did not disdain letters or disparage culture at Harvard any more than at the Lowell Institute. Indeed, there was widespread agreement as to the utility of culture for business families and of business perspectives for cultural personnel. Unlike latter-day capitalists, the Boston industrialists did not simply purchase intellect in an immediate utilitarian sense, although their benefactions did shift the focus of instruction and research decisively and irreversibly toward science and society and away from morals and religion. Their objective was to shape not merely a business elite but a durable upper class within a capitalist order — a task for which intellect and profits should be mutually tolerant and supportive. After 1830, moreover, there was a rapid merging of cultural personnel with the broader elite, producing a fusion of interest and outlook which partially erased the pecuniary-nonpecuniary division within the group and reduced much of the objective basis for even latent dissatisfaction, much less overt revolt. There was above all the Corporation. Aware that profits, like profiteers, were ultimately sovereign, the Fellows (and their equivalents elsewhere in the cultural complex) also esteemed the realm of culture and philanthropy and were at times as experienced in these areas as in the commercial. They thus formed a link among the different spheres and helped preserve the elite peace through sympathetic contact where mutual interests, common goals, and administrative power might not alone have sufficed.

Class stature, however, connoted not only differentiated attainment and style but persistence, the transgenerational maintenance of place. Hence one of the striking features of Boston's institutional development: the extent to which its promoters aspired to durability and took the long view. This characteristic was much in evidence among financial institutions such as the Suffolk Bank, which for decades was a quasi–central bank and clearinghouse fostering stable regional growth, or the Massachusetts Hospital Life Insurance Company, a "Savings Bank for the rich" which was the first American corporation to hold fortunes in lifetime trust. The Athenaeum sold its shares in perpetuity, as Mount Auburn did its plots; the Lowell Institute trustee had to add a tenth of annual earnings to principal forever. Harvardians sought to evoke a sense of permanence through memorials which would stand against "all vicissitudes"; tributes to dead leaders and benefactors; insistence on institutional autonomy and the inviolability of benefactions; gatherings of several generations of graduates. In this way culture, like fortunes, became a trust. Institutions became a counterweight to social flux and intergenerational mobility. For the domineering yet anxious elite, the cultural constellation served as conservative traditionalism served other countries — as a "center," so to speak, "that would hold."[1]

The "other country" was invariably England. The inspiration for the Athenaeum and Lowell Institute was the network of English gentlemen's libraries and lecture institutions of the early nineteenth century, creations of the urban entrepreneurs, politicians, and intellectuals whom the Bostonians admired and sought to emulate. Elite leaders were highly conscious, too, of the role of the English universities in shaping English "society," and while many internal developments at Harvard were suggested by Continental or even American examples, a significant number derived from Oxbridge, transplanted to New England with the hope of producing a class of comparable wealth, power and elegance. American conditions were obviously very different from those of Britain, with its landed nobles, great churchmen, centralized government, and restricted suffrage, and Oxford and Cambridge themselves could in any case not be copied so directly as, say, libraries or lecture organizations because of their traditionalism, clerical connections, and collegial organization, all rejected at Harvard in the 1820s. That the mimicry was still so omnipresent and the appreciation of

England so forthright only underscores the class ideal lurking beneath the surface of elite institutionalism. Institutional attachments — an Athenaeum share, a Mount Auburn plot, a place at Harvard — became, in the parlance of the day, "emblems of nobility." Brahmin Boston, therefore, assumed its vaunted English hue — and its vaunted class stature — not from mere ethnic and economic coincidence but by design.

Cultural institutions, including Harvard, contributed to elite development in crucial ways during the formative era before 1850: shaping, defining, linking, solidifying, absorbing, preparing. Yet this was only a part of the story, the first phase of the contribution. The second came with the crisis years after 1850, when the entire hard-wrought infrastructure of the elite seemed in danger of dilution, seizure, and collapse. The political dimension of this crisis phase has long been evident in broad outline, with the once-ascendant Whig party, splintered over slavery, losing its preponderance to Free-Soilers and Democrats, then to Know-Nothings, and finally to early Republicans. Each party was clearly more egalitarian than the Whigs on both national and local issues — more adamant against slavery but also more adamant against privileged and undemocratic institutions — and seemingly more lower-class, as a rule, in composition and leadership — farmers, immigrants and young professionals in the early 1850s, artisans, pentecostal ministers, and petty entrepreneurs later on. The elite ordeal was most striking at the state level, where non-Whigs elected most of the governors, sent their own senators to Washington, and captured the legislature; but there were similar problems in Boston, where by 1860 nonelite groups had sharply increased their share of elected officials. The city's paladins thus found themselves trying to pump life into a Whig corpse and, failing that, to wield indirect influence, via friendship, advice, and money, in the affairs of the insurgent parties.[2]

But the mid-century crisis involved more than politics, a fact which historians have not generally appreciated. The experience of the cultural institutions is a case in point. The medical complex, for example, encountered three types of difficulty. First, as noted in chapter 1, there was mounting criticism of the health and health care of the Boston population, prompted partly by the influx of migrants but partly directed, with some reason, at the long-suspect motives and attitudes of the extant institutions. At the same time, the rate of private financial contributions declined from over 20 percent of all charity funds between 1800 and 1830 to approximately 13 percent from then to 1860 — a larger absolute sum because of the greater charitable contributions but not sufficient to allow the complex to maintain its previous growth rate or keep pace with population expansion. The third problem, closely related to the others, was the appearance between 1855 and 1865 of hospitals founded and operated by nonelite elements: one by Catholics desiring to hold the loyalties of their fellow religionists; one by middle-class homeopathic doctors long at odds with the elite Massachusetts Medical Society; and one by the municipal authorities attempting to respond to the gathering pressure for better service to the poor.[3] That none of the new ventures even remotely rivaled the Massachusetts General group in size, status, or influence was doubtless only marginally reassuring at the time. What really mattered was that the hard-earned hegemony of the elite complex and its directors and staff seemed shaken, if not in jeopardy.

Institutional culture had its troubles as well: resentment over the monopolization of scarce resources, as at the Athenaeum; disgruntlement over doctrinal conservatism and authoritarian control, as at the Lowell Institute; attacks on exclusionary costs and self-perpetuating officers, as at Mount Auburn. In 1853 the Athenaeum shareholders narrowly averted a move by city authorities to commandeer the library's holdings for the use of common citizens; in 1856 the Mount Auburn proprietors beat back an attempt to democratize the institution's decision-making processes and reduce the price of its plots. The city then had the temerity to open its own library anyway, while middle-class elements, dissatisfied with or excluded from the dominant complex, initiated smaller cemeteries or historical organizations of their own.[4] Like elite medicine, therefore, elite cultural institutions encountered a demand for access, accountability, variety, and service which, given their long-range purposes, they could not satisfy; and the proliferation of small alternative institutions which they could influence, perhaps, but not control.

Nowhere was the ordeal more intense than at Harvard, whose size, fame, and governmental ties entangled it unavoidably with the public. Indeed, Harvard was involved in both the political and the institutional facets of this mid-century crisis. It suffered many of the same afflictions as the medical and cultural institutions which it led and helped bind together, and it also became itself a political issue that fed the fires of political contention. Criticism mounted, accordingly, over the elite monopolization of Harvard facilities; over the promulgation from Cambridge of dangerously conservative social and political doctrines or, conversely, dangerously permissive theological ones; over the arrogant rejection of cherished assumptions concerning community service and responsibility; over the accumulating evidence of an insulting disdain for nonelite, nongenteel values, behavior, and contact. In succession came a shrinkage of public dollars after 1825 and of private dollars after 1850; repeated attempts during the 1850s to democratize the university by asserting public authority and reversing conservative and exclusionary policies; and the establishment from 1855 to 1869 of a half-dozen lesser institutions — two Catholic, two lower-class Protestant, two technical — largely controlled, at least for the moment, either by government or by groups who had been denied influence and access at Harvard and did not like it.[5]

The college thus found its operations, autonomy, and, perchance, preeminence under siege from a host of foes. Ideologically defined, these foes included a hodgepodge of trinitarians, egalitarians, utilitarians, abolitionists, and democrats, not all in agreement with one another, by any means, but all similarly alienated from what Harvard had become. Sociologically defined, they included rural and small-town gentry in process of decline, petty urban capitalists in process of emergence, proletarians and immigrants being hammered into distinct (and aggrieved) groups, even blacks (who went to college in Amherst, not Cambridge).[6]

In general, these were precisely the forces seeking to undermine elite preponderance in politics and in the cultural complex elsewhere. They are more identifiable here from the closeness of the analysis rather than from the singularity of the case. In general, too, they were products, as regarded their social position and attitudes, of the very processes of industrialization and urban institution-building initiated by the elite early in the century. These were processes which, after all, had created hardpressed westerners, disgruntled workmen and militant Methodists as well as wealthy Unitarians, and had created them in considerably greater numbers. They were processes which inevitably antagonized groups, old or new, not sharing the benefits or appreciating the results.

The challenge which this disparate insurgency posed was all the more formidable for pressing at so many points simultaneously and in seeming sporadic concert. It came at a time, moreover, of considerable disunity and economic weakness within the ranks of the elite itself. The disunity appeared in the cotton-versus-conscience splintering of Whiggery and at times among the institutions (at Mount Auburn, for example). But it was also evident in areas such as religion, where during the 1850s Episcopalians multiplied somewhat more rapidly than Unitarians and even fading Orthodoxy held its own for a time. A large and growing non-Protestant population also appeared, not precisely of a radical or insurgent character, to be sure, but still aggrieved and certainly less responsive to established elite leadership than to its own hierarchy — with whose conservative elements the elite accordingly sought, as in the anticonstitutional campaign of 1853, to fashion ad hoc political alliances in the interest of stability.[7]

The weakness in business, which is even less well recognized and appreciated by historians than the institutional difficulties, may be discerned in four areas. First, after some forty flourishing years the shipping industry of Boston, which had still attracted substantial capital as late as the 1840s, fell off precipitously in the mid-1850s, carrying profits, at least temporarily, with it. Second, industrial dividends likewise declined sharply: in textile manufacturing, from a robust 14 percent a year on the average in the 1840s to barely 4 percent in the 1850s; in railroads by lesser but still significant rates. Third, whereas elite-dominated commercial banks had controlled almost 60 percent of the total banking capital of Boston in 1850, by 1860 they controlled only about 33 percent, having lost their enormous advantage here to a swarm of smaller banking establishments which had entered the marketplace in the preceding few years. Finally, the Suffolk Bank's position as regional regulator and clearinghouse, which had furnished elite financiers with handsome profits and weighty influence since 1820, was usurped in the late 1850s by a rival institution supported by resentful country bankers and upstart Bostonians.[8] Thus, with its control attenuated and its income diminished, the elite suddenly found itself pressed in business as in religion, politics, and culture — the falling rate of charitable benefactions doubtless a partial reflection of this fact.

The mid-century elite faced an ironic situation. Its enormous, invaluable institutional infrastructure was endangered by precisely those forces in American society which it was created in large part to combat: individualism (hence the internal divisions), capitalism (hence the falling rate of profit), and democracy (hence the popular attacks). The result of the convergence of these tendencies — lower-class insurgence, elite softness, broad-gauged confrontation — was to make the 1850s a period of intense struggle and a time of unparalleled crisis for the would-be aristocracy. Whether other metropolitan centers underwent the same sort of mid-century experience is unclear, although there is evidence that in some places perhaps they did.[9] For Boston, at any rate, the pattern is clear: challenge was the order of the day.

The end of the story is well known. The elite triumphed in every sphere, its victory doubtless all the sweeter after the bitterness of the fight. In politics this "thermidor" phase was naturally facilitated, and perhaps rendered inevitable, by the fragmented, unfocused character of the opposition, which was divided (as is well appreciated) between nativists and immigrants, proletarians and bourgeoisie, urbanites and rural people, most of them preoccupied with, among other things, the struggle against southern slavery and the Roman Church. The ultimate trend is perhaps clearest in politics. By 1860 there is evidence of strong elite movement toward Republicanism: Republican activists in that year were wealthier, as a rule, than their Democratic or Constitutional Unionist adversaries, while Beacon Hill's Ward 6 returned the largest majority in the city for Lincoln.[10] It would seem, therefore, that, as a Brahmin scholar later remarked, the "old-fashioned 'Cotton Whigs'. . . quietly captured" the Republican party "soon after its radical start."[11] Thanks in part to such machinations and in part to the inevitable unifying force of the war years, by 1865 Republicanism was almost the sole political vehicle of the upper class, which now had a strong and cohesive party through which to exert its authority. The minor deviations of Mugwumpery and Cleveland Democracy excepted, such Republican unity and strength was a fact of Brahmin life for the rest of the century.[12]

Unitarianism remained the leading upper-class religion. Boston was the national headquarters of the denomination, and no less than two-fifths of the leading businessmen of the metropolis were professing adherence to the faith as late as the early twentieth century.[13] More important, a steady ecumenical current had begun to flow even before the war. At the Unitarian-oriented Lowell Institute, for example, at least three non-Unitarians gave religious lectures during the 1850s, while a wealthy Episcopalian erected a nondenominational "Christ's Church" in the exclusive suburb of Brookline, for which he prepared his own liturgy and prayerbook. "If men will abstain," he wrote, "from obtruding into the act of worship those speculations which have no necessary connection with it, why may they not bow together before that God which they all adore?" This

particular church was not a great success, for denominational
distinctions were still too crucial to discard so easily; its existence, however, highlights the quest for an elite religious unity
beyond that provided by Unitarianism. When the scions of two
Brahmin families became leading postwar Episcopal bishops, it
was a cause for pride rather than alarm.[14] Orthodoxy, meanwhile, vanished as an upper-class sect virtually without a trace,
thus leaving the great Unitarian and small Episcopal wings of the
Brahmins at once amicable and ascendant.

The business experience was of a piece. In industry, railroad
and textile dividends surged upward after 1862, generally remaining at pre-1850 levels or more for at least the next decade,
while profitable new areas of investment opened in the form of
western railroads, nonferrous mining, and utilities.[15] Upper-
class commercial banks won back much of the ground lost prior
to the war. (The Suffolk Bank, to be sure, never again played a
major role, but the National Banking Act, modeled in part after
the Suffolk system, largely superseded such regional arrangements anyway.) Outside commercial banking there were still
greater gains, with institutions such as the Provident Institution
for Savings maintaining a high rate of growth and being joined
now by such well-known Brahmin-controlled trust and investment firms as the Boston Safe Deposit and Trust Company and
Lee, Higginson and Company.[16] The results were striking. As
of the 1890s over half the city's millionaires were listed in the
Social Register, with the proportion rising. By the early twentieth century Boston supplied more of the officers and trustees of
industrial firms listed on the New York Stock Exchange than
any other city save New York itself, and almost two-thirds of
them came from upper-class backgrounds.[14]

So, too, in the institutional realm, where the resurgence was
undoubtedly made easier by developments in politics and business and the release of pent-up pressure through the safety valve
of nonelite alternative institutions. In medicine the Massachusetts General Hospital complex reasserted itself in two ways:
first, through the establishment in the 1860s of the New England
Hospital for Women and the Children's Hospital, whose trustees

and personnel overlapped sufficiently with the Massachusetts General's to make them the first new components to be added to the extant group in thirty years and timely counterweights, therefore, to the new nonelite institutions; and second, via a sharp increase in the flow of private charity funds to the Massachusetts General (which attracted more money in the 1860s than in the previous three decades combined) and its satellites. Although additional medical facilities would appear on the Boston scene later in the century, including some which wound up in non-Brahmin hands, this sudden burst of renewed vigor served almost of itself to guarantee that the original medical complex would hold on to its central place of prestige and power, however the Boston medical world might develop. Indeed, by the early twentieth century the Massachusetts General and Lying-In hospitals controlled two of the three largest institutional endowments in Boston at a time when the area was well known for the magnitude of its long-settled charitable trusts.[18]

The cultural institutions exhibited a few variations on the same theme. For one thing, most of them had waged more or less successful struggles for autonomy and control rather early — the Athenaeum in 1853, Mount Auburn in 1856, the Lowell Institute throughout the 1850s, Harvard from 1850 to 1865, and so on. For another, while the cultural complex as a whole expanded enormously after 1860, far overshadowing any governmental or lower-class rivals, it did so, with one notable exception, less through the accumulation of new funds in the manner of the medical complex than through the proliferation of new upper-class institutions. These ranged from the Boston Symphony Orchestra, the Museum of Fine Arts, the Colonial Society of Massachusetts, the Gardner Museum, and Radcliffe College in the cultural realm proper to the Country, Myopia Hunt, Tavern, and other exclusive clubs of Brahmin society to, finally, the mature *Atlantic Monthly* and *Boston Evening Transcript* in the world of publishing.[19] So rapid and extensive was this spasm of creativity that it may be considered a kind of "third wave" of urban institutional formation, following the post-Revolutionary and antebellum waves in logical sequence.

The endowments of many of the original institutions increased impressively in these years, to be sure. Those of the Athenaeum and Lowell Institute tripled from 1850 to 1900, for example, and that of the smaller Horticultural Society grew still faster. There were also formal connections of a familiar sort. The Lowell Institute trustee served ex officio on the board of trustees of the Museum of Fine Arts, to which the Harvard Corporation and Athenaeum trustees named representatives as well; the Colonial Society held its quarterly meetings in the hall of the Academy of Arts and Sciences at the Athenaeum.[20] In general, however — and again with one exception — the cultural complex expanded by a process of institutional specialization and dispersal, with less propinquity and fewer interlocking trusteeships, so that while the aggregate endowment reached into the millions, no one or even two of these institutions exercised such sway as had the prewar Athenaeum and Lowell Institute.

The great exception to the pattern of growth via proliferation was, of course, Harvard, where charity funds accrued at the rate of $100,000 a year during the three decades after 1865, or more than quadruple the prewar rate. The university's assets multiplied sevenfold between 1870 and 1900, much the fastest growth ratio in the cultural constellation; its endowment by the early twentieth century was the single largest in Boston.[21] By now almost every dollar of this river of wealth came solely from wealthy Bostonians. Perhaps because of their greater numbers and residential propinquity, the university's patrons in this era revived the practice of giving large sums by subscription rather than by individual bequest. But these subscriptions should not be confused with the type of community subscription of the pre-1825 era. The latter was an expression of public support; the former, of class support.

Harvard was not merely larger. It was, if anything, even more interwoven with the Brahmin business establishment. Charles W. Eliot, who assumed the presidency in 1869 and remained president for forty years, was elected to the post as a scientist and an administrator and also as the scion of a patron family who was initially offered the treasurership of New England's largest textile mill.[22] Within a few years after 1865 the Corporation as a whole increased its number of businessmen (excluding Eliot) from two to three, while the median wealth of the Fellows rose steadily from $225,000 in 1850 to $400,000 in 1870 to $500,000 in 1890.[23] The single decade after 1865, moreover, saw the establishment of professorships of practical geology, mining, and political economy, inter alia, all created largely with the funds of men interested in western railroads, copper mining, and investment banking. In 1881 Eliot assured the Brahmin president of American Bell Telephone that a contribution to a new university physics laboratory would greatly benefit the company, which could profit from its discoveries in electricity, use its facilities for company research, and employ its professors for company work. "I trust," wrote Eliot, "that these reasons . . . will appear to your directors to warrant a contribution." The directors, understandably, contributed with some generosity.[24]

Eliot argued throughout his presidency that men aiming at a career in business — "which I understand to mean banking, transportation, manufacturing, mining, large-scale farming, and engineering" — required a "trained mind, and a deal of appropriate information" obtainable only in college. As evidence he pointed to the graduates of his own institution.[25] And well he might: by the 1890s, some 40 percent of them were becoming businessmen (excluding farming) as against 22 percent who became lawyers, 14 percent educators, 10 percent doctors, and 3 percent ministers.[26]

Since over half the incoming classes continued to come from the Boston area even at this late date and almost half took up careers there, it is hardly surprising to find the leading upper-class ventures headed increasingly by Harvard graduates. Thus:

> The proportion of presidents of Boston commercial banks with Harvard degrees rose from 14 percent in 1860 to 26 percent in 1880; and the proportion of Harvard-trained directors of selected noncommercial financial institutions increased from a third between 1831 and 1860 to 44 percent between 1870 and 1890.[27]

Of approximately 400 Boston millionaires in the 1890s, some 40 percent had attended Harvard; and of approximately 200 leading Boston industrialists of the early twentieth century, some 47 percent had Harvard degrees.

Of forty individuals named by two leading historians of late nineteenth-century Boston as *the* Brahmin leaders at the turn of the century, no fewer than 93 percent were Harvard men.[28]

The university was equally interwoven with and central to the prosperity of the late–nineteenth century cultural constellation. Again, the presence of university men among the officers and participants was perhaps the most significant factor. At most of the older institutions, where this presence had long been evident, it became even more evident. At the Boston Dispensary and the Horticultural Society, for example, 25 percent of the high officers elected before 1860 were Harvard graduates as opposed to 65 percent thereafter; at the Lowell Institute, whose trustee was always a Harvardian, Harvard graduates gave some 44 percent of the lectures before 1860 but 54 percent thereafter.[29] Among the newer institutions Harvard men tended to be preponderant from the start, although in most instances they became even more so as time passed. At the Museum of Fine Arts two-thirds of the original 1870 trustees were Harvard graduates as compared to nine-tenths of those elected in the 1890s. At Brookline's Country Club, founded in 1882, half the entire original membership had attended Harvard. At the Colonial Society, founded in 1892, 85 percent of the officers in the first decades were from Harvard.[30]

The civic institutions of this era were products, as one historian acknowledges, of the same basic objectives as their precursors: to provide their patrons with a sense of stability and order and to preserve culture and philanthropy from the excessive incursions of the populace.[31] Like their precursors, too, they were thought of in terms of their class function — as "our ultimate source of strength" — and their cohesiveness — as "in their nature inevitably corporate, cooperative."[32] Institutional consciousness seemed thus coextensive with Brahminism. Yet far more than before the war, it was Harvard alone which supplied this strength, cohesion, and consciousness, for the university attracted such wealth as to leave its institutional counterparts comparatively small. It exerted such influence, through its own activities and the role of its graduates in upper-class affairs, as to make them virtual institutional adjuncts. The tendency had been implicit in the developments of the antebellum era, when Harvard became primus inter pares. After the war it was no longer a tendency, for there were few, if any, *pares* to consider. "When Boston forgets Harvard," went a high Victorian stricture, "may her right hand forget its cunning."[33]

One further point may be noted: the degree to which the mid-century "crisis years" helped to shape Brahmin institutional attitudes and development. There is little doubt of the catalytic and energizing effect of this period. Of the 200 Harvard graduates among the original Country Club members, for example, some 38 percent had taken their degrees between 1851 and 1865, when the struggle for the university was most intense. Among the Harvardians on the Museum of Fine Arts board in the 1890s, the proportion of graduates from these years was 36 percent; for the original Colonial Society officers, 54 percent; for the forty select Brahmin luminaries, 47 percent; and for the Harvard Corporation itself from 1880 to 1900, more than 70 percent. To a remarkable extent, the men of mid-century Harvard created the late-century institutional constellation as a single cohort. And they molded it as befitted their experience. The university to which they owed primary fealty became its centerpiece; the complex as a whole remained almost wholly private, funded and controlled by the upper class without popular or governmental intervention to a degree unique even among the "private cities" of late–nineteenth century America.

This mature institutional constellation provided the Boston upper class with an interesting twofold staying power. One lay in its capacity to absorb and integrate parvenu families, who continued to arrive on the Boston scene in significant numbers (witness the Kennedys) and as continually to blend into the fabric of aristocratic life.[34] The variety of institutional activities doubtless facilitated this process of acculturation, making it looser and more flexible than in prewar days. The university's centrality likewise helped, the attendance there by the second generation making the accommodation — cooptation — more certain and secure. Meanwhile, Boston University, Tufts, and the other lesser colleges "took charge — each in its cheap way — of the cheap material."[35] So effective was the overall process that at the basic institutional level the upper class was, quite simply, never directly assaulted again.

The second source of strength lay in the influence of Harvard on the national scene, where economic, political, and social affairs were increasingly conducted. President Eliot was solicitous from the start of the number of New Yorkers at Cambridge (the South being temporarily powerless and therefore irrelevant), but he also took a broader view, holding it to be

> for the safety of Harvard College, and for the welfare of the country, that the College draw its material not from Massachusetts or New England alone; but from the whole country, and that the graduates of the College spread themselves over the whole country.[36]

Eliot opposed proposals to establish a federal university in Washington on the ostensible grounds that Americans instinctively preferred private institutions; but privately he suggested to New Haven that Harvard and Yale might offer coordinated admission examinations throughout the country in order to become the "Oxford and Cambridge" of the nation.[37] By 1900 Harvard, though still catering in the first instance to Boston, was attracting both the wealth and the sons of "Robber Barons" and non–New England business leaders generally.

A brief comparison with other late–nineteenth century metropolitan centers makes the Boston picture clearer. Philadelphia, for example, had had an affluent elite in the early decades of the century and a tradition of civic enterprise reaching back even further than Boston's, and it apparently experienced sociopolitical shocks in the 1850s not wholly dissimilar to those which awakened the New Englanders. By 1900, however, while there

was indisputably a Proper Philadelphia with ample fortunes and
high status, it did not compare to the Brahmins either economically, as measured by the number of millionaires or corporation officers,or socially, as measured by cohesiveness, continuity, sense of tradition, or cultural aura. Chicago, capital of
the Midwest, lacked a sense of tradition and continuity because
of its newness but fell short in all the other ways as well. While
vast size and rapid growth in Philadelphia and Chicago might
suffice to account for a part of the shortcomings, the close observer is struck especially by the great differences in the patterns
of civic institutional development — in Chicago more externally
oriented and preoccupied with social uplift and control than in
Boston during the formative years; in Philadelphia less centered
around a single entity such as Harvard and hence prone to cen-
trifugal fragmentation; in both cities far more localized as to
institutional interest and influence. Philadelphians and Chica-
goans might go to Harvard; Bostonians did not go to Penn or the
University of Chicago.[38]

The Brahmins thus formed a key element in the late–
nineteenth century national upper class by virtue of their genteel
bearing and economic prowess. Harvard provided them, however, with an invaluable reinforcement.

The foregoing will, it is hoped, serve as an addition to the growing literature on the evolution of nineteenth-century American
elites — in this instance, on the evolution of a relatively dispersed, relatively undifferentiated, preindustrial regional elite
into a distinctive, modern, urban upper class. The evidence
suggests that the process was not merely economic but cultural
as well, involving the symbiotic growth of urban civic institutions and the aspiring families who built, controlled and utilized
them; possessed a vision of their possible functions; and saw
them tested and tempered in the fires of struggle. In Boston, if
not elsewhere, the emergence of modern cultural and philanthropic institutions was inextricable from the emergence of a
modern upper class; the emergence of institutions and class,

inextricable from the larger patterns of urbanization and growth. Hence the durability of the Brahmin aristocracy. Hence, too, its distinctiveness.

Harvard, the centerpiece of the study, was likewise the centerpiece of the elite institutional constellation, more crucial, perhaps, than any other institution in molding its new constituency into a viable class and providing a focal point for its loyalties and more revealing, too, as to its motives and tenacity. Considered in this perspective, Harvard appears to have been even less typical of the "American college" of the era than once believed. But what made it atypical was not its independence or its liberalism, if by "liberal" is intended any of the term's recent connotations of egalitarianism, compassion, or intellectual iconoclasm. Indeed, it may be argued that Harvard's achievement of independence in 1865 was an effort to ward off the imposition by state and society of precisely this latter-day kind of liberalism. Nowhere else, certainly, was the faculty so subservient to the dictates of wealth and power or was its limited exercise of authority so contingent upon its own possession of wealth and connections.

The atypicality derived rather from a singularly close relationship to the nation's most entrepreneurial and ambitious metropolitan elite, the wealth and influence of which made Harvard at once the largest and richest of American universities and also the most secular, conservative and exclusive. Admitting the distinction between the quest for short-term profits and long-term power, one may observe nonetheless that the so-called "business invasion" came to Cambridge long before the age of Veblen.[39] That the invasion came so early made Harvard a harbinger of important future developments in American higher education, though not quite in the way sometimes supposed. That the invasion was so massive kept it forever in the lead.

The chief contention of the study, however, is that Harvard should be considered as much a civic institution as a college and as much an engine of class as an entity of culture. Its function, like that of its institutional counterparts, was to supply not education to the community but form and stability to the elite — a function which it eminently fulfilled. But what benefits a class may sometimes damage a society. It seems likely, in fact, that the emergence of overweening, elite-dominated institutions seriously exacerbated the regional and class divisions that already attended New England's nineteenth-century development. Excluded groups often managed to create alternative institutions, to be sure. Yet the insurgence of the 1850s suggests that pluralism of this sort was not simply a matter of preference. It was also a response to the growing institutional preponderance of a grasping elite on the part of excluded groups, who felt constrained (revolt having failed) to create separate, though hardly equal, facilities of their own. Once begun, such cultural fragmentation naturally fed upon itself and fed, too, the deepening social and economic rifts whence it had in part derived. Thereafter, people would peer at one another across vast gulfs of culture as well as of wealth. And insofar as the Proper Bostonians and their institutions were instrumental in the formation of a national upper class in the late nineteenth century, virtually the same observations would hold for this broader sphere.

For the forging of the Brahmin aristocracy, then, the consequences of the great institutional developments of the antebellum era were altogether happy. For the forging of a viable society with a coherent culture, they were far less so.

The Sources

It seems less necessary to itemize the thousands of sources consulted in the preparation of this study, for which the notes themselves should suffice, than to note the two principles which guided the research and indicate the major areas to which they led. The guiding principles were, first, to make every effort to look outside as well as within the various institutions under consideration in an effort to fuse the two spheres more thoroughly than had been done before; and secondly, not only to exhaust the standard manuscript and archival sources but to explore as many different types of material as could be disinterred. One principle naturally reinforced the other, resulting, it is hoped, in a more definitive and complete investigation than it might have been.

The major resource areas, with some of their chief components, are briefly, then, as follows:

1. Institutional Histories, Archives, and Publications

Of recent institutional historians, two scholars have produced what amount to oeuvres: Walter Muir Whitehill, with books on the Museum of Fine Arts, the Colonial Society of Massachusetts, and the Boston Public Library, as well as on the Provident Institution for Savings and the spatial permutations of the city of Boston itself; and Samuel Eliot Morison, who produced, besides a biography of Harrison Gray Otis and histories of Massachusetts shipping and the Plymouth Rope Works, the "official" history of Harvard, a collection of departmental histories of Harvard during the Eliot administration, a snatch of autobiography, and two valuable short pieces on the end of the Kirkland years and the controversy over Francis Bowen. All these works are reverential, useful more for loving antiquarian detail than for critical insight, but no less essential for that.

Elsewhere, the earlier institutional histories, with their lists of officers and contributors, thumbnail biographies, and closeness to nineteenth-century attitudes, were generally more helpful than the more recent ones. Thus, Harriette Smith was more informative than Edward Weeks on the Lowell Institute and Charles Warren much better than Arthur Sutherland on the Harvard Law School. Other good early works would include Nathaniel I. Bowditch on the Massachusetts General Hospital, William R. Lawrence on the Boston Dispensary, and Henry Jenks on the Boston Latin School; and especially the books by Josiah Quincy and Samuel A. Eliot on Harvard, both produced partly for polemical purposes and containing essential lists and numerous biographical sketches of early donors to the university, its schools, and its libraries. Useful among the later works was George Williams's edition of essays on the Harvard Divinity School. The institutional histories were profitably supplemented by Justin Winsor's multivolume history of Boston (1880) and early guidebooks and other bits of puffery such as those of Henry Dearborn and Moses King, published periodically with varying items of institutional information.

Institutional archives proved valuable in some cases: those of the Boston Public Library, the Boston Latin School, and the Boston Assemblies at the Boston Public Library, for example, and the financial records of the Lowell Institute at the Boston Athenaeum. At Harvard, where Jared Sparks established an official archive about 1850, there were four chief repositories: the letterbooks of the presidents, beginning with John Kirkland about 1810 and continuing through the Eliot years; and the College Papers and the Reports of the Corporation and the Board of Overseers, which were especially rich after about 1820. The letterbooks were helpful for relations with students, parents, faculty, and alumni. The Papers and Reports were invaluable for the transitional years after 1825 and the crisis years after 1850, on which latter there is little secondary literature of value. Also available were: manuscript faculty reports to the president, which were somewhat less useful than anticipated; a fine, massive compilation of Harvard bequests by A. T. Gibbs, which, together with Quincy, Eliot, and a few other sources, provided a near-complete record of university benefactions from the early seventeenth to the late nineteenth centuries; and the manuscript files of the class presidents, especially those of the classes before 1820, among which are superb materials on changing perceptions and values.

Among the printed institutional publications, the Harvardiana was most abundant. The basic volume, in some ways the very text of this study from which all else flowed, was the latest edition of the *Harvard Quinquennial Catalogue*, with its lists of all Harvard officers and overseers and all Harvard degree-holders both by year of graduation and by family name. Also helpful were the annual reports of the president and treasurer, first published in the 1820s and expanding in bulk and detail by the year. (The reports of President Eliot in the early 1870s were remarkably informative and suggestive about Harvard in the preceding twenty years.) The official catalogues which the university began to issue in the 1820s provided basic, if incomplete, information on costs and curriculum, and the official pamphlets of the administration during the 1850s were illuminating on the mid-century conflicts as perceived by the university leadership. Unofficial but institutionally sanctioned publications included the classbooks published from the 1820s on, useful for student backgrounds and future careers and for glimpses of the changing Cambridge scene; and the *Harvard Graduates Magazine*, a late-century journal devoted largely to recapturing the atmosphere of earlier days and producing studies on Harvard men in politics over the years, foreign language enrollments by decade, undergraduate religious preferences, and so on.

Outside the Yard the Athenaeum's annual printed reports were informative, as were those of the Mount Auburn Cemetery. In 1885 the Lowell Institute finally published its founder's will, together with several legal appendixes on the Trustee's powers and responsibilities; in the twentieth century appeared a newsletter (another project of Whitehill and before him of M. A. DeWolfe Howe) called *Athenaeum Items* which was informative on library history and controversies. Howe's edition of the *Monthly Anthology Proceedings* was informative as to Athenaeum antecedents; the *Athenaeum Centenary* volume of 1907 provided lists of members and contributors; Kenneth Cameron's amazing publication of the list of users of the library's circulating volumes in *Ralph Waldo Emerson's Reading* clarified the patterns of use. For the Massachusetts Historical Society and the American Academy of Arts and Sciences, the best sources on activities, leadership and patronage were the published *Memoirs*, *Proceedings*, and *Publications* of both societies.

2. Biographical Materials

The array of biographical materials is richer for this group than for perhaps any other of comparable size and significance in American history, thus allowing for an exceptionally close linkage of enterprise, institution, and family. The most extensive of these materials pertain, of course, to the Adams family: John Quincy's *Memoirs* and *Writings* and Charles Francis's early *Diary*, all available now in multivolume editions, plus the famed memoirs of Henry and Charles Francis II. Also valuable for this work was the typescript of "Extracts from the Diary of John Quincy Adams and His Son Charles Adams Relating to Harvard College," edited by William Roelker and Henry Adams and located in the Harvard archives. Of the recent biographies, the most useful were those of Edward Kirkland on Charles Francis II and of Ernest Samuels on the young Henry. The Adamses were gossipy, opinionated, and voluble, and their easily accessible writings have greatly influenced interpretations of elite Boston and nineteenth-century Harvard as well as of numerous other matters. For certain developments they comprise virtually the sole historical source. But the Adamses were also eccentric and occasionally misleading, and one must supplement extensively with the materials of other families in order to achieve any sort of balance.

For the Lowell family, certainly more influential in the affairs of elite Boston during these years than the Adamses, the published works of greatest value were Ferris Greenslet's superb family history; Edward Everett's lengthy eulogy of John Lowell, Jr., and A. Lawrence Lowell's of Edward Jackson Lowell; James Russell Lowell's three volumes of essays in the Riverside edition of his writings and the two volumes of his letters; and the collection of letters between James Russell Lowell, Robert Browning, and the William Wetmore Storys entitled *Browning to His American Friends.* For the Lawrences, whose benefactions were unmatched at antebellum Harvard and the Athenaeum, the key published sources were the biographies of Amos and Amos A. by their sons; the life of Abbott Lawrence by Hamilton Hill; and the fine autobiography by Amos A.'s son, William. For the Quincys, particularly the formidable Josiah, see the lengthy biography by his son, Edmund; the typescript "Autobiographical Notes" by Anna Waterston, now in the Harvard University Library; for occasional new detail, the recent study by Robert McCaughey; for inside household views, the selections from the diaries of Josiah's daughters published as *The Articulate Sisters;* and the reminiscences of Josiah's grandson, Josiah P. For the Storys, there were splendid modern biographies of Joseph by James McClellan and James Dunn, unquestionably the finest studies of an individual Bostonian to appear recently; plus a thorough life-and-letters by Joseph's son, William; plus Joseph's own *Miscellaneous Writings;* plus a memoir of William by Henry James and William's own letters in the Browning-Story-Lowell volume.

Less extensive but still considerable works were also available for other families. Kenneth Porter's classic compilation of business letters and memoranda on the Jacksons and Lees forms a solid core for those families, to which could be added volumes of the letters of Charles Jackson, Jr., and Henry and Mary Lee and an informative memoir of James Jackson by his grandson, James Jackson Putnam. Bliss Perry's life-and-letters of Henry Lee Higginson broadened the family connection somewhat, as did two autobiographies by Henry's cousin, Thomas Wentworth Higginson and a biography and compilation of Thomas's letters by his daughter. Another family branch was well covered in Vernon Briggs's massive genealogy of the Cabots, which concentrates on Samuel and Henry Cabot and on Samuel's father-in-law, Thomas Handasyd Perkins. The modern biography of Perkins himself by Carl Seaburg and Stanley Paterson proved more revealing than the older memoir by Perkins's son-in-law, Thomas G. Cary, who was himself a key figure in Louise Tharp's *Adventurous Alliance*, an engaging depiction of Cary's in-laws, the Agassizs.

The Agassiz literature is itself abundant. Besides Tharp, which deals with Louis and his son, Alexander, there is an excellent biography of Louis by Edward Lurie; an edition of Louis's letters by his wife; and a good life-and-letters of Alexander by his son, George. Of the additional family literature, the following were helpful enough to deserve special mention:

Holmes: Oliver Wendell Holmes's letters and his *Elsie Venner* and *The Autocrat of the Breakfast Table;* Mark Howe's study of the young Oliver Wendell Holmes, Jr.; and Holmes, Jr.'s letters to Frederick Pollock in *The Holmes-Pollock Letters*.

Prescott: Harvey Gardiner's biography of William Hickling Prescott; Gardiner's editions of Prescott's *Papers* and *Literary Memoranda;* and Roger Wolcott's edition of the Prescott correspondence.

Eliot: the biography of Charles W. Eliot by Henry James; Eliot's own reminiscences; and the history of Cambridge by his son, Samuel A.

Bowditch: the biography of Nathaniel by his son, Nathaniel Ingersoll; and the life-and-letters of Nathaniel's son, Henry, by Henry's son, Vincent.

Loring: the ample biography of Charles G. Loring by Theophilus Parsons; and the *Loring Genealogy* covering several generations of the family.

Forbes: the letters of John Murray Forbes; and the reminiscences of his brother, Robert.

Ware: a biography of Henry Ware, Jr., by his brother John; and a *Ware Genealogy* spanning six generations;

Everett: the five volumes of speeches by Edward Everett; the very able biography of Edward by Paul Frothingham; and the travel book, *On the Cam*, by Edward's son, William.

Of the hundreds of other memoirs, letters, and biographies consulted, the following are perhaps worth mention both for their usefulness and their comparative obscurity: the autobiographies and reminiscences of Frank P. Stearns, Andrew P. Peabody, and Sidney Willard; the letters of Barrett Wendell, Frederic D. Huntington, and the Minot family; and the biographies of Theophilus Parsons by his son and namesake, of Benjamin R. Curtis by his cousin, George Curtis, of Jacob Bigelow by George Ellis, and of Israel Thorndike and Thomas Hill by J. D. Forbes and William Land. The *Proceedings* of the Massachusetts Historical Society, to which most of these men belonged, provided eulogistic sketches of many of them, including especially valuable ones of James Walker, Francis Calley Gray, Samuel A. Eliot, John Lowell, James Perkins, and Josiah Quincy; the *New England Historic-Genealogical Society* volumes contained briefer sketches of several others, as did the historical society publications of Cambridge, Dedham, and Medford. Eulogistic contemporary pamphlets provided interesting details (often by ministers who were themselves accociated with the elite) in the cases of Nathaniel Bowditch, John Farrar, John T. Kirkland, and Henry Ware. Finally, for some of the most voluminous published commentaries on the Boston-Cambridge scene, see the *Memoirs and Letters of Charles Sumner* by Edward Pierce, which is considerably more helpful to the working historian than the recent two-volume biography by David Donald; and the *Life, Letters and Journals of George Ticknor* by George Hilliard, which for Ticknor, though not necessarily for Harvard itself, is, again, better than the modern study by David Tyack.

To these printed materials were added manuscript materials from the following collections in the following repositories:

Massachusetts Historical Society: Josiah Quincy, Nathan Appleton, Amos and Amos A. Lawrence, Charles Lowell, Thomas C. Amory, George Bancroft, Thomas H. Perkins, George W. Lyman, Lemuel Shaw, Thomas W. Ward, and Leverett Saltonstall.

Harvard University Archives: Samuel A. and Charles W. Eliot, Josiah Quincy, John Pickering, Daniel Treadwell, Edward Everett, Thomas W. Ward, Nathaniel Bowditch.

Houghton Library, Harvard: Charles G. Loring, John and James Russell Lowell.

University of Texas: Joseph and William Wetmore Story.

The papers of the Forbes and Bowditch families and of Daniel Webster, in addition, were consulted in microfilm editions. Of all the manuscripts, the most relevant and revealing for the purposes of this study were those of Quincy, Perkins, Ward, Saltonstall, and the Lawrences at the Massachusetts Historical Society; those of Treadwell, Bowditch, and the Eliots at the Harvard University Archives; those of the Storys at the University of Texas; and those of the Bowditches on microfilm. Every collection, of course, contained its nuggets.

3. *Economic Information*

The basic published works on elite economic interests are contained in note 10 of chapter 1 and notes 15 and 16 of chapter 9. In general the studies of particular firms — those notably of Ralph Hidy on the House of Baring and N. S. B. Gras and Caleb Stetson on the Massachusetts and State Banks, George Gibb on the Saco-Lowell machine shops, Stephen Salisbury and Charles Fisher on the Boston and Albany and the Old Colony railroads, George Browne and Evelyn Knowlton on the Amoskeag and Pepperell mills, Christopher Roberts on the Middlesex Canal, Morison on the Plymouth Rope Works — were better for tracing directorships, officers, and stockholdings than were the studies of the textile or other broad industrial sectors. Given the exceptional centrality of their institutions, D. R. Whitney and Fritz Redlich on the Suffolk Bank, Gerald White and Lance Davis on the Massachusetts Hospital Life Insurance Company, and Whitehill on the Provident Institution for Savings were particularly important.

Studies of other banks, factories and railroads were available, the most useful being the centennial "memorials" with their lists of directors and antiquarian tidbits. Also rich were the local histories. Vera Shlakman's study of Chicopee, which examines not only the mills and millowners of a particular town but all the main enterprises of the owners, is still in a league by itself after forty years. Older histories were also helpful, including Samuel Emery on Taunton, A. K. Teale on Milton, and Samuel A. Eliot on Cambridge. The Boston and Cambridge city directories from 1820 to 1870 were of immense value in tracing the officers and directors of financial institutions, the number of practicing doctors and lawyers in the area, and also the proliferation of the institutions themselves. The basic source for industrial earnings in the period, not yet superseded by any econometric contribution, was Joseph Martin's statistical compilation on Boston stock exchange companies in the nineteenth century. For the early twentieth century the *New York Stock Exchange Handbook* offered a singular insight into Bostonian business pursuits.

Supplementing the sources on enterprise were three major sources on wealth: the tax lists, the gossip sheets, and the probate records. The tax lists covered Boston holdings for the years 1833, 1848 and 1860, the first two summarized and analyzed in Edward Pessen's *Riches, Class, and Power*, the second available as printed by the city in 1860. The Cambridge city directory for 1850 provided additional tax data. The gossip sheets began with the anonymous *Our First Men* in 1846, a series of thumbnail sketches of the Boston rich with estimates of their wealth. This was followed by similar works by Thomas Wilson in 1848 and by Abner Forbes and J. W. Greene in 1851 and, in revised form, 1852. The wealth estimates seem to be based on the tax lists and are not unreliable; the accompanying notes on antecedents, activities, and attitudes are a historian's treasure trove.

Finally, there were the probate files of Suffolk, Norfolk, Middlesex, Essex, Worcester, and Plymouth Counties, wherein could be found the wills and inventories or executors' bonds for virtually every individual associated with the institutions discussed in this book. The files were important in several ways: first, as an indication of the specific industrial interests of the individual at the time of his death, and especially of his real estate, trade, and minor manufacturing concerns, all difficult to discover through other means; second, as a way of tracing kinship lines and the magnitude and direction of charitable bequests; and third, as an indicator, when taken with Horace Wadlin's very fine but woefully neglected 1885 study of nineteenth-century inventories, of the rank of the individual by wealth at the time of his death. In general the probate records appeared to be more reliable on actual estate value than the tax lists and had the additional benefit of providing significant biographical information. For the end of the century, tax lists were rare and inventories, for various reasons, less reliable guides to actual wealth. Here

Sidney Ratner's reprint of lists of millionaires for 1892 and 1902 was one possible substitute, a wealth equivalent of the stock exchange handbook's data on business connections.

4. Period Publications

The periodicals of the era covered many of the trends described in the text. Most helpful was the *North American Review*, a virtual house organ of Proper Boston wherein were debated such issues as academic reform in the 1820s, academic prerogative in the 1840s, and the general tendency of culture and society throughout the prewar decades. This journal was particularly useful on two points: the agitation of the faculty in the 1840s over exclusionary Corporation policies; and the magnitude and distribution of Boston philanthropy between 1800 and 1860 as estimated in Samuel A. Eliot's articles of 1845 and 1860, estimates which institutional sources, where available, generally corroborated. Also valuable was the *Christian Examiner*, the Unitarian journal of this era, which covered developments at Harvard and elsewhere from the elite religious perspective; and the *Monthly Anthology* and *Christian Disciple*, precursors of the *North American Review* and the *Examiner*, respectively. For other journals of the time with occasional usable data or opinion, see the list in note 32 of chapter 4. The many newspapers of the time, though consulted less systematically than the journals, proved highly informative on attitudes toward the dismissal of Kirkland in the late 1820s and as a record of the conflicts among the Mount Auburn and Athenaeum proprietors and in the legislature over Harvard during the 1850s. Perhaps the most helpful of the papers for this study were the *Boston Daily Advertiser*, which had a business orientation: the *Boston Atlas*, with a political bias; and the *Boston Daily Transcript*, devoted from the first to the realm of culture and society.

Official publications and pamphlets constituted a further important source. Of the official publications the most relevant were the proceedings of the Massachusetts constitutional conventions of 1820 and 1853; the documents of the Massachusetts House and Senate, especially for the years 1848–1857; the coverage of the state legislature and legislators in *Poole's Statistical View* for 1848 to 1855; and the state court proceedings and decisions as provided in *Pickering's Legal Reports*, particularly for the 1820s. Of the vast antebellum pamphlet literature the most pertinent of the polemical productions were those of John Lowell, George Ticknor, Joseph Story, and Edward Everett during the

Corporation-faculty controversy of the 1820s; those of Francis C. Gray, Josiah Quincy, and Samuel A. Eliot defending Harvard from political enemies between 1831 and 1851; and those of Benjamin Homer and Charles Eliot Norton concerning the Athenaeum in the 1850s. Of those in what might be termed the admonitory epistolary mode, the best were John Clark's *Letter to a Student* (1796), John Lowell's *A Father's Benediction* (1811), and William Atkinson's *Letter to a Young Man* (1849).

Two other contemporary sources yielded unexpectedly high dividends. One consisted of the society novels of the time, especially *The Barclays of Boston* (1854), *Fair Harvard* (1869), and *Hammersmith, His Harvard Days* (1878), which together provided a wealth of information about attitudes, values, manners, and mores both in the Yard and outside it. The other was the works of the Harvard faculty of the early and middle nineteenth century. The books of Story, Palfrey, and Bowen were particularly revealing as to legal precept, religious inclination, and economic assumption, although, as the reader will know by now, no effort was made to produce close intellectual history. Everywhere, the introductions, prefaces, and dedications of the books were suggestive. A checklist for all the books produced by these men was compiled from the card catalogue of the Widener Library at Harvard and from the National Union Catalogue of Pre-1956 Imprints.

5. Travel Literature

There were five major sources for tracing Boston attitudes to and contacts with Europe and especially with England. First in importance were probably the numerous articles published in the *Monthly Anthology*, *Christian Examiner*, and *North American Review*, some by cultural spokesmen such as Edward Everett and Francis Bowen, others by institutional patrons and officers ranging from the Lowells to the Brookses to the Eliots. Second came the older biographies, all containing great chunks of letters and diaries from England and the continent, of such luminaries as George Ticknor, Jared Sparks, Charles Sumner, and Edward Everett. Third, the manuscript collections of Thomas H. Perkins, Samuel A. Eliot, George W. Lyman, and Joseph Story were exceptionally rich in references to Oxbridge and the English scene.

A fourth source consisted of the travel writings of certain Bostonians which appeared in book form: Andrew Peabody and Robert C. Winthrop on Europe, Cornelius Felton on the Mediterranean area, Richard

Henry Dana on England, Theodore Lyman on Anglo-American relations, and William Everett on Cambridge University. Finally, a
number of secondary works contained usable information. Those of
Frank Thistlethwaite, Norman Buck, and Robert Spiller explored various aspects of the Anglo-American connection, including that between
Boston and England. The economic studies of Ralph Hidy, George
Gibb, and Evelyn Knowlton noted above contained many references to
the vast extent of the Anglo-Boston economic relationship. The Lowell
family studies of Ferris Greenslet and Edward Weeks and the Vernon
Briggs genealogical study of the Cabots were both rich and suggestive
on the evolution of Brahmin Anglicism, as was Mara Mayer's 1971
dissertation on Charles Eliot Norton, James Russell Lowell, and E. L.
Godkin.

On the other side of the coin, the immense travel literature left by
Europeans who visited the Boston area was informative for virtually
every phase of the research. Perhaps the most valuable were the letters
from the 1850s of Arthur Hugh Clough, English scholar and Boston
tutor, in the three volumes of his *Correspondence* and an additional volume of *Emerson-Clough Letters;* and the accounts by Charles Lyell,
Scottish scientist and Lowell Institute lecturer, of his two visits to the
United States in the 1840s. Of the journals and accounts of other
British visitors of the time, the most relevant were those of Basil Hall,
Harriet Martineau, and Richard Cobden for the 1830s; George T.
Barrett, Emmaline Stuart Wortley, and Marianne Finch for about
1850; and Edward Dicey and Anthony Trollope for the 1860s. Useful
works by non-British observers included the journals of Alexis
de Tocqueville and Charles Daubeny for the 1830s and Camille Pisani
and Ferenz Pulaszki for the period after 1850. Finally, the reviews of
scholarly and scientific works in the pages of the *Quarterly Journal of
Science* provided some insight into the surprisingly high international
standing of Boston professors in the early nineteenth century.

6. Paradigmatic Literature

Much of the most suggestive secondary literature has been noted in the
preceding paragraphs. Much more is mentioned and sometimes discussed in the footnotes. But a few titles deserve one additional word.

Every stage in the preparation of this work has been inspired by two
great classics of historical inquiry: E. Digby Baltzell's *Philadelphia Gentlemen* and Edward Thompson's *The Making of the English Working Class*.

Neither book deals directly with the topic or place discussed here, and neither is commonly conceived as bearing any very profound relationship to the other. The relationship is there, however, and these two models of scholarship were, for this study, of the essence. Fortunately, there now exists corresponding work which does, in fact, deal with antebellum New England and is capable of providing somewhat more immediate inspiration and directly applicable insight: for the elite, the New England sections of Edward Pessen's *Riches, Class, and Power* and the exemplary essays of Peter Hall in Rose Coser's 1974 edition of *The Family, Its Structure and Functions* and in the winter 1974 issue of the *History of Education Quarterly;* and for the nonelite, Alan Dawley's *Class and Community: The Industrial Revolution in Lynn* and Paul Faler's luminous article in the summer 1974 issue of *Labor History.* All this fine work, of course, ultimately flows together.

Beyond these studies were a few others worth noting by type. Among recent works on higher education in the nineteenth century, David Allmendinger's *Paupers and Scholars* was considerably more helpful and relevant than Barton Bledstein's *The Culture of Professionalism* or John Whitehead's *The Separation of College and State.* Among works on nineteenth-century Boston, Roger Lane's *Policing the City* was very useful; Peter Knight's *Plain People of Boston* and Stephan Thernstrom's *The Other Bostonians* much less so. Among cultural works, the dissertation of Richard Eddy Sykes, "Massachusetts Unitarianism and Social Change: A Religious Social System in Transition, 1780–1870," completed at the University of Minnesota in 1967, is superior in almost every way to Daniel Howe's *The Unitarian Conscience* or Stow Persons's *The Decline of American Gentility.*

Finally, there were two episodic works of exceedingly great value: Stanley Kutler's *Privilege and Creative Destruction: The Charles River Bridge Case,* an informative book of superb acuity; and Robert Sullivan's *The Disappearance of Dr. Parkman,* an informative book of superb charm. It need hardly be said that the grand synthesis, the final reckoning of the great class transformations and social crises of antebellum New England, is still in the scholarly inkwell, where it may remain for some time.

Notes

NAR	*North American Review*
CE	*Christian Examiner*
HUA	Harvard University Archives
MHS	Massachusetts Historical Society
BPL	Boston Public Library
MHSP	*Massachusetts Historical Society Proceedings*
CHSP	*Cambridge Historical Society Publications*
CSMP	*Colonial Society of Massachusetts Publications*
HGM	*Harvard Graduates Magazine*

Chapter 1

1. Edward Pessen, *Riches, Class, and Power before the Civil War* (Lexington, Mass., Toronto, London, 1973), p. 304.

2. Douglas T. Miller, *Jacksonian Aristocracy* (New York, 1967), p. 179.

3. Cf. Robert E. Callman, "Trends in the Size Distribution of Wealth in the Nineteenth Century: Some Speculation," in *Six Papers on the Size Distribution of Wealth and Income*, ed. Lee Soltow (New York and London, 1969), pp. 6–28; Stuart Blumin, "Mobility and Change in Ante-Bellum Philadelphia," in *Nineteenth-Century Cities*, eds. Stephan Thernstrom and Richard Sennett (New Haven and London, 1969), pp. 198–205; Jackson Turner Main, "Trends in Wealth Concentration before 1860," *Journal of Economic History* 31(June 1971):445–447.

4. Frederic Cople Jaher, "The Boston Brahmins in the Age of Industrial Capitalism," in *The Age of Industrialism in America*, ed. F. C. Jaher (New York and London, 1968), pp. 190–193. For data on the concentration of wealth in the Boston–New England area, see, e.g., James Henretta, "Economic Development and Social Structure in Colonial Boston," *William and Mary Quarterly* 22, s.3 (January 1965):75–92; Allan Kulikoff, "The Progress of Inequality in Revolutionary Boston," Ibid., 28, s.3 (July 1971):375–412; Alice Hanson Jones, "Wealth Estimates for the New England Colonies about 1770," *Journal of Economic History* 32(March 1972):98–127; Edward Pessen, "The Egalitarian Myth and the American Social Reality: Wealth, Mobility, and Equality in the 'Era of

the Common Man,' " *American Historical Review* 76(October 1971):989–1034; Richard Eddy Sykes, "Massachusetts Unitarianism and Social Change: A Religious Social System in Transition, 1780–1870" (Ph.D diss., University of Minnesota, 1967); Horace Wadlin, *Twenty-Fifth Annual Report of the Massachusetts Bureau of Statistics of Labor* (Boston, 1885), pp. 264–267.

5. Blumin, "Mobility and Change," p. 206. When Oliver Wendell Holmes first used the term "Brahmin" in *Elsie Venner* (Boston, 1861), he referred to the intellectual elite of New England rather than to its economic princes (pp. 17–19), although in other works from these years he clearly indicated that books also implied wealth and position, as I note in chapter 7. Just three years later, John Lothrop Motley employed the word to mean "rich, well-born, and virtuous" (*Memorial to Josiah Quincy* [Cambridge, 1864], p. 11). By 1869 the anonymous author of *Fair Harvard* (New York, 1869) means by "Brahmin" someone of inherited wealth and ascribed high status and assumes that his audience will understand and accept that usage without further explanation (pp. 269–270). For "Boston Associates" and "Whig Aristocracy," see e.g. Hannah Josephson, *The Golden Threads* (New York, 1949), p. 79–111.

As I note in the preface, an "upper class" may be said to differ from an "elite" in the greater proportion of community wealth it controls; in the greater cohesion of its occupational, familial, and generational components; and in its greater consciousness of its interests vis-à-vis antagonistic social elements. Different theorists have, of course, stressed different aspects of class development. For an emphasis on accumulation and economic engrossment, see e.g. G. William Domhoff, *Who Rules America?* (Englewood Cliffs, N.J., 1967), p. 5; for coherence and continuity, Edward N. Saveth, "The American Patrician Class: A Field for Research," in *American History and the Social Sciences*, ed. E. N. Saveth (New York and London, 1964), pp. 212–215; for conflict and consciousness, Eugene D. Genovese, *The World the Slaveholders Made* (New York, 1969), p. 5. In this study I have generally followed the usage of Frederic Jaher, employing "elite" when discussing developments before 1860 and "upper class" thereafter.

6. Lee Soltow, "Comment," in Soltow, *Six Papers*, p. 25. The "middle-class democracy" concept is from Robert E. Brown, *Middle-Class Democracy and the Revolution in Massachusetts, 1691–1780* (Ithaca, 1955), a much-maligned but meritorious work. For "common man" interpretations of the antebellum era per se, see, e.g., Marvin Meyers, *The Jacksonian Persuasion* (Stanford, 1957); Stanley Elkins, *Slavery* (New York, 1963), pp. 140–206; Lee Benson, *The Concept of Jacksonian Democracy* (Princeton, N.J., 1961), where it is suggested that the period be called the "Age of Egalitarianism."

7. Blumin, "Mobility and Change," p. 204.

8. Frederic Cople Jaher, "Nineteenth-Century Elites in Boston and New York," *Journal of Social History* 6(spring 1972):39.

9. Henry G. Pearson, "Frederic Tudor, Ice King," *MHSP* (November 1933):185–186.

10. The standard work on maritime commerce is Samuel Eliot Morison, *The Maritime History of Massachusetts, 1783–1860* (Boston, 1961); on textile manufacturing, Vera Shlakman, *Economic History of a Factory Town*, Smith College Studies in History, no. 20, October 1934–July 1935, pp. 39–42, 243, 247, passim, and Paul McGouldrick, *New England Textiles in the Nineteenth Century* (Cambridge, Mass., 1968); on railroads, Edward Chase Kirkland, *Men, Cities, and Transportation*, 2 vols. (Cambridge, Mass., 1948), Stephen Salisbury, *The State, the Investor, and the Railroad* (Cambridge, Mass., 1967), and Shlakman, *Ecomomic History*, p. 247.

For real estate ventures, see, e.g., Morison, *Maritime History*, pp. 237–246; Kirkland, *Men, Cities, and Transportation*, 1:153–155; Walter Muir Whitehill, *Boston: A Topographical History*, 2nd ed. (Cambridge, Mass., 1968), pp. 73–173; Arthur M. Johnson and Barry E. Supple, *Boston Capitalists and Western Railroads* (Cambridge, Mass., 1967), pp. 36–40, 54, 67–70, 122–125, 144–152; John Coolidge, *Mill and Mansion* (New York, 1941), pp. 168–169; George W. Browne, *The Amoskeag Manufacturing Co. of Manchester, New Hampshire* (Manchester, 1915), pp. 57, 77–78, 98–100.

For other industrial concerns, see, e.g., Christopher Roberts, *The Middlesex Canal, 1793–1860* (Cambridge, Mass., 1938); George S. Gibb, *The Saco-Lowell Shops: Textile Machinery Building in New England, 1813–1949* (Cambridge, Mass., 1950), pp. 39–40, 66; Samuel Eliot Morison, *The Ropemakers of Plymouth* (Boston, 1950), pp. 148–149; Shlakman, *Economic History*, pp. 82–84; "List of Stockholders of Boston Water Power Company Holding over 10 Shares," April 29, 1856, Amos A. Lawrence Papers, MHS; Daniel Treadwell–Francis C. Gray and Horace Gray, July 23, 1838, Daniel Treadwell Papers, HUA; George E. Ellis, *Memoir of Jacob Bigelow* (Cambridge, Mass., 1880), p. 33; Johnson and Supple, *Boston Capitalists*, pp. 121, 160; Carl Seaburg and Stanley Paterson, *Merchant Prince of Boston* (Cambridge, Mass., 1971), pp. 420–423.

For banking, the standard work is Shlakman, *Economic History*, 243–247, which may be supplemented by data from the Boston city directories for the years 1800 to 1870 and from Fritz Redlich, *The Molding of American Banking, 1781–1840* (New York, 1951). For the three most important financial institutions in antebellum Boston, see Walter Muir Whitehill, *The Provident Institution for Savings in the Town of Boston, 1816–1966* (Boston, 1966); Gerald T. White, *A History of the Massachusetts Hospital Life Insurance Company* (Cambridge, Mass., 1955); D. R. Whitney, *The Suffolk Bank* (Cambridge, 1878); Lance E. Davis, "The New England Textile Mills and the Capital Markets: A Study of Industrial Borrowing, 1840–1860," *Journal of Economic History* 20(March 1960):8–10. For the oldest and largest commercial banks, respectively, see N. S. B. Gras, *The Massachusetts First National Bank of Boston, 1784–1934* (Cambridge, Mass., 1964); and Caleb Stetson, *The State Bank* (Boston, 1870). For the leading British investment house, see Ralph W. Hidy, *The House of Baring in American Trade and Finance* (Cambridge, Mass., 1949).

11. For a graphic depiction of the interrelatedness of the economic enter-

prises, see Robert K. Lamb, "The Entrepreneur and the Community," in *Men in Business*, ed. William Miller (New York and Evanston, 1962), pp. 112–116; and Shlakman, *Economic History*. For the capitalization and dividends of incorporated ventures, see Joseph G. Martin, *A Century of Finance* (Boston, 1898), which suggests the remarkably high earning power of the elite ventures during the first half of the century.

12. See, e.g., Kenneth W. Porter, *The Jacksons and the Lees* (Cambridge, Mass., 1937), 1:98; Evelyn H. Knowlton, *Pepperell's Progress* (Cambridge, Mass., 1948), pp. 13–14.

13. Ferris Greenslet, *The Lowells and Their Seven Worlds* (Boston, 1946), p. 113; Pessen, *Riches, Class, and Power*, pp. 207–208, 215–216; Cleveland Amory, *The Proper Bostonians* (New York, n.d.), pp. 61–94.

14. Harrison Gray Otis–John Collins Warren, March 12, 1818, in Edward Warren, *The Life of John Collins Warren* (Boston, 1860), 1:146–147.

15. Peter Hall has made the important point that the most economically successful families were those whose cousinly marriage patterns united two unrelated husbands rather than two unrelated wives because this pattern was "most suited to generalized alliances and to capital combination." Peter Dobkin Hall, "Marital Selection and Business in Massachusetts Merchants' Families, 1700–1900," in *The American Family in Socio-Historical Perspective*, ed. Michael Gordon, 2nd ed. (New York, 1978), p. 112.

16. Thomas G. Cary, *The Dependence of the Fine Arts for Encouragement, in a Republic, on the Security of Property* (Boston, 1845), p. 15.

17. For the concept of party as class unifier, see Genovese, *The World the Slaveholders Made*, p. 136. For elite political affinities, see Morison, *Maritime History*, pp. 160, 299; Paul Goodman, *The Democratic Republicans of Massachusetts* (Cambridge, Mass., 1964), pp. 102–118; Robert Rich, " 'A Wilderness of Whigs': The Wealthy Men of Boston," *Journal of Social History* 4(spring 1971):263–276; Roger Lane, *Policing the City* (New York, 1971), p. 47; Thomas H. O'Connor, *Lords of the Loom* (New York, 1968); William G. Bean, "Party Transformation in Massachusetts with Special Reference to the Antecedents of Republicanism, 1848–1860" (Ph.D. diss., Harvard University, 1922).

18. On aspects of Whig programs and ideology, see, e.g., Richard N. Current, *Daniel Webster and the Rise of National Conservatism* (Boston and Toronto, 1955), pp. 189–202; Robert A. Lively, "The American System: A Review Article," *Business History Review* 29(1955):92–95; Ronald Story, "The Social and Religious Roots of Horace Mann's Involvement in the Massachusetts Common School Movement" (Master's thesis, University of Wisconsin, 1968), pp. 10–18; David Hackett Fischer, *The Revolution of American Conservatism* (New York, Evanston, London, 1969), pp. 29–49 and passim; and especially Daniel Calhoun, *The American Civil Engineer* (Cambridge, Mass., 1960), pp. 177–180.

19. These and other points are well adumbrated in two of the great classics of historical investigation: Lawrence Stone's *The Crisis of the Aristocracy* (Oxford, 1965), and E. Digby Baltzell's *Philadelphia Gentlemen* (New York, 1962).

20. Paul Goodman, "Ethics and Enterprise: The Values of a Boston Elite, 1800–1860," *American Quarterly* 18(fall 1966):446; Amory, *The Proper Bostonians*, pp. 12, 16; Alexis de Tocqueville, *Journey to America*, ed. J. P. Mayer (London, 1959), pp. 202–203.

21. Quoted in Walter Muir Whitehill, *Boston in the Age of John Fitzgerald Kennedy* (Norman, 1966), p. 33.

22. Cf. Conrad Wright, *The Beginnings of Unitarianism in America* (Boston, 1966), pp. 252–266; Sykes, "Massachusetts Unitarianism," pp. 114–149; Rich, " 'A Wilderness of Whigs'," p. 273; Octavius B. Frothingham, *Boston Unitarianism, 1820–1850* (New York, 1890).

23. On Unitarian doctrine, see Sykes, "Massachusetts Unitarianism," pp. 287–297; William R. Hutchison, *The Transcendentalist Ministers* (Boston, 1965), pp. 1–21; and especially E. L. Jones and G. E. Mingay, eds., *Land, Labour and Population in the Industrial Revolution* (London, 1967), p. 99. For the role of religion as a source of ideology and identity, see, e.g., Erik Erikson, *Young Man Luther* (London, 1959), pp. 22; Baltzell, *Philadelphia Gentlemen*, pp. 253–293; Lucien Goldman, *The Hidden God* (New York, 1964), p. 76; E. P. Thompson, *The Making of the English Working Class* (New York, 1963), pp. 26–54.

24. Lamb, "The Entrepreneur and the Community," pp. 94–98, 106–113.

25. Pessen, *Riches, Class, and Power*, pp. 253–255, 272–277.

26. Van Wyck Brooks, *The Flowering of New England* (New York, 1952), pp. 1–18.

27. The basic sources for antebellum charity are Samuel A. Eliot, "Public and Private Charities in Boston," *NAR* 61(July 1845):135–159; and Samuel A. Eliot, "Charities of Boston," Ibid. 91(July 1860):154–157. The Eliot figures include privately contributed charitable funds, exclusive of direct contributions to church parishes, and may be understated for want of complete reporting. In estimating proportions, I have omitted associations and organizations without endowments or facilities to provide them permanence, thus excluding such interesting but evanescent issue-oriented bodies as the various abolitionist or peace or temperance societies.

28. For brief sketches of most of the second-wave institutions, see, e.g., George S. Hale, "The Charities of Boston," in *The Memorial History of Boston*, ed. Justin Winsor (Boston, 1881) 4:658, 672–673; Nathaniel Dearborn, *Boston Notions* (Boston, 1848); *King's Handbook of Boston*, 9th ed. (Boston, Mass., 1884), pp. 121–166, 207–238, 301–312; Albert P. Langtry, *Metropolitan Boston* (New York, 1929), pp. 291–330, 959–992.

29. For characteristic treatments, see, e.g., C. Harvey Gardiner, *William Hickling Prescott* (Austin and London, 1969), p. 51; Robert F. Lucid, Introduction to *The Journal of Richard Henry Dana, Jr.*, ed. R. F. Lucid (Cambridge, Mass., 1968), 1:xxxi; Lewis P. Simpson, ed., *The Federalist Literary Mind* (n.p., 1962), p. 47; David B. Tyack, *George Ticknor and the Boston Brahmins* (Cambridge, Mass., 1967), pp. 174–175; Jaher, "The Boston Brahmins," pp. 196–243; Van Wyck Brooks, *New England: Indian Summer* (New York, 1965). Martin

Green provides a more judicious, though still very narrow, appraisal in *The Problem of Boston* (New York, 1966).

30. Norman Birnbaum, "Afterward," in Thernstrom and Sennett, *Nineteenth-Century Cities*, p. 421.

31. W. K. Jordan, *Philanthropy in England, 1480–1660* (New York and London, 1959), pp. 348–373; Baltzell, *Philadelphia Gentlemen*, pp. 327–403.

32. The basic history for this period is N. I. Bowditch, *A History of the Massachusetts General Hospital*, 2nd ed. (Boston, 1872), pp. 215–348, 434–455, 575, 576. For the physicians' training, see Rhoda Truax, *The Doctors Warren of Boston* (Boston, 1968), p. 171; Henry Viets, *A Brief History of Medicine in Massachusetts* (Boston and New York, 1930), p. 136; Thomas F. Harrington, *The Harvard Medical School* (New York and Chicago, 1905), 2:573.

33. For other components of the complex, see William R. Lawrence, *A History of the Boston Dispensary* (Boston, 1859); William D. Orcutt, *The Mirror of Life: Massachusetts Charitable Eye and Ear Infirmary* (Boston, 1920).

34. For the officers, trustees, and attending doctors, see Bowditch, *The Massachusetts General Hospital*, pp. 412–421. The manufacturers and merchants were Patrick Tracy Jackson, Francis Cabot Lowell, David Sears, Thomas Handasyd Perkins, Samuel Appleton, and Amos Lawrence. For the officers of the Massachusetts Medical Society, see Langtry, *Metropolitan Boston*, pp. 310–314. Here, as elsewhere throughout this work except where otherwise stated, estimates of wealth are based on inventories and executor's bonds from the probate courts of Suffolk, Norfolk, Middlesex, Essex, Franklin, Plymouth, and Worcester counties, Massachusetts; and on the *List of Persons, Copartnerships, and Corporations, Who Were Taxed on Ten Thousand Dollars and Upwards, in the City of Boston, in the Year 1860* (Boston, 1861). The probate records have proved much the most reliable and informative source and have been supplemented by material from other sources only where necessary. Lists of Boston's wealthiest individuals for years other than 1860 may be found in Pessen, *Riches, Class, and Power*, pp. 331–335. Lists of the directors of the leading banks are contained in the histories of those institutions cited in note 10.

35. Bowditch, *The Massachusetts General Hospital*, pp. 3–9, 454; Harold Schwartz, *Samuel Gridley Howe, Social Reformer* (Cambridge, 1956), p. 156; Dirk Struik, *Yankee Science in the Making*, rev. ed. (New York, 1962), pp. 281–292.

36. Francis Parkman, "Public Charities," *CE* 7(January 1830):390.

37. Eliot, "Public and Private Charities in Boston," pp. 155–156.

38. Bowditch, *The Massachusetts General Hospital*, p. 690.

39. Harrington, *The Harvard Medical School*, 2:565–566; Truax, *The Doctors Warren*, p. 144; Richard H. Shryock, *Medicine and Society in America, 1660–1860* (New York, 1960), p. 32.

40. For the scientific organizations, see Ralph S. Bates, *Scientific Societies in the United States* (New York and London, 1945), p. 51. For a convenient compilation of periodicals and cultural organizations, see Dearborn, *Boston Notions*, pp. 200–202, 381–386 and passim.

41. Josiah Quincy, *The History of the Boston Athenaeum* (Cambridge, 1851), pp. 22–24, 45–46, 53–56, 62–79, 95–105, 132–133, 248; Mabel Munson Swan, *The Athenaeum Gallery, 1827–1873* (Boston, 1940), pp. 3–4, 7–10; Charles K. Bolton, "The First One Hundred Years of Athenaeum History: A Chronological Sketch," in *Athenaeum Centenary* (Boston, 1907), pp. 28, 36–37, 44–47; Worthington C. Ford, "Introduction: The John Quincy Adams Library," in *A Catalogue of the Books of John Quincy Adams Deposited in the Boston Athenaeum* (Boston, 1938), p. 17; William L. Williamson, *William Frederick Poole and the Modern Library Movement* (New York, 1963), pp. 30–31.

42. For a list of proprietors, see *Athenaeum Centenary*, pp. 126–212. The Massachusetts probate records yield the following list of antebellum millionaires: Nathan and Samuel Appleton, Samuel D. Bradford, Josiah Bradlee, Peter C. Brooks, John P. Cushing, Samuel Eliot, Ebenezer Francis, William Gray, Gardiner Greene, Robert C. Hooper, Abbott Lawrence, John Parker, Joseph Peabody, Thomas H. Perkins, William Phillips, Dudley L. Pickman, William Pratt, David and Joshua Sears, Francis Skinner, Robert G. Shaw, William Sturgis, Israel Thorndike, John Welles, and John D. Williams. Only Bradford was not an Athenaeum patron. For contemporary estimates of the involvement of businessmen, see Quincy, *Boston Athenaeum*, pp. 24, 32–33; Josiah Quincy, "Massachusetts Institution," *NAR* 2(March 1816):313–314; Peter T. Homer, *To the Proprietors of the Boston Athenaeum* (Boston, 1851), unpaginated. For mill directors, see Shlakman, *Economic History*, pp. 39–42; for bank presidents, the Boston directory for 1850; for the wealthy men of 1848, Pessen, *Riches, Class, and Power*, pp. 331–333.

43. Amory, *The Proper Bostonians*, p. 339; *Boston Athenaeum Report for the Year 1927* (Boston, 1927), unpaginated.

44. For a list of founders, trustees, and officers, see *Athenaeum Centenary*, pp. 109–112, 115–121. Wealth estimates are from probate records, the 1860 Boston tax list, and A. Forbes and J. W. Greene, *The Rich Men of Massachusetts* (Boston, 1851). Here, as elsewhere throughout this study, estates have been ranked according to the distributions for 1829–31, 1859–61, and 1879–81 in Wadlin, *Twenty-Fifth Annual Report*. The particular distribution used is that which corresponds most closely to the date of death. For occupation and other biographical details, see *Athenaeum Centenary*, pp. 109–112; Simpson, *The Federalist Literary Mind*, pp. 1–25; Quincy, *Boston Athenaeum*; M. A. DeWolfe Howe, ed., *Journal of the Proceedings of the Society Which Conducts the Monthly Anthology and Boston Review* (Boston, 1910), pp. 1–27; *Our First Men* (Boston, 1846); Forbes and Greene, *Rich Men of Massachusetts*.

45. See the list of officers and trustees in *Athenaeum Centenary*, pp. 115–119. For the leading families, see, e.g., Edmund Quincy, *Life of Josiah Quincy* (Boston, 1868); Seaburg and Paterson, *Merchant Prince of Boston*; Greenslet, *The Lowells and Their Seven Worlds*; Edward Gray, *William Gray of Salem, Merchant* (Boston, 1914); Frances Gregory, "Nathan Appleton, Yankee Merchant (1779–1861)" (Ph.D. diss., Radcliffe College, 1949). The clans were as follows:

Quincy-Adams-Shaw; Perkins-Cary-Forbes-Cushing; Lowell-Jackson-Lee-Higginson-Cabot; Gray; Appleton.

46. For Lowell Institute regulations and procedures, see *Extracts from the Will and Codicil of John Lowell, Jr.*, *Concerning the Lecture Fund* (Boston, 1885), pp. 3–10. For a list of lectures and lecturers, see Harriette Knight Smith, *The History of the Lowell Institute* (Boston, New York and London, 1898), pp. 49–59. For the reputation of the Institute, see, e.g., Ralph W. Emerson, *The Journals and Miscellaneous Notebooks of Ralph Waldo Emerson*, ed. William Gilman et al. (Cambridge, Mass., 1960–1970) 8:80; Peter Lesley–Mrs. Peter Lesley, December 16, 1846, in *Life and Letters of Peter and Susan Lesley*, ed. Mary Lesley Ames (New York and London, 1909), 1:142–143; Josiah Dwight Whitney, Jr.–Josiah Dwight Whitney, October 20, 1841, in Edwin Tenney Brewster, *Life and Letters of Josiah Dwight Whitney* (Boston and New York, 1909), p. 53; Emmaline Stuart Wortley, *Travels in the United States etc.*, *During 1849 and 1850* (New York, 1851), p. 41; John Chipman Gray, Jr.–John Codman Ropes, November 13, 1862, in John Chipman Gray and John Codman Ropes, *War Letters, 1862–1865*, ed. Worthington Chauncey Ford (Boston, 1927), p. 23.

47. The Lowell men involved in Institute affairs included John (1769–1840), Charles (1782–1861), John Amory (1798–1881), John, Jr. (1799–1836), Francis Cabot II (1803–1874), James Russell (1819–1891), and Augustus (1830–1900). John, Jr. was the Institute's founder. John Amory and his son, Augustus, were trustees; Francis Cabot II was an alternate trustee and assisted his cousins in selecting and entertaining lecturers, as did John and Charles. James Russell was himself a lecturer on two occasions. For biographical details, see Greenslet, *The Lowells and Their Seven Worlds*, pp. 43–127, 220–221, and passim. Wealth estimates are from inventories and executors' bonds.

48. For the operations of the Institute, see Smith, *History of the Lowell Institute*, pp. 18–20, 37; Edward Weeks, *The Lowells and Their Institute* (Boston and Toronto, 1966), pp. 47–51, 56; Benjamin R. Curtis–George Ticknor, February 6, 1855, in George T. Curtis, *A Memoir of Benjamin Robbins Curtis* (Boston, 1879), p. 176; George Ticknor–Nathan Appleton, February 5, 1855, Nathan Appleton Papers, MHS; Alonzo Potter–William Appleton, June 9, 1845 and August 13, 1860, in M. A. DeWolfe Howe, *Memoirs of the Life and Services of the Rt. Rev. Alonzo Potter* (Philadelphia, 1871), pp. 126, 326–327; Charles Lyell, *Travels in North America* (New York, 1845), 1:iii; John Tyndall, *Lectures on Light* (New York, 1873), p. 186; Charles Goodrich, *The Science of Government* (Boston, 1853), p. v; A. K. Teele, *The History of Milton, Mass., 1640 to 1887* (n.p., 1887), p. 542.

For the Institute's recruitment and socializing functions, see, e.g., Edward Lurie, *Louis Agassiz, A Life in Science* (Chicago, 1960), pp. 116–131; A. Hunter Dupree, *Asa Gray, 1810–1888* (Cambridge, 1959), p. 120; Oliver Wendell Holmes, "Professor Jeffries Wyman, A Memorial Outline," in O. W. Holmes, *The Autocrat's Miscellanies*, ed. Albert Mordell (New York, 1959), p. 169; Charles Eliot Norton, *Letters of Charles Eliot Norton*, ed. M. A. DeWolfe Howe

(Boston, 1913), 1:119; J. C. Levenson, *The Mind and Art of Henry Adams* (Boston, 1957), pp. 40–41; Oliver Wendell Holmes and Frederick Pollock, *Holmes-Pollock Letters*, ed. Mark DeWolfe Howe, 2nd ed. (Cambridge, Mass., 1961), 1:14–15; Henry Cabot Lodge, *Early Memories* (New York, 1913), p. 268.

49. For Institute attendance, see Smith, *History of the Lowell Institute*, pp. 9, 24–26, 37; Weeks, *The Lowells and Their Institute*, pp. 40–42, 45–46; Ephraim Peabody, "Hopkins's Lectures Before the Lowell Institute," *CE* 41(September 1846):218; Lyell, *Travels*, pp. 86–87; Edward Everett Hale, *A New England Boyhood and Other Bits of Autobiography* (Boston, 1922), p. 126; Ednah D. Cheney, "The Women of Boston," in Winsor, *Memorial History of Boston*, 4:346; Julia Ward Howe, *Reminiscences, 1819–1899* (Boston and New York, 1900), p. 182; Elizabeth Cary Agassiz, ed., *Louis Agassiz: His Life and Correspondence* (Boston and New York, 1885), p. 407; William T. W. Ball, "The Old Federal Street Theatre," *The Bostonian Society Publications* 8(1911), pp. 82–83; Howe, *Alonzo Potter*, p. 122; Mark Hopkins, *Lectures on the Evidences of Christianity* (Boston, 1846), pp. 15–17.

50. *Extracts from the Will of John Lowell, Jr.*, pp. 6–8; M. A. DeWolfe Howe, "Abbott Lawrence Lowell," *Athenaeum Items* 27(February 1943).

51. Dearborn, *Boston Notions*, pp. 383–384; Smith, *History of the Lowell Institute*, pp. 55–65; Albert Emerson Benson, *History of the Massachusetts Horticultural Society* (Norwood, Mass., 1929), pp. 35–42; *The Boston Society of Natural History, 1830–1930* (Boston, 1930), pp. 7–11; *Handbook of the Principal Scientific Institutions of Boston and Vicinity* (Boston, 1898), pp. 32–35, 44–51, 53–54. The Lowells held positions in the Society of Natural History, the Massachusetts Historical Society, the American Academy of Arts and Sciences, the Mount Auburn Cemetery, and the more transient Society for the Diffusion of Useful Knowledge as well as the Athenaeum and the Lowell Institute.

52. Walter Muir Whitehill, *Boston Public Library* (Cambridge, 1956), pp. 8, 15; *Boston Daily Advertiser*, March 25, 1853; Edward Warren, *Life of John Collins Warren* (Boston, 1860), 2:234–235; William H. Prescott–Mary E. Lyell, March 28, 1853, in W. H. Prescott, *The Papers of William Hickling Prescott*, ed. C. Harvey Gardiner (Urbana, Ill., 1964), p. 322.

53. George Ticknor Curtis, *History of the Origins, Formation, and Adoption of the Constitution of the United States* (New York, 1854), pp. 12–14, 36; "Bowen's Lowell Lectures," *CE* 48(January 1850):89; Smith, *History of the Lowell Institute*, p. 30; Weeks, *The Lowells and Their Institute*, pp. 90, 96; Goodrich, *The Science of Government*, pp. v–vi, 339.

54. *Annual Report of the Trustees of the Mount Auburn Cemetery, January, 1856* (Boston, 1856), pp. 2–4; *Boston Evening Transcript*, June 20, November 1, 4, 5, 1856, January 28, 29, 31, February 3, 4, 1857; *Boston Daily Courier*, June 17, 23, 24, 1856, February 2, 4, 1857; *Boston Atlas*, June 20, 24, 40, 1856; *Boston Daily Advertiser*, February 2, 3, 1857.

55. G. W. Greene, "Libraries," *NAR* 45(July 1837):134; Vincent Y. Bowditch, *Life and Correspondence of Henry Ingersoll Bowditch* (Boston, 1902), 1:50;

204 The Forging of an Aristocracy

Horace Mann, *Lectures and Annual Reports on Education* (Cambridge, 1867), p. 300.

56. Quoted in *Athenaeum Centenary*, pp. 31–32.

57. Smith, *History of the Lowell Institute*, pp. 9, 24–26, 37; Peabody, "Hopkins's Lectures," p. 218; "Lowell Lectures," CE 36(May 1844), pp. 439–440.

58. Henry David Thoreau, *The Journals of Henry David Thoreau*, ed. Bradford Torrey et al. (Boston, 1949), 2:327–328 (November 16, 1858).

59. For the contours of the antebellum city, see, e.g., Allan R. Pred, *Urban Growth and the Circulation of Information: The United States System of Cities, 1790–1840* (Cambridge, Mass., 1973), pp. 239–283 and passim; Lane, *Policing the City;* Paul Boyer, *Urban Masses and Moral Order in America, 1820–1920* (Cambridge, Mass., 1978), pp. 3–122; Sam Bass Warner, Jr., *The Private City* (Philadelphia, 1968), pp. 49–160.

60. Athenaeum trustees also serving the Massachusetts General Hospital between 1820 and 1850 were Nathan Appleton, Charles Amory, William T. Andrews, Henry Codman, Samuel A. Eliot, John and John Amory Lowell, Amos and Samuel Lawrence, Theodore Lyman, Jr., Samuel May, Thomas and James Perkins, Josiah Quincy, William Sturgis, David Sears, George Ticknor, Joseph Tilden, Edward Wigglesworth, and Thomas W. Ward. Dispensary trustees with Historical Society ties were Charles Amory, John G. Coffin, Joseph Coolidge, Jr., Uriel Crocker, Pliny Cutler, Thomas A. Dexter, Nathaniel L. Frothingham, William Gray, Samuel E. Guild, Stephen Higginson, Jr., Abbott and William Lawrence, Charles Lowell, Francis Parkman, Jonathan Phillips, Thomas Phillips, Edward Phillips, William Phillips, Samuel Salisbury, William Smith, Samuel and George Snelling, Edward Tuckerman, Joseph Tilden, Henry Ware, Henry A. Whitney, and J. Huntington Wolcott.

61. The work of Samuel Eliot Morison long marked the boundaries of most intense scholarly interest. For the colonial era, see Morison's exhaustive *The Founding of Harvard College* (Cambridge, 1935) and *Harvard College in the Seventeenth Century*, 2 vols. (Cambridge, 1936). For the later period, see Samuel Eliot Morison, ed., *The Development of Harvard University since the Inauguration of President Eliot, 1869–1929* (Cambridge, Mass., 1930). For colonial times, see also Kenneth B. Murdock, *Increase Mather* (Cambridge, 1925); and more recently Margery Somers Foster, *"Out of Smalle Beginnings . . .": An Economic History of Harvard College in the Puritan Period* (Cambridge, Mass., 1962) and Jurgen Herbst, "The First Three American Colleges: Schools of the Reformation," *Perspectives in American History* 8(1974):7–54.

For the recent period, see, besides Morison, Lawrence Veysey, *The Emergance of the American University* (Chicago and London, 1968), pp. 81–98 and passim; Hugh Hawkins, *Between Harvard and America* (New York, 1972); and the standard presidential biographies: Henry James, *Charles W. Eliot*, 2 vols. (Boston and New York, 1930); and Henry Yeomans, *Abbott Lawrence Lowell* (Cambridge, Mass., 1948).

The chief source for the antebellum period has been the relevant section of

Samuel Eliot Morison, *Three Centuries of Harvard* (Cambridge, Mass., 1936). The imbalance has been partially redressed of late by biographical studies such as Tyack, *George Ticknor*, and especially Robert A. McCaughey, *Josiah Quincy 1772–1864: The Last Federalist* (Cambridge, 1974).

62. Cf. Frederick Rudolph, *The American College and University* (New York, 1962); Burton Bledstein, *The Culture of Professionalism* (New York, 1976).

63. Cf. Morison, *Three Centuries of Harvard*, pp. 226–259.

64. Greenslet, *The Lowells and Their Seven Worlds*, pp. 235–236; Morison, *Three Centuries of Harvard*, p. 420; Tyack, *George Ticknor*, p. 181; Amory, *The Proper Bostonians*, p. 173.

65. Peter French, *The Long Reach* (New York, 1962), pp. 27, 208.

66. Josiah Quincy, *Speech of February 25, 1845, on the Minority Report of Mr. Bancroft* (Boston, 1845), p. vi. For the text of the charter and a succinct account of the governing structures and their composition, see *Harvard University Quinquennial Catalogue of the Officers and Graduates, 1636–1930* (Cambridge, Mass., 1930), pp. 3–22.

Chapter 2

1. Compiled from Morison, *Three Centuries of Harvard*, pp. 238–241, 279–280, 241–244; Samuel A. Eliot, *A Sketch of the History of Harvard College and of Its Present State* (Boston, 1848), pp. 167–190; Josiah Quincy, *History of Harvard University* (Cambridge, 1840), 2:538–558; *Education, Bricks, and Mortar: Harvard Buildings and Their Contributions* (Cambridge, Mass., 1949), p. 95; *Harvard Quinquennial Catalogue*, pp. 23–28; A. T. Gibbs, "Gifts and Bequests, 1638–1870," vol. 2, ms., HUA; William J. Rhees, *Manual of Public Libraries, Institutions, and Societies* (Philadelphia, 1859), p. 605; Keyes Metcalf, "The Undergraduate and the Harvard Library, 1765–1877," *Harvard Library Bulletin* 1(1947):361; Jared Sparks, *Twenty-Sixth Annual Report on Harvard College, 1850–1851* (Cambridge, 1851), p. 30. The figures for total assets include rough estimates of the value of the physical plant and non-income-producing real property.

2. Estimated from Eliot, *Sketch of Harvard College*, pp. 167–185; Gibbs, "Gifts and Bequests, 1638–1870."

3. For Williams and Amherst, see J. Lothrop Motley, "Memorial of the Presidents of Harvard, Williams and Amherst Colleges," Massachusetts House Document no. 92, March 1849, pp. 24–27. For Yale, see *Yale University Treasurer's Report, 1851* (New Haven, n.d.), pp. 1–4; Bernard C. Steiner, *The History of Education in Connecticut* (Washington, 1893), pp. 153–156.

4. William D. Whitney–Josiah Dwight Whitney, April 6, 1845, in Brewster, *Josiah Dwight Whitney*, p. 74; John Fiske–Mary Green, August 10, 1859, in John Fiske, *The Letters of John Fiske*, ed. Ethel F. Fisk (New York, 1940), p. 27.

5. Edward Everett, "University of Virginia," *NAR* 10(January 1820):36; Edward Everett, *Orations and Speeches on Various Occasions* (Boston, 1859–65), 2:521–522.

6. James Walker, Lemuel Shaw, Charles G. Loring, *Report on the Rights and Duties of the President and Fellows of Harvard College in Relation to the Board of Overseers* (Cambridge, 1856), p. 41.

7. Computed from Eliot, *Sketch of Harvard College,* pp. 153–185.

8. Computed from Ibid., pp. 181–185; Quincy, *History of Harvard University,* 2:542–543, 546–553, 564–565; "Subscribers to Scholarship Fund," March 27, 1841, Corporation Papers, HUA.

9. See the library donation list in Quincy, *History of Harvard University,* 2:569–585.

10. Derived from Eliot, *Sketch of Harvard College,* pp. 180–185; Gibbs, "Gifts and Bequests." The purposes have been summarized to facilitate comparison and analysis.

11. Useful sketches of most contributors may be found in Quincy, *History of Harvard University,* Vol. 2; *Our First Men;* Thomas L. V. Wilson, *The Aristocracy of Boston* (Boston, 1848); Forbes and Greene, *The Rich Men of Massachusetts* (Boston, 1851), and 2nd ed. (Boston, 1852). Other helpful biographical studies include J. D. Forbes, *Israel Thorndike: Federalist Financier* (New York, 1953); "Benjamin Bussey," *Dedham Historical Register* 10(July 1899):71–76; Carlton A. Staples, "Samuel Dexter," Ibid. 3(April 1892):50–59; Robert Sullivan, *The Disappearance of Dr. Parkman* (Boston and Toronto, 1971); Howard Doughty, *Francis Parkman* (New York, 1962); Robert L. Weis, *Abiel Smith and Lydia Otis* (Lincoln, R.I., 1923); Robert C. Winthrop, *Memoir of the Hon. David Sears* (Cambridge, 1886); Truax, *The Doctors Warren; Dictionary of American Biography,* 2nd ed. s.v. "Dane, Nathan"; Helen Reisinger Pinckney, "Christopher Gore: A Federalist of Massachusetts, 1758–1827" (Ph.D. diss., Radcliffe College, 1942); Hamilton A. Hill, *Memoir of Abbott Lawrence,* 2nd ed. (Boston, 1884). For Perkins, Eliot and McLean, see also L. Vernon Briggs, *History and Genealogy of the Cabot Family, 1475–1927* (Boston, 1927), 1:160–161; Samuel Eliot, "Being Mayor of Boston a Hundred Years Ago," *MHSP* 66(1934–41):154–173; "Harvard College and Massachusetts General Hospital versus Francis Amory," Octavius Pickering, *Pickering's Legal Reports,* (Boston, 1804–1840) 9:446–465.

12. The five non-Bostonians were Nathan Dane (Beverly), Samuel Dexter (Mendon), Joshua Fisher (Beverly), Samuel Livermore (New Hampshire), Benjamin Thompson (Europe). Samuel Dexter accumulated his estate in the eighteenth century; Abbott Lawrence, Israel Thorndike, John C. Warren, Benjamin Bussey, and Israel Munson accumulated theirs mostly in the nineteenth century; the families of Jonathan Phillips and David Sears seem to have been wealthy prior to the Revolution. Nonbusinessmen included lawyers Nathan Dane, Samuel Livermore, and Christopher Gore; doctors George Parkman, John C. Warren, and Joshua Fisher; and minister Francis Parkman. Samuel A. Eliot was both businessman, with substantial banking and manufacturing interests, and politician, serving as mayor of Boston and Massachusetts legislator.

13. The Episcopalians were John C. Warren and David Sears. The non-

Notes

207

Whig was John Parker, Jr. For Thorndike and Webster, see Josiah P. Quincy, *Figures from the Past* (Boston, 1883), p. 118.

14. Charles Francis Adams, July 16, 1857, in "Extracts from the Diaries of John Quincy Adams (1787) and his son Charles Francis Adams (1825) Relating to Harvard College. From 1786 to 1880," selected and transcribed by Henry Adams and William G. Roelker, typescript, HUA.

15. For mid-twentieth century philanthropy, see, e.g., F. Emerson Andrews, *Philanthropic Giving* (New York, 1950), pp. 53, 59–60.

16. Jared Sparks, Lemuel Shaw, James Walker, Charles G. Loring, B. R. Curtis, Samuel A. Eliot, "Harvard College Memorial," Massachusetts House Document no. 10, January 14, 1851, p. 4.

17. Walker et al., *Rights and Duties of the President and Fellows*, p. 41.

18. Theophilus Parsons, "Argument of Chief Justice Parsons on the Subject of the Visitors of Harvard College," ca. 1812, ms., HUA, pp. 2–3, 12–13.

19. Quincy, *History of Harvard University*, 2:416–417.

20. *Harvard Quinquennial Catalogue*, pp. 10–12; Truax, *The Doctors Warren*, pp. 181–210; Paul Revere Frothingham, *Edward Everett, Orator and Statesman* (Boston, 1925).

21. Alexander Young, *A Discourse on the Life and Character of the Reverend John Thornton Kirkland* (Boston, 1840), p. 59. Theodore Lyman and Nicholas Boylston had contributed substantially to Harvard between 1800 and 1825 but in sums less than $5,000. Lyman in particular — and the Lymans generally — were considered to be important patrons and backers of the university.

22. Quincy, *History of Harvard University*, 2:596.

23. The same general references which were most helpful in tracing the donors were also helpful in tracing the members of the Corporation; these are listed at the beginning of note 11 of this chapter. For the Fellows the *Dictionary of American Biography* and the *National Cyclopedia of American Biography* were also of use. For additional biographical details, see, e.g., Frothingham, *Edward Everett;* Herbert B. Adams, *Life and Writings of Jared Sparks* (Boston and New York, 1893); Madeleine H. Rice, *Federal Street Pastor: The Life of William Ellery Channing* (New York, 1961); Theophilus Parsons, *Memoir of Theophilus Parsons* (Boston, 1861); George T. Curtis, *A Memoir of Benjamin Robbins Curtis* (Boston, 1879). Additional references are cited below as appropriate.

24. The Episcopalians were Francis C. Gray, Amos A. Lawrence, and Benjamin R. Curtis. The ministers were John T. Kirkland, Samuel C. Thacher, William E. Channing, Charles Lowell, Eliphalet Porter, George Putnam, James Walker, and Samuel Webber; Edward Everett and Jared Sparks preached briefly before becoming a politician and scholar, respectively.

25. Cf. Andrew P. Peabody, *Harvard Reminiscences* (Boston, 1888), pp. 9, 160; Andrew P. Peabody, *Harvard Graduates Whom I Have Known* (Boston and New York, 1890), p. 98.

26. F. W. P. Greenwood, "Memoir of the Rev. Samuel C. Thacher," in

Samuel C. Thacher, *Sermons* (Boston, 1824), pp. xv–xxx; Rice, *Federal Street Pastor*, pp. 102–104; Sidney Ahlstrom, "The Middle Period (1840–1880)," in *The Harvard Divinity School*, ed. George H. Williams (Boston, 1954), p. 82; Octavius B. Frothingham, "Memoir of Rev. James Walker," *MHSP*, s.2, vol. 6(1890–91):448.

27. Peabody, *Harvard Graduates*, pp. 107–108; Charles Francis Adams; *The Diary of Charles Francis Adams*, ed. Aida DiPace Donald et al. (New York, 1967–1976), 4:25–26 (April 10, 1831); Frothingham, "James Walker," pp. 455–457; Robert S. Peabody, *A New England Romance* (Boston and New York, 1920), p. 121.

28. The exception was Ebenezer Rockwood Hoar, a moderate Republican discussed more fully in chapter 8.

29. Parsons, *Theophilus Parsons*, p. 132.

30. John Quincy Adams–Ward Nicholas Boylston, May 24, 1819, in John Quincy Adams, *The Writings of John Quincy Adams*, ed. Worthington C. Ford (New York, 1913–1917), 6:552. Fisher Ames, moreover, was offered the Harvard presidency but declined. See Fisher Ames, *Works of Fisher Ames*, ed. Seth Ames (Boston, 1854), 1:346–348. The other men mentioned by Parsons — Josiah Strong, George Cabot, Timothy Pickering — were members of the so-called Essex Junto, well-known Federalist conservatives.

31. Dana, *Journal of Richard Henry Dana, Jr.*, 1:110–111 (December 23, 1842); Edward Everett–Thomas W. Ward, February 18, 1834, Thomas W. Ward Papers, MHS; Frothingham, *Edward Everett*, p. 105; Theophilus Parsons, *Memoir of Charles Greely Loring* (Cambridge, 1870), p. 11.

32. Bowditch, *Life of Henry Ingersoll Bowditch*, 1:100, 203; Curtis, *Benjamin Robbins Curtis*, pp. 74, 122–123, 335; George S. Boutwell, *Reminiscences of Sixty Years in Public Affairs* (New York, 1902), 1:112; James McClellan, *Joseph Story and the American Constitution* (Norman, 1971), pp. 48, 224, 232–234; John Greenleaf Whittier–William Lloyd Garrison, May 13, 1850, in John Greenleaf Whittier, *The Letters of John Greenleaf Whittier*, ed. John B. Pickard (Cambridge, Mass., London, 1975), 2:155. Story began his legal and political career as a Jeffersonian, but even before 1810, according to his latest biography, he entertained "doubts about the wisdom of popular assemblies and unchecked popular sovereignty." The radicalism of "Jean Jacques" was thus displaced by "the unruffled conservatism of Blackstone." McClellan, *Joseph Story*, pp. 13–15, 38.

33. This assignment of occupations places Harrison Gray Otis among the lawyers despite his extensive entrepreneurial activities in land and textile manufacturing; and Samuel A. Eliot, Francis C. Gray, and Josiah Quincy among the businessmen even though Quincy and Gray studied law (without practicing) and all three held political office. For Otis, see Samuel Eliot Morison, *Harrison Gray Otis, 1765–1848* (Boston, 1969), pp. 218–223, 449–454. For Eliot, see, e.g., Shlakman, *Economic History*, pp. 26–28; Samuel H. Emery, *History of Taunton, Massachusetts* (Syracuse, 1893), pp. 647–658; Eliot, "Being Mayor of Boston," p. 164. Both Gray and Quincy are discussed at greater length in chapter 3.

34. Alexander Young, *The Varieties of Human Greatness: A Discourse on the Life and Character of the Hon. Nathaniel Bowditch* (Boston, 1838), p. 61.

35. Parsons, *Charles Greely Loring*, pp. 7–10; Morison, *The Ropemakers of Plymouth*, p. 15; "Boston Water Power Co. Stockholder List," 1856, Amos A. Lawrence Papers, MHS; Curtis, *Benjamin Robbins Curtis*, pp. 84–85, 184, 268; Benjamin R. Curtis, "Executor's Inventory," File 56115, Suffolk County (Mass.) Probate Court.

36. Greenslet, *The Lowells and Their Seven Worlds*, pp. 232–233; Lamb, "The Entrepreneur and the Community," p. 116.

37. Ralph Waldo Emerson, *The Journals and Miscellaneous Notebooks*, ed. William Gilman et al. (Cambridge, Mass., 1960–1977), 9:81 (May 1, 1846).

Chapter 3

1. In 1850 the Corporation also included a scholar, President Jared Sparks; in 1860 a scholar, President Cornelius Felton, and a vacancy; and in 1870 an administrator, President Charles W. Eliot. As in the preceding chapters and throughout the book, the data on wealth derive from Massachusetts probate records.

2. For the reforms and debate of this period, see, e.g., Samuel Eliot Morison, "The Great Rebellion in Harvard College, and the Resignation of President Kirkland," *CSMP* 27(April 1928):65–112; Morison, *Three Centuries of Harvard*, pp. 222–245.

3. Young, *John Thornton Kirkland*, p. 73; Francis Parkman, *A Discourse Occasioned by the Death of Rev. John T. Kirkland* (Boston, 1840), pp. 9–10; Charles Francis Adams, August 27, 1845, in "Extracts from the Diaries of John Quincy Adams and Charles Francis Adams," p. 26.

4. John T. Kirkland–William Emerson, September 19, 1788, John T. Kirkland–William Emerson, June 16, 1790, John T. Kirkland–Stephen Palmer, October 17, 1790, in Young, *John Thornton Kirkland*, pp. 28–29, 31, 44–45.

5. Elfrieda A. Kraege, "The Life of John Thornton Kirkland, A President of Harvard, 1770–1840," typescript, BPL; Young, *John Thornton Kirkland*, p. 73.

6. John G. Palfrey, "Quincy's History of Harvard University," *NAR* 52 (April 1841):375–376; "Letter to Kirkland," *Boston Daily Advertiser*, April 23, 1828; Young, *John Thornton Kirkland*, p. 73; James Russell Lowell, "Cambridge Thirty Years Ago," in James Russell Lowell, *Literary Essays* (Boston and New York, 1890), 1:83.

7. Thomas J. Mumford, *Memoir of Samuel Joseph May* (Boston, 1873), p. 63; Peabody, *Harvard Reminiscences*, pp. 17–18.

8. Josiah Quincy, 1827, in Josiah Quincy, "Memorandum Books, 1825–1847," Josiah Quincy Papers, MHS.

9. Quincy, *Josiah Quincy*, pp. 34–58; Allen Chamberlain, *Beacon Hill* (Boston and New York, 1925), pp. 215–216; Edward Everett Hale, *James Russell Lowell and His Friends* (Boston and New York, 1899), p. 17; Charles P. Huse, *The*

Financial History of Boston (Cambridge and London, 1916), pp. 30–33, 49.

10. Josiah Quincy, "Journal and Common-place Book," February 11, 17, 24, 1827, passim, Josiah Quincy Papers, MHS; Orville Dewey, *Autobiography and Letters of Orville Dewey*, ed. Mary Dewey (Boston, 1883), pp. 52–53; Mary Van Meter, "Bay Village, or the Church-Street District," *The Bostonian Society Proceedings* (1969), pp. 19–21; Anna Waterston, "Autobiographical Notes," typescript, Harvard College Library, pp. 7–8, 34–35; Daniel Webster–Joseph Story, April 5, 1822, April 6, 1822, Daniel Webster Papers, MHS (microfilm edition); Charles Francis Adams, *Diary*, 3:11–12 (September 11, 1829); Leverett Saltonstall–James C. Merrill, April 9, 1822, Leverett Saltonstall Papers, MHS.

11. Thomas Cushing, "Undergraduate Life Sixty Years Ago," *HGM* 1(July 1893):547.

12. Quincy, *Josiah Quincy*, p. 430; Samuel Atkins Eliot, *A History of Cambridge, Massachusetts (1630–1913)* (Cambridge, Mass., 1913), p. 109; Hale, *James Russell Lowell*, p. 17.

13. Josiah Quincy, "Executor's Inventory," File 45572, Suffolk County (Mass.) Probate Court; Barrett Wendell–Sir Robert White–Thompson, December 13, 1908, in M. A. DeWolfe Howe, *Barrett Wendell and His Letters* (Boston, 1924), p. 198. The remark concerning the "considerable" fortunes of Harvard presidents after Quincy must be qualified to a degree. When Barrett Wendell made the statement in 1908, he was thinking mainly of Charles W. Eliot, who possessed an estate of some $400,000, much of it inherited, and of Eliot's heir-apparent, Abbott Lawrence Lowell, a multimillionaire. But the observation holds up surprisingly well even for the quarter-century between Quincy and Eliot, which witnessed the brief tenures of Edward Everett, Jared Sparks, and James Walker, all with estates in the $50,000–$100,000 range; and that of Cornelius Felton, who enjoyed the considerable properties of his wife, a Perkins in-law. Only Thomas Hill, among this string of short-term presidents, possessed neither personal fortune nor wealthy wife. Wendell, then, was basically right: Quincy did set a new style in this respect as in so many others.

14. Joseph Buckingham, "Seventh Annual Report of the President of Harvard University," *New-England Magazine* 4(February 1833):171–172; Benjamin Waterhouse, June 3, 1837, in William Roscoe Thayer, "Extracts from the Journal of Benjamin Waterhouse," *CHSP* 4(January 1909):30; James Walker, "Memoir of Josiah Quincy," *MHSP* (March 1866), p. 125; *Proceedings of the Government of Harvard University on the Death of the Hon. Josiah Quincy, July 5, 1864* (Cambridge, Mass., 1864), unpaginated.

15. Young, *Nathaniel Bowditch*, p. 24; Daniel Appleton White, *An Eulogy on the Life and Character of Nathaniel Bowditch* (Salem, 1838), pp. 23, 33; Nathaniel Ingersoll Bowditch, *Memoir of Nathaniel Bowditch* (Lowell, 1839), pp. 79–84; Nathaniel Bowditch, "Executor's Inventory," File 31807, Suffolk County (Mass.) Probate Court.

16. J. H. Morison, "Finished Lives," *NAR* 80(January 1855):46.

17. Nathan Reingold, ed., *Science in Nineteenth-Century America* (New York, 1964), p. 12.

18. Young, *Nathaniel Bowditch*, pp. 24, 33, 67–68, 77; Bowditch, *Nathaniel Bowditch*, pp. 77, 130; Nathaniel Bowditch–Eliza Clarke, August 3, 1813, *Papers of James Murray Forbes*, The Forbes Papers (Reel 38, MHS Microfilm Edition); Nathan Appleton–Nathaniel Bowditch, March 7, 1838, Nathan Appleton Papers, MHS; Maud Howe Elliott,*Uncle Sam Ward and His Circle* (New York, 1938), p. 72.

19. Nathaniel Bowditch, "College History," 1828, ms., HUA, p. 11; Eliza Susan Quincy, June 3, 1825, in Archibald Murray Howe, "Journal of Eliza Susan Quincy," *CHSP* 4(October 1909):90–92.

20. Wilson, *The Aristocracy of Boston*, p. 16; Forbes and Greene, *Rich Men of Massachusetts*, 2nd ed., 1852, p. 29.

21. Robert Mason, *A Sketch of the Life of Ebenezer Francis* (New York, 1859), p. 32; Curtis Guild, "Bits of Old Boston and Word-Pictures of the Past," *The Bostonian Society Publications*, s.2, vol. 1 (1916):26–28; Ebenezer Francis, "Executor's Inventory," File 7313, Norfolk County (Mass.) Probate Court; Bowditch, "College History," p. 49; Quincy, *History of Harvard University*, 2:364–368.

22. Charles K. Bolton, "Memoir of Francis Calley Gray," *MHSP* 47(June 1914):529–530.

23. Wilson, *The Aristocracy of Boston*, p. 17; Daniel Treadwell–F. C. Gray and Horace Gray, July 23, 1838, Daniel Treadwell Papers, HUA; Lurie, *Louis Agassiz*, pp. 196–198; Thomas W. Ward–Joshua Bates, December 12, 1830, Thomas W. Ward Papers, MHS.

24. Shlakman, *Economic History*, pp. 39–41, 146; James Jackson Putnam, *A Memoir of James Jackson* (Boston and New York, 1905), pp. 375–376.

25. Gerald T. Dunne, *Justice Joseph Story and the Rise of the Supreme Court* (New York, 1970), pp. 267–268, 283; McClellan,*Joseph Story*, p. 257; Charles Warren, *History of the Harvard Law School* (New York, 1908), 2:45–46.

26. Dunne,*Joseph Story*, pp. 112, 283; Stanley I. Kutler, *Privilege and Creative Destruction; The Charles River Bridge Case* (Philadelphia, New York, Toronto, 1971), pp. 99–100; Willard Phillips, *The Law of Patents for Inventions* (Boston and New York, 1837), p. iii; Joseph Story, *Commentaries on the Law of Promissory Notes*, 3rd ed. (Boston, 1851), p. vii; Arthur Sutherland, *The Law at Harvard* (Cambridge, Mass., 1967), p. 136.

27. Dudley L. Pickman–Ebenezer Francis, October 10, 1827, College Papers, s.2, vol. 2, HUA; Peabody, *Harvard Reminiscences*, pp. 68–69; Charles Sanders, "Executor's Inventory," File 41118, Middlesex County (Mass.) Probate Court.

28. Thomas W. Ward–Joshua Bates, December 29, 1831, April 27, 1842, Thomas W. Ward Papers, MHS.

29. Thomas W. Ward–Joshua Bates, January 6, 1839, Thomas W. Ward Papers, MHS.

30. Hidy, *The House of Baring*, pp. 98–101; Thomas W. Ward–Jonathan Goodhue, April 23, 1814, Thomas W. Ward–Joshua Bates, December 12, 1830, Thomas W. Ward–Joshua Bates, July 13, 1846, Thomas W. Ward Papers, MHS.

31. The reform thrust is treated in general terms in Morison, "The Great Rebellion in Harvard College," pp. 65–112; and Morison, *Three Centuries of Harvard*, pp. 222–245.

32. Hale, *James Russell Lowell*, pp. 128–130; Bowditch, "College History," pp. 11, 14–15, 21, 25–26, 37, 58–59, 212–213; Thomas W. Ward, "Suffolk Bank Account Book, 1830–1834," HUA; Quincy, *Josiah Quincy*, p. 472; *Treasurer's Statement, Harvard University, 1830–1831* (Cambridge, Mass., 1832), p. 4.

33. David Greenough–Ebenezer Francis, April 1, 1828, College Papers, s.2, vol. 2, HUA; John Lowell–Samuel Hubbard, December 3, 1828, Samuel Hubbard–Ebenezer Francis, December 5, 1828, College Papers, s.2, vol. 3, HUA; "Corporation Resolution," April 27, 1827, College Papers, s.2, vol. 1, HUA; Pickering, "Harvard College and Massachusetts General Hospital versus Francis Amory," pp. 446–465. Policy with regard to faculty and students is considered in detail in chapters 4 through 7.

34. Bowditch, "College History," pp. 128–131; Young, *John Thornton Kirkland*, p. 52; Briggs, *History of the Cabot Family*, 1:187–193; Robert C. Winthrop–Board of Overseers, April 29, 1828, interleaf insert in Bowditch, "College History."

35. Charles Francis Adams, *Diary*, 2:226 (March 3, 1828); John Lowell–James Jackson, November 22, 1831, Corporation Papers, HUA; *Boston Courier*, April 5, 1828; *Boston Daily Advertiser*, April 23, 1828.

36. Hale, *A New England Boyhood*, p. 358; Peabody, *Harvard Reminiscences*, pp. 24–25; Ralph Waldo Emerson–William Emerson, April 3, 1928, in Ralph Waldo Emerson, *The Letters of Ralph Waldo Emerson*, ed. Ralph Rusk (Cambridge, Mass., 1939), 1:230.

37. For the texture of this remarkable relationship, see, e.g., Martha Nichols, ed., *George Nichols, Salem Shipmaster and Merchant* (Salem, n.d.), pp. 71, 79; Peabody, *Harvard Reminiscences*, pp. 24–25; Dudley L. Pickman–Ebenezer Francis, October 10, 1827, College Papers, s.2, vol. 2, HUA; Charles Sanders, "Last Will and Testament," File 41118, Middlesex County (Mass.) Probate Court; "Last Will and Testament of Thomas Sanders of Salem," 1833, Leverett Saltonstall Papers, MHS; Thomas W. Ward–Josiah Quincy, July 10, 1834, College Papers, s.2., vol. 6, HUA; Joseph Story, "Last Will and Testament," File 42571, Middlesex County (Mass.) Probate Court; Thomas W. Ward–William Ward, September 2, 1808, Martha Ward–Thomas W. Ward, March 2, 1834, "College Bond, July 1, 1835," Thomas W. Ward Papers, MHS; Bolton, "Francis Calley Gray," p. 534; Young, *Nathaniel Bowditch*, p. 19; Bowditch, *Nathaniel Bowditch*, p. 122; Andrew P. Peabody, *Sketch of the Life of J. Ingersoll Bowditch* (Cambridge, 1909), pp. 3, 7; S. K. Lathrop, *Memoir of Nathaniel Ingersoll Bowditch* (Boston, 1862), pp. 3–6; Allan Forbes, *Ebenezer Francis, 1775–1858* (n.p., n.d.), pp. 3–7.

38. *Remarks Concerning the Late Dr. Bowditch, by the Reverend Dr. Palfrey, with the Replies of Dr. Bowditch's Children* (Boston, 1840), p. 4; Bowditch, "College History," pp. 128–131; Young, *Nathaniel Bowditch*, pp. 18–19; Hall Gleason, "Colonel Ebenezer Francis," *Medford Historical Register* 18(June 1925):34–35; Forbes, *Ebenezer Francis*, p. 5; *Boston Evening Gazette*, April 5, 1828.

39. Samuel A. Eliot–Andrews Norton, August 1, 1842, Samuel A. Eliot Papers, HUA; Walker, "Josiah Quincy," p. 125; Charles Francis Adams, *Theodore Lyman (1833–1897) and Robert Charles Winthrop, Jr. (1834–1905)* (Cambridge, 1906), p. 166.

40. See, e.g., Nathaniel Silsbee, Dudley L. Pickman, Leverett Saltonstall, Willard Pyle, Gideon Barstow, George Peabody, Theophilus King–Joseph Story, August 21, 1829, Joseph Story Papers, University of Texas; John Pickering, "Overseer Memoranda," January 21, February 3, 4, 1825, John Pickering Papers, HUA; Abbot Lawrence–Josiah Quincy, January 14, 1829, Daniel Appleton White–Josiah Quincy, March 25, 1845, Josiah Quincy Papers, MHS; Nathaniel I. Bowditch–Daniel Appleton White, May 28, 1838, "The Papers of James Murray Forbes," The Forbes Papers (microfilm reel 38), MHS; Charles P. Curtis–Josiah Quincy, September 18, 1834, College Papers, s.2, vol. 6, HUA; Boutwell, *Reminiscences*, 1:113; Amos Lawrence–N. I. Bowditch, December 11, 1840, interleaf insert in Bowditch, "College History;" Bowditch, "College History," pp. 49–59, 126–127.

41. Daniel Webster–Joseph Story, April 18, 1828, in Dunne, *Joseph Story*, p. 275; Edward Everett–Nicholas Biddle, July 19, 1828, Edward Everett Papers, HUA; Warren, *The Harvard Law School*, 1:365–370; George Ticknor–Daniel Treadwell, July 24, 1835, Daniel Treadwell Papers, HUA.

42. Josiah Quincy–James T. Austin, June 6, 1834, John Lowell–Josiah Quincy, December 15, 1834, College Papers, s.2, vol. 6, HUA; Samuel Cabot–Josiah Quincy, August 24, 1830, College Papers, s.2, vol. 4, HUA; Francis Boott–Josiah Quincy, February 2, 1835, College Papers, s.2, vol. 7, HUA; Joseph Story–John Lowell, October 10, 1843, Corporation Papers, HUA.

43. Thomas Jefferson Wertenbaker, *Princeton, 1746–1896* (Princeton, N.J., 1946), pp. 239, 377; Edward P. Cheyney, *History of the University of Pennsylvania, 1740–1940* (Philadelphia, 1940), pp. 180–256; Mather Brooks Kelley, *Yale: A History* (New Haven and London, 1974), pp. 273, 325.

44. Cornelius C. Felton, "Notice," in *The Inauguration of Jared Sparks as President of Harvard University* (Cambridge, Mass., 1850), p. 3; Thomas W. Ward–Joshua Bates, August 31, 1842, Thomas W. Ward Papers, MHS; Francis Bowen–Amos A. Lawrence, November 12, 1859, Tyler Bigelow–Amos A. Lawrence, February 3, 1867, Amos A. Lawrence Papers, MHS.

45. For this phenomenon, see, e.g., David N. Smith, *Who Rules the Universities?* (New York and London, 1974), pp. 61–138.

46. Emerson, *Journals and Miscellaneous Notebooks* 9:380–381 (May 1, 1846).

47. Thomas W. Ward–Joshua Bates, February 27, 1850, Thomas W. Ward Papers, MHS.

Chapter 4

1. Among the more important of these studies are Tyack, *George Ticknor*, pp. 85–128, passim; and Robert A. McCaughey, "The Transformation of American Academic Life: Harvard University, 1821–1892," *Perspectives in American History* 8(1974):239–334. Biographies of Harvard scientists are also of relevance here, notably Lurie, *Louis Agassiz*; Jeannette Graustein, *Thomas Nuttall, Naturalist* (Cambridge, Mass., 1967); Dupree, *Asa Gray*.
2. For professiorial appointments and tenures, see *Harvard Quinquennial Catalogue*, pp. 23–162. The list of faculty members appointed in these years is as follows:

John Quincy Adams	Rhetoric & Oratory	1806–09
Louis Agassiz	Zoology	1847–73
John H. Ashmun	Law	1829–33
Charles Beck	Latin	1831–50
Henry J. Bigelow	Surgery	1849–82
Jacob Bigelow	Applied Science/Materia Medica	1815–55
George P. Bond	Astronomy	1846–65
William C. Bond	Astronomy	1840–59
Henry I. Bowditch	Clinical Medicine	1859–67
Francis Bowen	Philosophy/Civil Polity	⎰1836–39 ⎱1853–89
Joseph S. Buckminster	Biblical Literature	1811–12
Edward T. Channing	Rhetoric & Oratory	1819–51
Walter Channing	Obstetrics & Medical Jurisprudence	1815–54
William E. Channing	Biblical Literature	1812–13
Francis J. Child	Rhetoric & English	1848–76
Josiah P. Cooke	Chemistry & Mineralogy	1850–94
Henry L. Eustis	Engineering	1849–85
Edward Everett	Greek Literature	1815–26
John Farrar	Mathematics & Natural Philosophy	1807–36
Cornelius Felton	Greek Literature	1833–60
Convers Francis	Pulpit Eloquence & Pastoral Care	1842–63
Levi Frisbie	Latin/Philosophy & Civil Polity	1811–22
William W. Goodwin	Greek Literature	1860–1901
John Gorham	Chemistry & Materia Medica	1809–27
Asa Gray	Natural History	1842–88
Simon Greenleaf	Law	1833–48
George Hayward	Surgery	1835–49
Levi Hedge	Logic & Metaphysics/Philosophy & Civil Polity	1810–32
Oliver W. Holmes	Anatomy & Physiology	1847–82
Eben Horsford	Applied Science	1847–63

Frederic D. Huntington	Christian Morals	1855–60
James Jackson	Physic	1812–36
John B. S. Jackson	Morbid Anatomy	1847–79
George M. Lane	Latin	1851–94
Henry W. Longfellow	Modern Languages	1836–54
Joseph Lovering	Mathematics & Natural Philosophy	1835–88
James R. Lowell	Modern Languages	1855–86
Joseph McKean	Rhetoric & Oratory	1809–18
Andrews Norton	Biblical Literature	1813–30
George R. Noyes	Oriental Languages	1840–68
Thomas Nuttall	Natural History	1825–34
John G. Palfrey	Biblical Literature	1830–39
Isaac Parker	Law	1815–27
Joel Parker	Law	1847–68
Theophilus Parsons	Law	1848–70
Andrew P. Peabody	Christian Morals	1860–81
William D. Peck	Natural History	1805–22
Benjamin Peirce	Mathematics	1833–80
John S. Popkin	Greek Literature	1815–33
George C. Shattuck	Physic/Clinical Medicine	1855–74
Jared Sparks	History	1838–49
Asahel Stearns	Law	1817–29
Joseph Story	Law	1829–45
George Ticknor	Modern Languages	1817–35
Henry W. Torrey	History	{ 1844–48 / 1856–86
Daniel Treadwell	Applied Science	1824–45
James Walker	Philosophy & Civil Polity	1838–53
Henry Ware	Divinity	1805–40
Henry Ware, Jr.	Pulpit Eloquence & Pastoral Care	1829–42
John Ware	Physic	1832–58
John C. Warren	Anatomy & Surgery	1809–47
Emory Washburn	Law	1855–76
John W. Webster	Chemistry & Mineralogy	1824–50
Sidney Willard	Oriental Languages	1807–31
Jeffries Wyman	Anatomy	1847–74
Morrill Wyman	Physic	1853–56

The list includes only men appointed to professorships, not tutors or lecturers. Most of these were endowed chairs, although a few, such as Latin and mathematics in the early years, were university professorships supported from general income.

3. See, e.g., Graustein, *Thomas Nuttall*, p. 185; I. Bernard Cohen, *Some Early Tools of American Science* (Cambridge, Mass., 1950), pp. 62–63, 82–83; Anna

Haddow, *Political Science in American Colleges and Universities, 1636–1900* (New York, 1969), pp. 57–58. The advent of new course offerings may also be found in the printed college catalogues from 1826 to 1870.

4. See, e.g., Mary Orne Pickering, *Life of John Pickering* (Boston, 1887), p. 47; A. H. Everett, "Phillip's Manual of Political Economy," *NAR* 32(January 1831):233; Edward Everett, "Louis Say's Political Economy," Ibid. 17(October 1823):426; Caleb Cushing, *Summary of the Practical Principles of Political Economy* (Cambridge, 1826), pp. 62–63.

5. Anna Ticknor, *James G. Cogswell* (Cambridge, Mass., 1874), p. 44.

6. Andrew P. Peabody, "The Condition and Wants of Harvard College," *NAR* 60(January 1845):50–53; Leverett Saltonstall–Leverett Saltonstall, Jr., August 22, 1841, Leverett Saltonstall Papers, MHS.

7. Josiah Quincy–John Farrar, June 29, 1832, Josiah Quincy Papers, HUA; Thomas G. Cary, *Memoir of Thomas Handasyd Perkins* (Boston, 1856), p. 9; William P. Atkinson, *A Letter to a Young Man Who Has Just Entered College* (Boston, 1849), p. 29; George R. Sampson, *Address Delivered at the Dedication of the New Rooms of the Mercantile Library Association* (Boston, 1856), pp. 38–41.

8. Cf. Cohen, *Some Early Tools of American Science*, p. 94; Ernest Samuels, *The Young Henry Adams* (Cambridge, Mass., 1948), p. 19. For perhaps the most forceful contemporary expression of the "common culture" thesis, see the presidential reports of Jared Sparks from 1850 to 1852 and especially Jared Sparks, *Inaugural Address* (Cambridge, Mass., 1849).

9. John Ware, "Gorham's Chemistry," *NAR* 9(June 1819):113–114; Joseph Lovering, "Elementary Works on Physical Science," Ibid. 72(April 1851): 364–366. For the inception of the lecture system, see, e.g., Morison, *Three Centuries of Harvard*, pp. 224–238.

10. For the continental inspiration, see, e.g., Tyack, *George Ticknor*, pp. 85–92; Morison, *Three Centuries of Harvard*, pp. 224–230.

11. John Chipman Gray, "Wayland on College Education in America," *NAR* 72(January 1851):76–77. The spread of electives may be traced with some accuracy in the annual catalogues through 1870.

12. Jared Sparks–John T. Kirkland, September 3, 1825, American mss., BPL; Charles K. Bolton, "The Harvard University Library," *New England Magazine* 9(December 1893):440–441; Quincy, *Josiah Quincy*, pp. 441–442; Quincy, *History of Harvard University*, 2:320–361, 369–370; Edwin D. Sanborn, "European and American Universities," *NAR* 80(January 1855):129, 137; Jared Sparks–Francis Bowen, August 21, 1850, Jared Sparks Papers, HUA; Tyack, *George Ticknor*, p. 120; Emilio Goggio, "The History of Modern Language Teaching at Harvard University from Its Origins to 1850," *HGM* 38 (March 1930):286–291.

13. Leverett Saltonstall–Leverett Saltonstall, Jr., September 6, 1840, Leverett Saltonstall Papers, MHS; "Harvard Parents Memorial," July 1865, Thomas Hill Papers, HUA.

14. See, e.g., John Clarke, *Letter to a Student in the University at Cambridge*,

Massachusetts (Boston, 1796), pp. 34–87, passim; Samuel Eliot Morison, *Life and Letters of Harrison Gray Otis* (Boston and New York, 1913), 1:24; William W. Story, *Life and Letters of Joseph Story* (Boston, 1851), 1:49; Samuel D. Bradford, *Works of Samuel Dexter Bradford* (Boston, 1858), p. 369.

15. Peabody, *Harvard Reminiscences*, p. 137; Artemas Bowers Muzzey, "Harvard, 1820–1824," *The Harvard Monthly* 13(February 1892):88; Theodore Lyman–Eliza Pratt, April 3, 1821, George W. Lyman Papers, MHS; Morison, "The Great Rebellion in Harvard College," p. 62.

16. For disruptive episodes in this period, see, e.g., Muzzey, "Harvard, 1820–1824," p. 86; T. Prentiss Allen and Thomas Cushing, "Town and Gown in Old Times," *HGM* 8(September 1899), pp. 15–18; Quincy, *History of Harvard University*, 2:344–353; Morison, *Three Centuries of Harvard*, pp. 175–176.

17. John Lowell, *A Father's Benediction, and Advice* (Roxbury, 1811), pp. 1–7.

18. Theodore Lyman–Eliza Pratt, April 3, 1821, George W. Lyman Papers, MHS.

19. Leverett Saltonstall–Leverett Saltonstall, Jr., August 30, 1840, Leverett Saltonstall Papers, MHS.

20. Lowell, *A Father's Benediction*, p. 6; Amos Lawrence–Amos A. Lawrence, March 13, 1832, Amos A. Lawrence Papers, MHS; Peabody, *Harvard Reminiscences*, p. 2; Morison, "The Great Rebellion in Harvard College," p. 62.

21. Octavius Brooks Frothingham, *Recollections and Impressions, 1822–1890* (New York, 1891), pp. 22–23; Mary Thacher Higginson, *Thomas Wentworth Higginson* (New York and London, 1971), pp. 29–30; Susanna Willard, "Letters of Rev. Joseph Willard," *CHSP* 11(October 1916):31; Joseph Story, *Miscellaneous Writings* (Boston, 1835), pp. 134–146; John Ware, *Memoir of the Life of Henry Ware, Jr.* (Boston and London, 1846), p. 377; William C. Gannett, *Ezra Stiles Gannett* (Port Washington, New York and London, 1971), p. 276.

22. Hale, *James Russell Lowell*, p. 20.

23. Higginson, *Thomas Wentworth Higginson*, pp. 29–30; Frothingham, *Recollections and Impressions*, pp. 22–23.

24. Since the prevailing impression is that faculty-student relations in antebellum years were strained or nonexistent, the overwhelming evidence for the contrary view is especially notable. See, e.g., Boutwell, *Reminiscences*, 1:260; Edward Everett Hale, *Memories of a Hundred Years* (New York, 1904), p. 148; Hale, *A New England Boyhood*, p. 344; Hal Bridges, *Iron Millionaire: Life of Charlemagne Tower* (Philadelphia, 1952), pp. 21, 33; Higginson, *Thomas Wentworth Higginson*, pp. 24, 28; Thomas Wentworth Higginson, *Cheerful Yesterdays* (Boston and New York, 1898), pp. 49–53; *Addresses in Commemoration of Josiah Parsons Cooke* (Cambridge, 1895), pp. 20–21; Louis Agassiz, *Lake Superior* (Boston, 1850), p. iii; S.J. Spalding, "Memoir of Henry Coit Perkins," *Essex Institute Historical Collections* 12(1874):6–7; Graustein, *Thomas Nuttall*, pp. 188–192; Horatio J. Perry, "Harvard and Vacation Fifty Years Ago," *New England Magazine* 9(October 1893):208–209; Arria S. Huntington, *Memoirs and Letters of Frederic Dan Huntington* (Boston and New York, 1906), p. 49.

25. Charles W. Eliot, *Sixtieth Annual President's Report for 1884–85* (Cambridge, Mass., 1885), p. 48.

26. George F. Hoar, *Autobiography of Seventy Years* (New York, 1903), 1:91.

27. George A. Torrey, *A Lawyer's Recollections In and Out of Court* (Boston, 1910), pp. 50–51.

28. Henry Adams, "Harvard College, 1786–87," *NAR* 114(January 1872): 137–143.

29. Higginson, *Cheerful Yesterdays*, p. 55; Sullivan, *The Disappearance of Dr. Parkman* (Boston and Toronto, 1971), pp. 27–28.

30. Gray, "Wayland on College Education," p. 83.

31. Richard Hofstadter and Wilson Smith, eds., *American Higher Education: A Documentary History* (Chicago and London, 1961), 2:749.

32. For *North American Review* essays and Lowell Institute lectures, see William Cushing, *Index to the North American Review, 1815–1877* (Cambridge, 1878); Smith, *History of the Lowell Institute*, pp. 49–59. The list of scholarly publications was compiled from entries in the National Union Catalogue of Pre-1956 Imprints and the card catalogue of the Widener Library, Harvard University. The list of periodicals came principally from Frank Luther Mott, *A History of American Magazines, 1850–1865* (Cambridge, Mass., 1967), and the biographical essays on the faculty in the *Dictionary of American Biography*, 2nd ed. The faculty-edited periodicals included the following at least: *The American Almanac and Repository of Useful Knowledge* (Francis Bowen), *The American Monthly Review* (Sidney Willard), *The Atlantic Monthly* (James Russell Lowell), *The Boston Journal of Philosophy and the Arts* (Daniel Treadwell et al.), *The Boston Medical and Surgical Journal* (Walter Channing et al.), *Botany* (Asa Gray), *The Cambridge Miscellany of Mathematics, Physics, and Astronomy* (Joseph Lovering et al.), *Christian Disciple* (Henry Ware, Jr.), *Christian Examiner* (James Walker et al.), *The Church Monthly* (F. D. Huntington), *The General Repository and Review* (Andrews Norton), *The Law Reporter* (Asahel Stearns), *The Monthly Religious Magazine* (F. D. Huntington), *The New England Journal of Medicine* (J. B. S. Jackson et al.), *The North American Review* (Jared Sparks et al.), *The Select Journal of Foreign Periodical Literature* (Andrews Norton), *The United States Literary Gazette* (Theophilus Parsons).

33. There are *Dictionary of American Biography* sketches for every professor except Ashmun, J. B. S. Jackson, McKean, Popkin, and Torrey. These provide much relevant information as to scholarly achievement and reputation, although additional and sometimes fuller references are provided in chapter 5. That professors were generally expected to do scholarly work — that they did not merely pursue it as a quaint and irrelevant idiosyncracy — is suggested by the research time which was explicitly allotted to Story, Sparks, Gray, and other instructors at the time of their appointments as well as by the overall concern with academic excellence as a desirable trait for a professorial candidate.

34. The tabular version of the data is as follows:

Professors appointed	Scholarly books per professor	% books produced while at Harvard	Average number of editions	% books in more than 10 editions
1800–30	3.7	63	3.5	8
1831–60	5.6	77	7.1	20

Works were considered to have been produced while at Harvard if they appeared within five years after the termination of tenure. Only nineteenth-century editions are included in the compilation, which also excludes mere reminiscences, travel accounts, or works outside the field of expertise, broadly construed. In the case of the poet, Longfellow, only the epic-length works issued during his Harvard years were included.

35. Cf. McCaughey, "The Transformation of American Academic Life," pp. 246–269, passim; George H. Daniels, *American Science in the Age of Jackson* (New York, 1968), p. 35.

36. Quoted in Huntington, *Memoirs of Frederic Dan Huntington*, pp. 114–115.

37. Willard Phillips, "Seybert's Statistical Annals," *NAR* 9(September 1819):236.

38. Josiah Quincy, May 2, 1820, "Journal and Common-place Book, 1818–1828," Josiah Quincy Papers, MHS; Edward Everett–Joseph Story, April 13, 1821, in Frothingham, *Edward Everett*, p. 71.

39. Andrews Norton, *Speech Delivered Before the Overseers of Harvard College, February 3, 1825, in Behalf of the Resident Instructors of the College* (Boston, 1825), p. vii; Henry Ware et al., "Memorial of Professors and Tutors relative to the mode in which, according to the Charter of the institution, the Corporation of the same ought of right to be constituted," ms., HUA, pp. 3–4, 29.

40. Edward Everett, *A Letter to John Lowell, Esq.* (Boston, 1824), pp. 48–50, 74–75.

41. Norton, *Speech Delivered Before the Overseers*, p. xxi; Ware et al., "Memorial of Professors and Tutors," pp. 32–33; Andrews Norton, *Remarks on a Report of a Committee of the Overseers of Harvard College* (Cambridge, Mass., 1824), pp. 17, 25.

42. For biographical details, see Frothingham, *Edward Everett;* Kermit Vanderbilt, *Charles Eliot Norton* (Cambridge, Mass., 1959).

43. John T. Kirkland–Henry Ware, April 16, 1824, ms., HUA; Joseph Story–Edward Everett, January 4, 1825, in Story, *Joseph Story,* 1:447.

44. John Lowell, *Remarks on a Pamphlet Printed by the Professors and Tutors of Harvard University* (Boston, 1824); John Lowell, *Further Remarks* (Boston, 1824); George Ticknor, *Remarks on Changes Lately Proposed or Adopted, in Harvard University* (n.p., 1825); Joseph Story, *Report of the Chairman of the Committee of the Overseers of Harvard University* (Boston, 1824); William Ellery Channing–[?], September 27, 1824, ms., HUA; Quincy, *History of Harvard University*, 2:341–348.

45. Lowell, *Remarks on a Pamphlet*, pp. 31, 39–43. See also Ticknor, *Remarks on Changes*, pp. 27–28, 30–32.

46. Lowell, *Remarks on a Pamphlet*, p. 33.

47. Everett, *Letter to Lowell*, p. 96.

48. Lowell, *Remarks on a Pamphlet*, pp. 46–47.

49. Everett, *Letter to Lowell*, pp. 74–75.

50. Overseer records do not indicate the ease or margin of the Corporation's victory over the professors, but the intensity and extent of the public debate would seem to indicate some degree of sympathy with the faculty position among at least a portion of the Overseers, a view perhaps substantiated by the conflicts over the advent and policies of the Bowditch-Quincy regime.

51. Quincy, *History of Harvard University*, 2:343–353.

52. The eleven signers were Henry Ware, Levi Hedge, John S. Popkin, Asahel Stearns, Sidney Willard, John Farrar, Andrews Norton, Edward Everett, George Otis, James Hayward, and Nathaniel Wood. Ware et al., "Memorial of Professors and Tutors." Only Ware and Farrar remained after 1833.

53. The outlines of this debate may be followed in John G. Palfrey, "Quincy's History of Harvard University," *NAR* 52(April 1841):338–384; Francis Bowen, "Classical Studies at Cambridge," Ibid. 54(January 1842):35–73; Francis Bowen, "College Education," Ibid. 55(October 1842):302–343; Peabody, "The Condition and Wants of Harvard College," pp. 38–63; Francis Bowen, "Eliot's Sketch of Harvard College," *NAR* 68(January 1848):99–128.

54. John G. Palfrey, *Notice of Professor Farrar* (Boston, 1853), p. 11.

55. Harrington, *The Harvard Medical School*, 2:517; Jared Sparks–Francis Bowen, August 21, 1850, Jared Sparks Papers, HUA; [?]–Thomas Hill, September 16, 1865, John Amory Lowell–Thomas Hill, October 20, 1865, Corporation Papers, HUA.

56. Bowen, "College Education," p. 324.

57. Hofstadter and Smith, *American Higher Education*, 2:751.

58. Hale, *A New England Boyhood*, p. 354. See also George Herbert Palmer, *Autobiography* (Boston, 1930), p. 41.

Chapter 5

1. Joseph Henry–Louis Agassiz, August 13, 1864, in Reingold, *Science in Nineteenth-Century America*, p. 216.

2. The rejected benefactor of 1855 was William J. Walker. The law benefactor was Nathan Dane, who tapped Joseph Story; the scientific donors were Thomas Lee, who wanted and got Jeffries Wyman, and Abbot Lawrence, who selected Louis Agassiz. Merle Curti and Roderick Nash, *Philanthropy in the Shaping of American Higher Education* (New Brunswick, N.J., 1965), pp. 47–48; Sutherland, *The Law at Harvard*, pp. 92–98; Lurie, *Louis Agassiz*, pp. 139, 167–168; Henry and Mary Lee, *Letters and Journals with Other Family Letters, 1802–1860*, ed. Frances Rollins Morse (Boston, 1926), p. 28.

3. Walker, "Josiah Quincy," p. 131. Cf. also Jared Sparks–George Putnam, November 29, 1849, Jared Sparks Papers, HUA; James Walker–James Russell Lowell, January 30, 1855, James Walker Papers, HUA.

4. Joseph A. Willard, *Half a Century with Judges and Lawyers* (Boston and New York, 1895), p. 35.

5. Higginson, *Cheerful Yesterdays*, pp. 107–110.

6. Henry Wadsworth Longfellow, *The Letters of Henry Wadsworth Longfellow, 1814–1843*, ed. Andrew Hilen (Cambridge, Mass., 1969), 3:313; Arthur Hugh Clough, *The Correspondence of Arthur Hugh Clough*, ed. F. L. Mulhauser (Oxford, 1957), 2:474–475.

7. Raymond Calkins, *The Life and Times of Alexander McKenzie* (Cambridge, Mass., 1935), p. 76.

8. Peabody, *Harvard Reminiscences*, pp. 47–48; Leo Lesquereux–J. P. Lesley, March 21, 1866, in Reingold, *Science in Nineteenth-Century America*, p. 222.

9. Warren, *The Harvard Law School*, 1:361; Kutler, *Privilege and Creative Destruction*, pp. 76–77.

10. John Quincy Adams, *Memoirs of John Quincy Adams*, ed. Charles Francis Adams (Philadelphia, 1877), 8:546; Thayer, "Extracts from the Journal of Benjamin Waterhouse," p. 28; Peabody, *Harvard Reminiscences*, p. 106.

11. Cf. Palfrey, *Notice of Professor Farrar*, p. 11; Peabody, *Harvard Reminiscences*, p. 136.

12. Quoted in Kutler, *Privilege and Creative Destruction*, p. 80.

13. Thayer, "Extracts from the Journal of Benjamin Waterhouse," p. 28; David Donald, *Charles Sumner and the Coming of the Civil War* (New York, 1960), pp. 112, 129; Warren, *The Harvard Law School*, 2:98.

14. Jared Sparks–Richard Hildreth, September 24, 1851, Jared Sparks–Samuel A. Eliot, December 1, 1851, Jared Sparks Papers, HUA.

15. Frank Preston Stearns, *Cambridge Sketches* (Philadelphia and London, 1905), p. 99; James Walker–James Russell Lowell, January 30, 1855, James Walker Papers, HUA; Noel G. Annan, *Leslie Stephen* (Cambridge, Mass., 1952), pp. 58–59.

16. Teele, *The History of Milton, Massachusetts*, p. 262; Stearns, *Cambridge Sketches*, p. 25.

17. Quoted in Clough, *Correspondence*, 2:335, 399.

18. Morison, *Three Centuries of Harvard*, p. 254; Ware, *Life of Henry Ware, Jr.*, p. 361; Walker, "Josiah Quincy," pp. 130–131.

19. Charles Francis Adams, August 26, 1846, in "Extracts from the Diaries of John Quincy Adams and Charles Francis Adams," p. 53; Higginson, *Cheerful Yesterdays*, p. 51.

20. Stearns, *Cambridge Sketches*, pp. 38, 62.

21. Ibid., pp. 48, 51, 79. The antislavery moderates of the 1850s included Charles Beck, Henry W. Longfellow, James Russell Lowell, Francis J. Child, Henry I. Bowditch, Asa Gray, Frederic D. Huntington, and George R. Noyes.

222   The Forging of an Aristocracy

22. Hoar, *Autobiography*, 1:98–99; Moncure D. Conway, *Autobiography, Memoirs and Experiences* (Boston and New York, 1904), 1:165; Longfellow, *Letters*, 3:4.

23. Huntington, *Memoirs of Frederic Dan Huntington*, p. 127.

24. Annan, *Leslie Stephen*, pp. 57–58.

25. Charles G. B. Daubeny, *Journal of a tour through the United States, and in Canada, made During the Years 1837–38* (Oxford, 1843), p. 67.

26. Williams, *The Harvard Divinity School*, p. 87; Lucius R. Paige, *History of Cambridge, Massachusetts, 1630–1877* (Boston and New York, 1877), p. 306.

27. Truman Nelson, "Theodore Parker as Revolutionary Moralist: From Divinity Hall to Harper's Ferry," *Unitarian Historical Society Proceedings* 13 (1960):71–83; George Smalley, *Anglo-American Memories* (London, 1911), p. 53; Amos Lawrence–Henry I. Bowditch, May 28, 1842, Amos Lawrence–George Putnam, April 12, 1846, Abbott Lawrence–T. K. Lothrop, April 18, 1844, Amos Lawrence Papers, MHS.

28. Samuel Lawrence–Amos Lawrence, August 28, 1844, Amos Lawrence Papers, MHS.

29. Stearns, *Cambridge Sketches*, p. 33; Samuels, *The Young Henry Adams*, pp. 22–25; Paige, *History of Cambridge*, pp. 309–310; Thomas W. Ward–Joshua Bates, December 10, 1844, Thomas W. Ward Papers, MHS. The non-Unitarian faculty included Theophilus Parsons, Simon Greenleaf, William C. and George P. Bond, Asa Gray, Joel Parker, Emory Washburn, and Eben Horsford.

30. Cf. Edwin P. Whipple, *Recollections of Eminent Men, with Other Papers* (Boston, 1887), p. 93; Lurie, *Louis Agassiz*, pp. 255–265; Calkins, *Alexander McKenzie*, pp. 154–156; Camille Ferri Pisani, *Prince Napoleon in America*, tr. G. J. Joyaux (London, 1960), p. 275.

31. George R. Minot–William Minot, June 17, 1801, in Katharine Minot Channing, *Minot Family Letters, 1773–1871* (Sherborn, Mass., 1957), p. 196; Palfrey, *Notice of Professor Farrar*, pp. 12–13.

32. John Quincy Adams, August 30, 1821, "Extracts from the Diaries of John Quincy Adams and Charles Francis Adams," p. 19; George B. Emerson, *Reminiscences of an Old Teacher* (Boston, 1878), p. 29; Daubeny, *Journal of a Tour*, pp. 67, 69. See also Richard Cobden, *The American Diaries of Richard Cobden*, ed. E. H. Cawley (Princeton, 1952), pp. 114–115.

33. Edward Dicey, *Spectator in America*, ed. Herbert Mitgang (Chicago, 1971), pp. 265–266.

34. Ruth Huntington Sessions, *Sixty-Odd: A Personal History* (Brattleboro, Vt., 1936), p. 11. See also Pisani, *Prince Napoleon in America*, p. 271.

35. Leslie Stephen–Lady Jane Stephen, July 21, 1863, in Frederic William Maitland, *The Life and Letters of Leslie Stephen* (New York and London, 1906), p. 113–116.

36. Thorstein Veblen, *The Theory of the Leisure Class* (New York, 1953), pp. 250–251.

37. Edward Sylvester Morse, October 22, 1860, in Louise Hall Tharp, *Adventurous Alliance* (Boston and Toronto, 1959), p. 150.

38. *Cambridge Directory for 1863–4* (Cambridgeport, Mass., 1863), map facing p. i, pp. 219–223; Charles W. Eliot, *Views Respecting the Present Exemption from Taxation of Property Used for Religious, Educational, and Charitable Purposes* (Cambridge, Mass., 1875), p. 380; Vanderbilt, *Charles Eliot Norton*, p. 21.

39. Quoted in George W. Smith and Charles Judah, eds., *Life in the North During the Civil War* (Albuquerque, N. Mex., 1966), p. 280.

40. James, *Charles W. Eliot*, 1:129. The reference was to Louis Agassiz.

41. Longfellow, *Letters*, 3:123.

42. Sullivan, *The Disappearance of Dr. Parkman*, p. 27.

43. Thomas Wentworth Higginson, *Old Cambridge* (New York and London, 1900), p. 32.

44. Clough, *Correspondence*, 2:338.

45. Boston bank salaries have been estimated from data in Redlich, *The Molding of American Banking*, p. 257; Stetson, *The State Bank*, pp. 44–49. The salaries of state officials may be found in *Lists of Officers with Their Deputies etc., Who Have Been in Commission, in Massachusetts, Since 1833* (Boston, 1843); the salaries of mill treasurers, from "Commission data on 18 textile firms, August 1, 1848," Amos A. Lawrence Papers, MHS.

46. Hale, *A New England Boyhood*, p. 361.

47. Peabody, "The Condition and Wants of Harvard College," p. 55; Edward E. Hale, "Longfellow at Harvard," *HGM* 15(March 1907):368; Calkins, *Alexander McKenzie*, p. 69.

48. Faculty members who were also Corporation members or patrons included William Ellery Channing, Joseph Story, John C. Warren, George Hayward, C. C. Felton, and James Walker. The sons and brothers were James Jackson, Edward T. and Walter Channing, James R. Lowell, Theophilus Parsons, and Nathaniel I. Bowditch. Sons-in-law and brothers-in-law included John Gorham, Edward Everett, George Ticknor, Andrews Norton, Oliver Wendell Holmes, and Asa Gray. The nephews were George Otis and J. B. S. Jackson.

49. For examples of elite influence in the hiring process, see e.g. George E. Ellis, *Memoir of Jacob Bigelow* (Cambridge, 1880), p. 35; Charles Pope and Katharine Peabody Loring, *Loring Genealogy* (Cambridge, Mass., 1917), p. 97; *Addresses in Commemoration of Josiah Parsons Cooke*, pp. 1–4; Martin Duberman, *James Russell Lowell* (Boston, 1966), p. 141; Palfrey, *Notice of Professor Farrar*, pp. 8–10; John G. Palfrey, *A Discourse on the Life and Character of the Reverend Henry Ware* (Cambridge, 1845), pp. 30–31; Charles Lowell–[?], ca. 1845, Charles Lowell Papers, MHS; Warren, *The Harvard Law School*, 1:290–291; Putnam, *James Jackson*, p. 43; Hoar, *Autobiography*, 1:113; Morison, *The Development of Harvard University*, p. 153; John Amory Lowell–Nathan Appleton, December 6, 1834, Samuel A. Eliot–Nathan Appleton, December 9, 1847, Nathan Appleton Papers, MHS; John Lowell–Josiah Quincy, December 15, 1834, College

Papers, s.2, vol. 6, HUA; Jared Sparks–George Putnam, November 29, 1849, Jared Sparks Papers, HUA; A. P. Peabody–John Amory Lowell, March 18, 1862, C. C. Felton Letters, HUA.

50. James Russell Lowell–William Wetmore Story, September 23, 1849, in Gertrude R. Hudson, ed., *Browning to His American Friends: Letters Between the Brownings, the Storys and James Russell Lowell, 1841–1890* (New York, 1965), p. 248; Arthur Hugh Clough–Blanche Smith, April 29, 1853, in Clough, *Correspondence,* 2:424.

51. The most active faculty businessmen were probably Willard and Treadwell. Other directors, consultants, and entrepreneurs from the early period included Joseph Story, Isaac Parker, Walter Channing, Asahel Stearns, Aaron Dexter, George Ticknor, and William Ellery Channing; and Simon Greenleaf, Charles Beck, Joel Parker, Emory Washburn, Josiah Parsons Cooke, Benjamin Peirce, and Eben Horsford after 1830. The basic sources for faculty business participation are the lists of directors, officers, and investors in the major firms cited in chapter 1, note 10.

See also the city directories for Boston and Cambridge, which provide the names of bank and insurance company directors and officers, plus the following sources: Paige, *History of Cambridge,* pp. 200, 230; Eliot, *History of Cambridge,* p. 286; Willard, *Half a Century,* p. 36; *Report of the Joint Standing Committee on Boston Harbor, for the Year 1852* (Boston, 1853), pp. 36–50; Longfellow, *Letters,* 3:5; James Russell Lowell, *New Letters of James Russell Lowell,* ed. M. A. DeWolfe Howe (New York and London, 1932), p. 112; Tharp, *Adventurous Alliance,* pp. 253–254; *The Merchants National Bank of Salem* (Salem, 1908), p. 57; *The Worcester National Bank* (Worcester, Mass., 1904), p. 29; Charles E. Fisher, *The Story of the Old Colony Railroad* (n.p., 1919), p. 170; Daniel Treadwell–Francis C. Gray and Horace Gray, July 23, 1838, Daniel Treadwell, "Financial Statement," 1845, Daniel Treadwell Papers, HUA.

52. Information on stockholding and real estate as a percentage of total wealth comes principally from probate court inventories, which were available for approximately 80 percent of the antebellum professors. For elite gifts, loans, and advice, see, e.g., N. I. Bowditch–Daniel Treadwell, July 8, 1831, Daniel Treadwell Papers, HUA; Levi Frisbie–Leverett Saltonstall, February 13, 1822, Leverett Saltonstall Papers, MHS; Henry W. Longfellow–Amos A. Lawrence, February 15, 1854, Amos A. Lawrence Papers, MHS; Charles G. Loring–William G. Gardiner, September 29, [year?], Charles Greely Loring Papers, Houghton Library; Stearns, *Cambridge Sketches,* p. 35.

53. Francis J. Grund, *Aristocracy in America* (New York, Evanston, and London, 1959), p. 156.

54. Ferencz Pulszky, *White, Red, Black: Sketches of Society in the United States* (New York, 1968), 2:165. For examples of beneficial faculty marriages, see, e.g., Lowell, *New Letters,* p. 80; Clough, *Correspondence,* 2:396; John G. Palfrey, "Professor Farrar," *CE* 55(July 1853):121–136; Truax, *The Doctors Warren,* pp. 131–133; Robert Hallowell Gardiner, *Early Recollections, 1782–1864* (Hallowell,

Me., 1936), p. 45; Putnam, *James Jackson*, pp. 104, 128; John T. Morse, *Life and Letters of Oliver Wendell Holmes* (Boston and New York, 1896), 1:171; Tharp, *Adventurous Alliance*, p. 150; Robert B. Forbes, *Personal Reminiscences*, 2nd ed. (Boston, 1882), p. 29; Frothingham, *Edward Everett*, p. 75; Adams, *Life and Writings of Jared Sparks*, 1:340–345; Dupree, *Asa Gray*, p. 110; Newton Arvin, *Longfellow* (Boston, 1963), p. 51.

Chapter 6

1. For a summary of these early circumstances and expectations, see John Whitehead, *The Separation of College and State* (New Haven and London, 1973), pp. 9–52.
2. Samuel A. Eliot, *A Letter to the President of Harvard College* (Boston, 1849), pp. 33–34; William G. Land, *Thomas Hill, Twentieth President of Harvard* (Cambridge, Mass., 1933), p. 137; Sidney Willard, *Memories of Youth and Manhood* (Cambridge, 1855), 1:98. Professors in the medical, law, and scientific schools gave lectures to undergraduates in chemistry, anatomy, law, and geology during this period, as the divinity faculty gave sermons; all professional lectures were in turn open to any undergraduate, as were the facilities of the observatory. Moreover, a third of all Harvard College graduates from 1820 to 1850 also earned Harvard professional degrees, constituting in turn about a third of all those receiving such degrees. The Corporation did, however, prepare an 1832 edition of the university laws in which those applying to undergraduates were listed separately, and in 1846 the president's report discussed the professional schools separately for the first time. Cf. Josiah Quincy–Lemuel Shaw, July 11, 1832, Lemuel Shaw Papers, MHS; Edward Everett, *President's Report for 1845–1846* (Cambridge, Mass., 1846).
3. Curtis, *Benjamin Robbins Curtis*, p. 49; Hale, *A New England Boyhood*, p. 360.
4. Horatio R. Storer, "Thomas Jefferson Coolidge," *HGM* 29(March 1921):409–410.
5. Mark Sibley Severance, *Hammersmith, His Harvard Days* (Boston, 1878), p. 44.
6. Morison, *Three Centuries of Harvard*, pp. 219–220; Frederick Robinson, "A Letter to the Hon. Rufus Choate" (1831), in *The Golden Age of American Law*, ed., Charles M. Haar (New York, 1965), pp. 90–92.
7. Peabody, "The Condition and Wants of Harvard College," p. 41.
8. Bowen, "Eliot's Sketch of Harvard College," pp. 117–118.
9. Bowen, "College Education," p. 303; Bowen, "Classical Studies at Cambridge," p. 48; Peabody, "The Condition and Wants of Harvard College," p. 52; Quincy, *Josiah Quincy*, p. 438.
10. Theodore Parker, "The Position and Duties of the American Scholar," August 8, 1849, in *The Works of Theodore Parker*, ed. Frances P. Cobbe (London, 1876),7:221.

11. The names used for comparison, together with the number of graduates per period, are as follows: Bigelow (2–17), Bowditch (0–3), Brimmer (0–4), Brooks (4–15), Cabot (5–9), Choate (1–5), Codman (1–7), Crowninshield (0–3), Curtis (4–9), Derby (3–7), Dexter (3–7), Francis (0–3), Gardiner (0–3), Gray (9–14), Greene (2–6), Greenough (0–7), Higginson (1–4), Hoar (2–5), Holmes (1–9), Lawrence (4–10), Loring (7–11), Lowell (6–11), Lyman (0–9), Otis (7–10), Peabody (5–12), Perkins (5–17), Richardson (7–13), Sargent (2–13), Sears (0–5), Shaw (9–14), Swett (1–6), Thayer (6–11), Thorndike (1–7), Tuckerman (1–3), Ware (2–11), Weld (5–8). Some elite families — Quincy, Amory, Eliot — were roughly equal in both periods. Others — Adams, Appleton, Lee, Jackson, Phillips — have names too common for meaningful comparison. Some of the names listed — Gray, Bigelow, Richardson, Thayer — obviously include more than one family. The trend is nonetheless clear, particularly since some families with relatively high eighteenth-century totals — Loring, Lowell, Otis — accumulated them mainly in the post-Revolutionary era.

12. Thomas Wentworth Higginson–Nancy Storrow, May 17, 1844, in Thomas Wentworth Higginson, *Letters and Journals of Thomas Wentworth Higginson*, ed. Mary Thacher Higginson (New York, 1969), p. 1.

13. Fathers' occupations for the early years are estimated from surviving classbooks and other fragmentary data and must be considered tentative. The figure for the 1860s is from Charles W. Eliot, *President's Report for 1874–1875* (Cambridge, Mass., 1875), p. 10. Of the twenty-five antebellum millionaires as derived from probate records (see chapter 1, note 42), only Thomas H. Perkins (whose son was retarded), William Pratt, Francis Skinner, John Welles, and Samuel Bradford did not send sons to Harvard.

14. John Randolph–Josiah Quincy, December 1, 1813, in Quincy, *Josiah Quincy*, p. 341.

15. Overseer Report, April 27, 1819, Overseers Reports, vol. 1, HUA.

16. William G. Stearns–Amos A. Lawrence, July 4, 1860, Amos A. Lawrence Papers, MHS.

17. E. R. Hoar, J. W. Churchill, L. N. Thayer, January 28, 1858, Overseer Miscellaneous Reports, vol. 1, HUA.

18. Cf. Brewster, *Josiah Dwight Whitney*, 1:75; Severance, *Hammersmith*, p. 13.

19. Parsons, *Theophilus Parsons*, pp. 286–287; William H. Channing, *The Life of William Ellery Channing* (Boston, 1890), p. 22.

20. Joseph Story–William H. Channing, September 23, 1843, in Story, *Joseph Story*, 1:51.

21. Palfrey, *The Reverend Henry Ware*, p. 9.

22. Quincy, *Josiah Quincy*, p. 439.

23. Longfellow, *Letters*, 2:125–126; "1845 Subscribers," November 18, 1845, Boston Assembly, BPL.

24. Leverett Saltonstall–Leverett Saltonstall, Jr., September 27, 1840, Leverett Saltonstall Papers, MHS. See also Huntington, *Memoirs of Frederic*

Dan Huntington, p. 17; Eliza Susan Quincy, April 21, 1819, in M. A. DeWolfe Howe, ed., *The Articulate Sisters* (Cambridge, Mass., 1946), p. 34.

25. Morison, *Three Centuries of Harvard*, pp. 208, 312–313.

26. The study of law per se did not mean, of course, the practice of law, so the figure for lawyers may be slightly overstated. As a student wrote to his mother at mid-century, "Father says I should study law whether I practice it or not. Every man . . . should know how to attend to his own private business, and for this end Law is indispensable." Nicholas Longworth Anderson–Catherine Anderson, December 28, 1857, in Nicholas Longworth Anderson, *The Letters and Journals of General Nicholas Longworth Anderson*, ed. Isabel Anderson (New York, London, Edinburgh, 1942), p. 120. The pattern of Harvard careers was very different from that of most antebellum colleges in any case. At Williams College, for example, some 45 percent of the graduates between 1821 and 1840 became ministers and 90 percent either ministers or lawyers. Eben Burt Parsons, "Williams College," in *History of Higher Education in Massachusetts*, ed. George G. Bush (Washington, 1891), p. 228. At Yale only 10 percent of the graduates pursued business careers even as late as mid-century. Brooks Mather Kelley, *Yale, A History* (New Haven and London, 1974), p. 279.

27. The proportion of Boston doctors and lawyers holding a Harvard bachelor's degree is derived from a comparison of the list of degreeholders in the *Harvard Quinquennial Catalogue* with the occupational lists in the Boston city directory for 1849–1850. For Harvard judges, see Charles P. Ware, "Harvard Graduates in the Public Service," *HGM* (July 1893)1, pp. 564–570. The early textile directors include thirty-seven individuals from the boards of the largest mills in seven New England manufacturing centers; for 1870, see Frances Gregory and Irene Neu, "The American Industrial Elite in the 1870's," in Miller, *Men in Business*, p. 203. Financial institutions selected for analysis include: the State Bank, the Suffolk Bank, and the Bank of Commerce, plus the Provident Institution for Savings, the Massachusetts Hospital Life Insurance Company, and the Boston Manufacturers Mutual Fire Insurance Company. On the preeminence of Harvard professionals, see also Gray, "Wayland on College Education," pp. 71–72; Warren, *The Harvard Law School*, 1:153–154. Lists of the wealthy men of Boston in 1833 and 1848 are provided in Pessen, *Riches, Class and Power*, pp. 331–335; for 1860, in *List of Persons, Copartnerships, and Corporations . . . in the Year 1860*.

28. For political and religious affiliations, see Francis Gordon Caffey, "Harvard's Political Preferences Since 1860," *HGM* (April 1893)1, p. 407; F. M. Weld, ed., *Harvard College Report of the Class of 1860, 1860–1880* (New York, 1880), which lists fifty-eight Unitarians, seventeen Episcopalians, fourteen Orthodox Congregationalists, nine Baptists, three Methodists, three Spiritualists, two Swedenborgians, and one Dutch Reformed. The same class had seventy-five Republicans, twenty-three Constitutional Unionists, and nine Democrats. Both sets of figures are for the years of graduation.

29. Piano manufacturer Jesse Chickering, for example, placed his sons in

business positions after they had completed secondary school, not feeling, as his eulogist has it, "above having his sons become mechanics, laboring with their own hands as he had done." "Jesse Chickering," in Freeman Hunt, ed., *Lives of American Merchants* (New York, 1855), 1:517–519. Nathaniel Bowditch sent three of his four sons to Harvard, whence they emerged to become lawyers or doctors; the fourth, however, moved directly into a mercantile firm.

30. John Murray Forbes–Paul Siemen Forbes, March 23, 1848, in Sarah Forbes Hughes, *Letters and Recollections of John Murray Forbes* (Boston and New York), 1:182–183.

31. Quoted in John Crosby Brown, *A Hundred Years of Merchant Banking: A History of Brown Brothers* (New York, 1909), p. 252.

32. Cf. Henry Adams, *The Education of Henry Adams* (Boston, 1961), p. 65; Henry Cabot Lodge, *Early Memories* (New York, 1913), p. 208; Bliss Perry, *Life and Letters of Henry Lee Higginson* (Boston, 1921), pp. 23–24; Theodore Lyman, *Theodore Lyman, Jr.* (Boston, 1886), p. 17.

33. Land, *Thomas Hill*, pp. 134–135.

34. Curtis, *Benjamin Robbins Curtis*, p. 49; George Bancroft–Board of Overseers, January 1845, Overseer Reports, vol. 7, HUA.

35. Kelley, *Yale*, p. 144.

36. For tuition and other officially estimated costs, see the Harvard catalogues for 1825, 1835, 1845, and 1860; and William R. Thayer, "The Tuition Fee," *HGM* 23(December 1914):228.

37. [?]–Amos Lawrence, December 22, 1837, Amos Lawrence Papers, MHS.

38. Quoted in Sarah H. Emerson, *Life of Abby Hopper Gibbons* (New York and London, 1897), 1:177.

39. Anthony Trollope, *North America* (Baltimore, 1968), p. 143.

40. Samuel H. Walley, Jr., January 20, 1848, Overseer Reports, vol. 8, HUA.

41. Theodore Parker, "A Sermon of Merchants," November 22, 1846, in *Works of Theodore Parker*, 7:9; Curtis, *Benjamin Robbins Curtis*, pp. 15–17; Harold F. Williamson, *Edward Atkinson* (Boston, 1934), pp. 1–2; Horatio Greenough, *Letters of Horatio Greenough to His Brother, Henry Greenough*, ed. Francis B. Greenough (Boston, 1887), p. 17.

42. Mrs. Harrison Gray Otis, *The Barclays of Boston* (Boston, 1854), p. 46.

43. See, e.g., Ruth H. Sessions, "A Harvard Man's Budget in 1790," *HGM* 42(December 1933):141; Peabody, *Harvard Graduates*, p. 82; Anderson, *Letters and Journals of General Nicholas Longworth Anderson*, pp. 129–131; William Everett, "Harvard in 1855," *The Harvard Monthly* 3(November 1887):46; George L. Locke–Amos A. Lawrence, July 14, 1858, Amos A. Lawrence Papers, MHS; George Torrey, *A Lawyer's Recollections* (Boston, 1910), p. 63; Robert Grant, *Fourscore* (Boston and New York, 1934), p. 90. Data is less adequate for the professional schools, but these, too, were comparatively expensive. Theodore Parker estimated the minimum cost of a year at the divinity

school at $200 in 1834; tuition alone at the new Lawrence Scientific School was $150 plus laboratory fees; in 1854 Mrs. Otis assumed that it would take $1,000 to spend a year as a law student in Cambridge. Tuition at other colleges was considerably less, and probably expenses as well. At Yale, for example, tuition was only $39 a year as late as 1860. Kelley, *Yale*, p. 193.

44. George Bancroft–Board of Overseers, January 1845, Overseer Reports, vol. 7, HUA.

45. Bowen, "Eliot's Sketch of Harvard College," p. 118.

46. E. R. Hoar, J. W. Churchill, L. N. Thayer, January 28, 1858, Overseer Miscellaneous Reports, vol. 1, HUA.

47. See, e.g., Quincy, *History of Harvard University*, 2:434–435; Foster, *"Out of Smalle Beginnings,"* p. 206; note by Eliza Susan Quincy, May 20, 1868, inserted in Josiah Quincy, "Letter Book, 1829–1833," Josiah Quincy Papers, HUA; Morison, "The Great Rebellion in Harvard College," p. 96; Edmund Quincy Sewall, "Complaints and Calumnies Against Harvard University," *The Unitarian Advocate, and Religious Miscellany* n.s., vol. 3(1831):281; Jared Sparks–Cyrus A. Royston, January 15, 1851, Jared Sparks Papers, HUA; Henry Seidel Canby, *Thoreau* (Boston, 1939), p. 58.

48. See the Harvard catalogue for 1860–61 for scholarship aid available at that time.

49. For admission requirements and the system of examinations, see the university catalogues for 1825, 1835, 1845, 1855, and 1865, and the annals of the Harvard classes of 1835 and 1852, which provide excellent glimpses into the admission examination. Also relevant are John T. Kirkland, "Literary Institutions," NAR 7(July 1818), p. 270–271; Bowen, "Classical Studies at Cambridge," p. 48; "Harvard University," *Monthly Chronicle* 2(February 1841):64; Horatio J. Perry, "Harvard and Vacation Fifty Years Ago," *New England Magazine* 9(October 1893):208; Samuel G. Ward–Thomas W. Ward, September 9, 1839, Thomas W. Ward Papers, MHS; Fiske, *Letters*, p. 27; Severance, *Hammersmith*, pp. 31, 36–37; John A. Garraty, *Henry Cabot Lodge* (New York, 1953), p. 21.

50. For the average ages of New England college students generally, see David Allmendinger, Jr., *Paupers and Scholars: The Transformation of Student Life in Nineteenth-Century New England* (New York, 1975).

51. George Bancroft–Board of Overseers, January 1845, Overseer Reports, vol. 7, HUA.

52. Cushing, "Undergraduate Life Sixty Years Ago," p. 553.

53. James C. White, "An Undergraduate's Diary I," HGM 21(March 1913):423.

54. Severance, *Hammersmith*, p. 36.

55. See also Samuel A. Eliot, ed., *Heralds of a Liberal Faith*, 4 vols. (Boston, 1910), a biographical compilation covering dozens of early Unitarian ministers, most of whom attended Harvard; and *Harvard Memorial Biographies*, 2 vols. (Cambridge, Mass., 1866), which sketches members of Harvard classes from

1828 to 1865 who died in the Civil War. Charles W. Eliot's *Forty-Ninth Report of the President of Harvard, 1873–74* (Cambridge, Mass., 1875), pp. 82–84, produces an invaluable table on which schools prepared how many entering students from 1867 through 1874. Useful school histories are cited in note 56, as are some of the hundreds of pertinent articles and biographical studies on preparatory schooling in the period. The percentages in table 14 are of course estimates only. In deriving them I have generally excluded the southern students, who bulked large in several antebellum years.

56. For the Boston Latin School, see Grant, *Fourscore*, p. 31; Henry Jenks, *Catalogue of the Boston Public Latin School, with an Historical Sketch* (Boston, 1886), p. 71; Joseph Power and Lee Dunn, "Brief History of the Boston Latin School," typescript, Boston Latin School Papers, BPL; "Records of Subscribers to Association Funds," Boston Latin School ms. no. 186, BPL. For the Phillips academies, see *Biographical Catalogue of the Trustees, Teachers and Students of Phillips Academy, Andover, 1798–1830* (Andover, 1903); Claude M. Fuess, *An Old New England School* (Boston and New York, 1917); *Catalogue of the Officers and Students of Phillips Exeter Academy, 1783–1883* (Boston, 1883); Edward Echols, *The Phillips Exeter Academy* (Exeter, 1970); L. M. Crosbie, *The Phillips Exeter Academy* (Exeter, 1923). For Round Hill, see John S. Bassett, "The Round Hill School," *American Antiquarian Society Proceedings* n.s., vol. 27 (April 1917): 18–35; J. G. Cogswell, *Outline of the Round Hill School* (Boston, 1831); George Bancroft–Ebenezer Francis, March 19, 1827, College Papers, s.2, vol. 1, HUA. For other important schools, see, e.g., A. K. Teele, *History of Milton Academy, 1798–1879* (Boston, 1879); *A General Catalogue of the Trustees, Teachers, and Students of Lawrence Academy, Groton, Massachusetts, 1793–1893* (Groton, 1893); *The Jubilee of the Lawrence Academy* (New York, 1855); Higginson, *Old Cambridge*, p. 154; William Lawrence, *Memories of a Happy Life* (Boston and New York, 1926), p. 12; Frothingham, *Recollections and Impressions*, p. 20; Emerson, *Reminiscences of an old Teacher*, pp. 24–64; George Wright, "The Schools of Cambridge, 1800–1870," *CHSP* 13(June 1918):89–112.

57. Besides the above histories and catalogues, which contain information on costs, see, e.g., *Report of the Roxbury School Committee, 1840* (Boston, 1840); *Report of the Roxbury Preambulating Committee, 1866* (Boston, 1866); *Annual Catalogue of the Teachers and Pupils of Chauncy-Hall School* (Boston, 1835); Thomas Cushing, *Memoir of Gideon Thayer* (n.p., 1865); Henry B. Fearon, *Sketches of America*, 2nd ed. (London, 1818), pp. 112–113; Rufus Ellis, "The Academies and Public High Schools of Massachusetts," *CE* 50(January 1851):27.

58. Cf. Michael Katz, *The Irony of Early School Reform* (Boston, 1970), pp. 19–112.

59. Jenks, *Catalogue of the Boston Public Latin School*, p. 71; Amos French, ed., *Exeter and Harvard Eighty Years Ago* (Chester, N.H., 1932), p. 68.

60. Cf. Fischer, *The Revolution of American Conservatism*, for a persuasive analysis of "covert elitism" in early American politics.

61. The sum most often mentioned was $100,000. The participants included John Quincy Adams, Jacob Bigelow, Charles P. Curtis, William H. Gardiner,

Benjamin A. Gould, George Hayward, Hosea Hidreth, John Lowell, Stephen C. Phillips, Leverett Saltonstall, Joseph Story, Jonathan Wainwright, Thomas B. Wales, Sidney Willard, and Robert C. Winthrop. "Extracts from the Diaries of John Quincy Adams and Charles Francis Adams," pp. 27–33.

62. Charles Francis Adams, *Diary*, 1:10 (December 18, 1823); Parker, "A Sermon of Merchants," November 22, 1846, in *Works of Theodore Parker*, 7:9.

63. James E. Cabot, "Bigelow's Classical and Utilitarian Studies," *NAR* 104 (April 1867):616.

64. George Santayana, *Character and Opinion in the United States* (New York, 1920), p. 40. The tendency of the exclusionary forms was to make the university exclusive by class rather than, say, religion as with Oxford. The Unitarian preponderance simply reflected the denominational stratification of the society. The first Irish Catholic attended in the early 1850s, however — the son of an East Boston land developer. There were even one or two Negroes around 1850, at least in the law and medical schools, although blacks who could afford college were obviously rare and in any case seem to have preferred other instutitions, especially Amherst. The sharpest line was drawn between the sexes, where the university adopted official policy excluding women as it never did Catholics, blacks, or the poor.

65. For Child, see the very good essay in the *Dictionary of American Biography*, 1st ed.; for Parker, the sketch in the *Twenty-Fifth Anniversary Classbook of the Harvard Class of 1841* (Cambridge, 1866).

66. Professor Colin Burke, whose study of antebellum higher education will shortly appear under the title "The Quiet Influence: American Liberal Arts Colleges and Students in the Early Nineteenth Century," has reported the following impressions: that even in the 1850s Harvard was a "creature of the Boston area" whose students were "more likely" than those of other institutions to "remain in their home regions," more likely to enter "secular occupations such as business, banking, manufacturing," and more likely to have "businessmen fathers." I am indebted to Professor Burke for sharing his findings with me.

Chapter 7

1. Cf., e.g., Stow Persons, *The Decline of American Gentility* (New York and London, 1973), based mainly on literary evidence and using examples chiefly from the Boston area. Other standard treatments are cited in notes 20 through 29 of chapter 1; the names of Green, Goodman, Amory, and Jaher are worth reiteration. For another treatment of elite style within a different context, see Ronald Story, "Class and Culture in Boston: The Athenaeum, 1807–1860," *American Quarterly* 27(May 1975):178–192.

2. Mary Lyman–Charles Lyman, April 21, 1821, George W. Lyman Papers, MHS.

3. William R. Lawrence, ed., *Extracts from the Diary and Correspondence of the Late Amos Lawrence* (Boston, 1855), p. 87.

4. Bridges, *Charlemagne Tower*, pp. 22–23; Donald, *Charles Sumner and the Coming of the Civil War*, p. 18.

5. Edward Everett, *Twenty-First Presidential Report for 1845–46* (Cambridge, Mass., 1846), p. 12.

6. C. C. Perkins, "Memoir of James Perkins," *MHSP* 1(April 1823):362–364; Howe, *The Articulate Sisters*, p. 34; Peabody, *Harvard Graduates*, pp. 78–79; Hale, *James Russell Lowell*, p. 18.

7. See, e.g., Peabody, *Harvard Reminiscences*, pp. 26, 34, 59; Quincy, *Josiah Quincy*, p. 440; Cushing, "Undergraduate Life Sixty Years Ago," p. 549; Mason, *Ebenezer Francis*, pp. 10–11; Samuel F. Batchelder, *Bits of Harvard History* (Cambridge, 1924), pp. 143–152.

8. I. J. Austin, "The Military Academy," *NAR* 57(Oct. 1843):278.

9. Amos Lawrence–Amos A. Lawrence, March 17, 1833, Amos A. Lawrence Papers, MHS.

10. Frothingham, *Edward Everett*, pp. 291–292; Benjamin W. Crowninshield, *A Private Journal, 1856–1858*, ed. Francis B. Crowninshield (Cambridge, 1941), p. 58.

11. *Statutes and Laws of the University in Cambridge, Massachusetts* (Cambridge, Mass., 1826), p. 25; Tyack, *George Ticknor*, pp. 96–98; Anderson, *Letters and Journals of General Nicholas Longworth Anderson*, p. 56; Lowell, *Literary Essays*, 2:306.

12. F. O. Vaille and H. A. Clark, eds., *The Harvard Book* (Cambridge, Mass., 1875), 2:186–191.

13. See, e.g., Higginson, *Cheerful Yesterdays*, p. 118; Grant, *Fourscore*, pp. 22–23.

14. Charles Francis Adams, *Diary*, 3:105; Young, *John Thornton Kirkland*, p. 53.

15. Haddow, *Political Science*, p. 110; Adams, "Harvard College," p. 114; William Bentley, *The Diary of William Bentley, D.D.* (Gloucester, Mass., 1962), 3:543; Francis C. Gray, *Letter to Governor Lincoln in Relation to Harvard University*, 2nd ed. (Boston, 1831), pp. 24–25.

16. C. C. Felton, "Classical Learning in England," *NAR* 54(April 1842):276; Mary Lyman–Charles Lyman, George W. Lyman Papers, April 7, 1821, MHS.

17. Edward T. Channing, "The Abuses of Political Discussion," *NAR* 4 (January 1817):195–199; C. C. Felton, "Professor Channing and His Lectures," Ibid. 84(January 1857):38–39.

18. Morison, *Three Centuries of Harvard*, pp. 216–217.

19. Vaille and Clark, *The Harvard Book*, pp. 64–83.

20. Charles P. Curtis–Josiah Quincy, April 5, 1833, College Papers, s.2, vol. 5, HUA; Higginson, *Thomas Wentworth Higginson*, p. 18; Otis, *The Barclays of Boston*, p. 21; Rutherford B. Hayes, *Diary and Letters of Rutherford B. Hayes, Nineteenth President of the United States* (Columbus, 1922), 1:112, 114; Howe, *Barrett Wendell*, p. 201.

Notes

233

21. Willard Phillips–Octavius Pickering, October 1, 1848, in Archibald Murrary Howe, "Letters from Willard Phillips," *CHSP* 4(October 1909):86–89.

22. Thomas Bulfinch, "Record of Class of 1814," 1861, ms., HUA, pp. 12–14.

23. See, e.g., Talbot Hamlin, *Greek Revival Architecture in America* (New York, 1964), pp. 10–11; A. Lawrence Lowell, *Memoir of Edward Jackson Lowell* (Cambridge, 1895), p. 4; Nathaniel I. Bowditch–Jonathan Ingersoll, February 18 and June 1, 1838, "Papers of James Murray Forbes," (MHS microfilm reel 38); Lodge, *Early Memories*, pp. 60–61; Oliver Wendell Holmes, *The Autocrat of the Breakfast Table* (New York, 1961); Carl L. Cannon, *American Book Collectors and Collecting from Colonial Times to the Present* (New York, 1941), pp. 1–14, 57–63; Seymour De Ricci, *English Collectors of Books and Manuscripts* (Cambridge, 1930), pp. 93–94; Raymond Irwin, *The Heritage of the English Library* (London, 1964), pp. 50–51.

24. C. C. Felton, "Young England," *NAR* 61(July 1845):235–236; Atkinson, *Letter to a Young Man*, pp. 47–49.

25. Perry, "Harvard and Vacation Fifty Years Ago," p. 209; Sarah S. W. Blake, *Diaries and Letters of Francis Minot Weld, M.D., With a Sketch of His Life* (Boston, 1925), p. 76; Harrington, *The Harvard Medical School*, 1:467–468; Warren, *John Collins Warren*, 1:232–234; John T. Kirkland–Charles Follen, September 25, 1827, John T. Kirkland Letterbooks, HUA; Brewster, *Josiah Dwight Whitney*, 1:75; John A. Blanchard, ed., *The "H" Book of Harvard Athletics, 1852–1922* (Cambridge, Mass., 1923), pp. 12–14, 18–24; Anderson, *Letters and Journals of General Nicholas Longworth Anderson*, pp. 80, 126; James Walker–F. E. Parker, April 22, 1856, James Walker Papers, HUA; James Freeman Clarke, *Autobiography, Diary and Correspondence*, ed. Edward Everett Hale (Boston and New York, 1891), pp. 43–44.

26. Severance, *Hammersmith*, p. 14.

27. Quincy, *Josiah Quincy*, p. 438.

28. Quincy, *History of Harvard University*, 2:330–353; Muzzey, "Harvard, 1820–1823," p. 188; Ticknor, *Remarks on Changes*, p. 8; Adams, *Memoirs of John Quincy Adams*, 9:160–184, Quincy, *Josiah Quincy*, pp. 464–465; Josiah Quincy–Leverett Saltonstall, June 8, 1834, Leverett Saltonstall Papers, MHS. After 1830 rustication was resorted to in occasional extreme cases, but never again on so massive a scale.

29. Atkinson, *Letter to a Young Man*, p. 27.

30. One argument against faculty autonomy in the 1820s was that wealthy lay Fellows could shield professors wishing to discipline the "children of powerful families." Lowell, *Remarks on a Pamphlet*, pp. 46–47.

31. See, e.g., William Coolidge Lane, "The Building of Holworthy Hall," *CHSP* 7(April 1912):64; Quincy, *Josiah Quincy*, p. 440; Henry Ware, Jr.–James Walker, December 8, 1836, Corporation Papers, HUA; Edward Everett, *Presidential Report for 1846–47* (Cambridge, Mass., 1847).

32. Willard Reed, "An Excommunication in Harvard Square," *CHSP* 29

(1943):68–69; D. Hamilton Hurd, *History of Middlesex County, Massachusetts* (Philadelphia, 1890), 1:52–53; Franklin Sanborn, *Recollections of Seventy Years* (Boston, 1909), 2:315; George W. Greene, "Libraries," *NAR* 45(July 1837):139–140; Milton Meltzer and Walter Harding, *A Thoreau Profile* (Concord, 1962), pp. 266–268.

33. Peabody, *Harvard Reminiscences*, pp. 26–34, 59–60; Quincy, *Josiah Quincy*, p. 440; Cushing, "Undergraduate Life Sixty Years Ago," p. 549; Mason, *Ebenezer Francis*, pp. 10–11; Hale, *A New England Boyhood*, p. 205.

34. Willard, *Memories of Youth and Manhood*, 2:2; Charles Francis Adams, *Charles Francis Adams, 1838–1915: An Autobiography* (Boston and New York, 1916), p. 30; Clarke, *Autobiography*, pp. 42–43.

35. C. C. Felton, "Peirce's History of Harvard College," *CE* 15(January 1834):330.

36. Sparks, *Inaugural Address*, pp. 43–47.

37. Willard, *Memories of Youth and Manhood*, 2:2; Morison, *Three Centuries of Harvard*, pp. 202–204, 310–311; Vaille and Clark, *The Harvard Book*, 2:341–408.

38. Walter Raymond Spaulding, *Music at Harvard* (New York, 1935), p. 40; Milton Goldin, *The Music Merchants* (London, 1969), pp. 123–124.

39. Cf. Annan, *Leslie Stephen*, pp. 31–33.

40. Quincy, *History of Harvard University*, 2:639–708; Walker, "Josiah Quincy," p. 125; Edward Everett, *Orations and Speeches*, 1:179; Daniel Walker Howe, "A Massachusetts Yankee in Senator Calhoun's Court: Samuel Gilman in South Carolina," *New England Quarterly* 44(June 1970):197–220.

41. Benjamin Peirce, *A History of Harvard University* (Cambridge, 1833); Quincy, *History of Harvard University*; Eliot, *Sketch of Harvard College*. Among the major reviews were John G. Palfrey, "Quincy's History of Harvard University," *NAR* 52(January 1841):338–384; Francis Parkman, "History of Harvard University," *CE* 30(March 1841):338–359; Sidney Willard, "Peirce's History of Harvard College," *American Monthly Review* 4(October 1833):301–312; George E. Ellis, "Eliot's History of Harvard College," *CE* 45(November 1848):338–356; Bowen, "Eliot's Sketch of Harvard College," pp. 99–128. For statements of purpose, see, e.g., John Pickering, "Peirce's History of Harvard University," *NAR* 38(April 1834):381; Quincy, *History of Harvard University*, 1:vi–x.

42. Higginson, *Cheerful Yesterdays*, p. 43; Bentley, *Diary*, 4:192 (August 25, 1813); Hale, *A New England Boyhood*, p. 191; Morison, *Three Centuries of Harvard*, pp. 200, 317.

43. William Hickling Prescott, *The Literary Memoranda of William Hickling Prescott*, ed. C. Harvery Gardiner (Norman, Okla., 1961), 2:128–129.

44. Leverett Saltonstall–Leverett Saltonstall, Jr., August 22, 1841, Leverett Saltonstall Papers, MHS.

45. Amos A. Lawrence, "Remarks on Confirmation of A. P. Peabody," February 1860, ms., Amos A. Lawrence Papers, MHS.

46. John Lowell, "Letter from Europe," *Monthly Anthology* 5(April 1808):191.

47. For examples of such attitudes, see, e.g., Storer, "Thomas Jefferson Coolidge," p. 410; Allen and Cushing, "Town and Gown in Old Times," pp. 15–18; Warren, *The Harvard Law School*, 2:12; Hoar, *Autobiography*, 1:92; Crowninshield, *A Private Journal*, pp. 32–33; Anderson, *Letters and Journals of General Nicholas Longworth Anderson*, p. 56.

48. Storer, "Thomas Jefferson Coolidge," p. 410; Allen and Cushing, "Town and Gown in Old Times," pp. 15–18; Reed, "An Excommunication in Harvard Square," pp. 68–69; Hurd, *History of Middlesex County*, 1:52–53; Sanborn, *Recollections*, 2:315.

49. Grace Williamson Edes, *Annals of the Harvard Class of 1852* (Cambridge, Mass., 1922), pp. 329–330; Robert Grant, "Harvard College in the Seventies," *Scribner's Weekly* 21(May 1897):558–559.

50. Truax, *The Doctors Warren*, pp. 105, 110.

51. Henry Wadsworth Longfellow–Stephen Longfellow, March 27, 1842, in Longfellow, *Letters*, 2:394.

52. Atkinson, *Letter to a Young Man*, pp. 19; Storer, "Thomas Jefferson Coolidge," p. 410; Crowninshield, *A Private Journal*, pp. 32–33; Anderson, *Letters and Journals of General Nicholas Longworth Anderson*, p. 56.

53. See, e.g., John G. Palfrey, "Harvard College," *CE* 17(September 1834):93.

54. Leverett Saltonstall–Leverett Saltonstall, Jr., December 12, 1840, Leverett Saltonstall Papers, MHS.

55. Charles P. Curtis–Ebenezer Lane, October 10, 1836, File of the Class of 1811, HUA.

56. Clarke, *Autobiography*, pp. 42–43.

57. Charles P. Curtis–Ebenezer Lane, October 10, 1836, File of the Class of 1811, HUA.

58. Charles Jackson, Jr.–Charles Jackson, April 15, 1831, in Charles Jackson, *Memoir of Charles Jackson, Jr.* (Boston, 1835), p. 19.

59. William Lawrence, *Life of Amos A. Lawrence* (Boston and New York, 1899), p. 23.

60. Marianne Finch, *An Englishwoman's Experience in America* (n.p., 1853), p. 46.

61. *Fair Harvard*, p. 99.

62. Palfrey, "Harvard College," p. 93.

63. Quincy, *Josiah Quincy*, p. 438.

64. Bowen, "College Education," p. 303.

65. "Harvard University," *Monthly Chronicle* 2(February 1841):67.

66. Morison, *Three Centuries of Harvard*, pp. 200–201.

67. Cf. Story, "Class and Culture in Boston," pp. 184–188.

68. See, e.g., Samuel Lawrence–Amos A. Lawrence, October 12, 1861, Amos A. Lawrence Papers, MHS; Lowell, *Remarks on a Pamphlet*, pp. 25–36.

69. For manufacturing connections, see, e.g., Weeks, *The Lowells and Their Institute*, pp. 4–16; Josephson, *The Golden Threads*, pp. 39–40; Gibb, *The Saco-Lowell Shops*, p. 8; Knowlton, *Pepperell's Progress*, pp. 55–56; Samuel Batchelder, *Introduction and Early Progress of the Cotton Manufacture in the United States* (Boston, 1863), p. 65; William Bagnall, *Samuel Batchelder, 1784–1879* (Lowell, 1885), p. 16; George L. Vose, *A Sketch of the Life and Works of Loammi Baldwin, Civil Engineer* (Boston,1885), pp. 6–9. For banking connections, see Hidy, *The House of Baring*, pp. 82–84; *Some Merchants and Sea Captains of Old Boston* (Boston, 1918), pp. 1–8. For the Unitarian connection, see Frank Thistlethwaite, *America and the Atlantic Community* (New York and Evanston, 1963), p. 79; Robert Spiller, *The American in England During the First Half Century of Independence* (New York, 1926), pp. 30–33; Mrs. Eliza Buckminster Lee, *Memoirs of Reverend Joseph Buckminster, D.D., and of His Son, Reverend Joseph Stevens Buckminster* (Boston, 1849), pp. 261–262; Jones and Mingay, *Land, Labour and Population*, pp. 92–94.

70. Thornton K. Lothrop, "Memoir of John Lowell," *MHSP* s.2, vol. 14 (May 1900):177–178; John Lowell, "Letter from Europe," *Monthly Anthology* 6 (January 1809):10–11, passim; Edward L. Pierce, *Memoirs and Letters of Charles Sumner* (Boston, 1877–1893), 1:360; Weeks, *The Lowells and Their Institute*, pp. 19–20.

71. John Lowell–John Amory Lowell, August 11, 1817, in Greenslet, *The Lowells and Their Seven Worlds*, pp. 178–179.

72. Weeks, *The Lowells and Their Institute*, pp. 19–20; Mara Nacht Mayer, "Norton, Lowell and Godkin: A Study of American Attitudes Toward England, 1865–1885" (Ph.D. diss., Yale University, 1969), pp. 13–73, passim.

73. Henry James, *William Wetmore Story and His Friends* (London, 1903), pp. 12–13; Howe, *The Articulate Sisters*, p. 228.

74. Charles G. Loring–William H. Gardiner, March 6, 1853, Charles Greely Loring Papers, Houghton Library; George Tuthill Barrett, *Letters from Canada and the United States* (London, 1865), pp. 191–192.

75. Samuel A. Eliot–Catherine Eliot, May 16, 1823, Samuel A. Eliot Papers, HUA; Samuel A. Eliot, "Mackintosh's History of England," *CE* 11 (January 1832):347.

76. Thomas H. Perkins, "Journal," May 9, 1826, Thomas H. Perkins Journals, MHS; Hidy, *The House of Baring*, pp. 82–84; *Some Merchants and Sea Captains*, pp. 4–7.

77. Edward Brooks, "Foreigner's Opinion of England," *NAR* 15(July 1822):56–57.

78. Nathan Appleton, "Abbott Lawrence," in Freeman Hunt, *Lives of American Merchants* (New York, 1856) 2:337.

79. Amos Lawrence–Amos A. Lawrence and Charles Mason, January 13, 1840, Amos A. Lawrence Papers, MHS.

80. "Miscellaneous and Literary Intelligence," *NAR* 2(May 1816):137–138.

81. Briggs, *History and Genealogy of the Cabot Family*, 1:467–469; Pierce, *Memoirs and Letters of Charles Sumner*, 2:78; George S. Hillard, *Life, Letters and Journals of George Ticknor* (Boston, 1876), 1:270–271, 404–406, passim.

82. Andrew P. Peabody, *Reminiscences of European Travel* (New York, 1868), p. 17.

83. Harriet Martineau, *Society in America* (London, 1837), 2:171–172.

84. For Roscoe, see George Ticknor–Charles S. Daveis, May 1815, in Hillard, *Life, Letters and Journals of George Ticknor*, 1:51; Arthur M. Walter–William S. Shaw, December 22, 1802, in Joseph B. Felt, *Memorials of William Smith Shaw* (Boston, 1852), p. 162; Ware, *Life of Henry Ware, Jr.*, p. 265; Adams, *Life and Writings of Jared Sparks*, 2:52; George Livermore, "Last Will and Testament," File 36509, Middlesex County (Mass.) Probate Court; William Roscoe Thayer–Frederick Allen, 1919, in William Roscoe Thayer, *The Letters of William Roscoe Thayer*, ed. Charles Downer Hazen (Boston and New York, 1926), p. 3.

For the manufacturing classes and politicians, see C. C. Felton, "An Address Pronounced on the Anniversary of the Concord Lyceum, November 4, 1829," in Kenneth W. Cameron, ed., *The Massachusetts Lyceum During the American Renaissance* (Hartford, 1969), p. 44; Willard Phillips, "Brougham on Natural Theology," *NAR* 42(April 1836):464–488; A. H. Everett, "Sir James Mackintosh," Ibid. 35(October 1832):472; Andrew P. Peabody, "Sir James Mackintosh," Ibid. 66(April 1848):279–280; Jeremiah Mason–George Ticknor, April 3, 1836, in George S. Hillard, *Memoir and Correspondence of Jeremiah Mason* (Cambridge, 1873), p. 359.

For the City men, see Spiller, *The American in England*, pp. 125–130; Hidy, *The House of Baring*, pp. 82–84, 395; Richard Henry Dana, *Hospitable England in the Seventies* (Boston and New York, 1921), pp. 2–3. These models, and that of Roscoe in particular, are treated more fully in Story, "Class and Culture in Boston," pp. 184–188.

85. George W. Lyman–[?], September 26, 1820, George W. Lyman–Mrs. Theodore Lyman, October 4, 1820, George W. Lyman Papers, MHS.

86. William Everett, *On the Cam* (Cambridge, 1865), p. 308.

87. George S. Hillard, "Sears, Edwards and Felton on Classical Studies," *NAR* 57(July 1843):187; Ticknor, February 1819, in Hillard, *Life, Letters and Journals of George Ticknor*, 1:270–271; Adams, *Life and Writings of Jared Sparks*, 2:124.

88. James Russell Lowell–Charles F. Briggs, January 30, 1846, in Lowell, *New Letters*, p. 18.

89. Francis Parkman, "Life of Wilberforce," *CE* 26(May 1839):193.

90. Charles Sumner–George S. Hillard, March 9, 1839, in Pierce, *Memoirs and Letters of Charles Sumner*, 2:78; Theodore Lyman, Jr., *The Diplomacy of the United States*, 2nd ed. (Boston, 1828), 1:351.

91. John Pickering–Timothy Pickering, August 24, 1800, in Mary Orne Pickering, *Life of John Pickering* (Boston, 1887), p. 177; Joseph S. Buckminster–

John Pickering, March 22, 1802, John Pickering–Joseph S. Buckminster, April 22, 1802, in Ibid., pp. 208–210.

92. Edward Everett, February, 1819, in Frothingham, *Edward Everett*, p. 51.

93. Hillard, *Life, Letters and Journals of George Ticknor*, 1:404–406.

94. Charles Sumner–George S. Hillard, December 11, 1838, in Pierce, *Memoirs and Letters of Charles Sumner*, 1:501.

95. Charles Eliot Norton, May 1873, in Charles Eliot Norton, *Letters of Charles Eliot Norton*, ed. M. A. DeWolfe Howe (Boston, 1913), 1:501.

96. Edward Everett, "The English Universities," *NAR* 12(January 1821):3.

97. Hillard, *Life, Letters and Journals of George Ticknor*, 2:169; Pierce, *Memoirs and Letters and Charles Sumner*, 2:30.

98. Hillard, *Life, Letters and Journals of George Ticknor*, 2:156–158; Felton, "An Address Pronounced on the Anniversary of the Concord Lyceum," pp. 40–41.

99. Bowen, "College Education," p. 303.

100. John G. Palfrey, "Unitarians of England," *CE* 4(July–August 1827):295.

101. Arthur H. Clough–Ralph Waldo Emerson, November 26, 1847, in Howard Lowry and Ralph L. Rusk, eds., *Emerson-Clough Letters* (New York, 1968), letter 1.

102. Theodore Lyman, Jr.–Edward Everett, July 20, 1817, in Lyman, *Theodore Lyman, Jr.*, p. 18.

103. Joseph Romilly–Josiah Quincy, March 27, 1843, Josiah Quincy Papers, MHS.

104. George Tuthill Borrett, *Out West: A Series of Letters from Canada and the United States* (London, 1866), p. 200.

105. Samuel A. Eliot–[James Walker ?], June 13, 1853, College Papers, s.2, vol. 20, HUA. For recipients of honorary degrees, see *Harvard Quinquennial Catalogue*, pp. 1155–1169.

106. "Sketch of the Literary Institutions of Edinburgh," *Monthly Anthology* 5 (July 1808):360–366; Peabody, "The Condition and Wants of Harvard College," pp. 58–60; Walter H. Kilham, *Boston After Bulfinch* (Cambridge, 1946), pp. 11, 27, 45, 75; *Education, Bricks, and Mortar*, pp. 12–14.

107. Adams, "Harvard College," pp. 112–114; *Fair Harvard*, p. 32.

108. Spaulding, *Music at Harvard*, pp. 45, 122–123; Josiah Quincy–Jared Sparks, June 7, 1849, Josiah Quincy Papers, HUA.

109. Felton, "Classical Learning in England," pp. 269–276; C. C. Felton–Lewis H. Clark, April 9, 1860, C. C. Felton Letters, HUA.

110. Anderson, *Letters and Journals of General Nicholas Longworth Anderson*, p. 16; Morison, *Three Centuries of Harvard*, pp. 216–217.

111. C. C. Felton, "University of Cambridge, England," *NAR* 44(January 1837):179.

112. Daniel Appleton White, *An Address Delivered Before the Society of the Alumni of Harvard University* (Cambridge, 1844), p. 28.

113. Bowen, "Classical Studies," p. 48; Francis Wayland, "Life and Correspondence of Dr. Arnold," *NAR* 59(October 1844):402–403.

114. Sidney Willard, "Graduates of Harvard University," *American Monthly Review* 4(September 1833):252; Felton, "University of Cambridge, England," p. 179.

115. Cf. F. M. L. Thompson, *English Landed Society in the Nineteenth Century* (London and Toronto, 1963), pp. 85–86; O. F. Christie, *The Transition from Aristocracy, 1832–1867* (New York and London, 1928), p. 309; Dacre Balsdon, *Oxford Then and Now* (New York, 1970), pp. 32–33.

116. Basil Hall, *Travels in North America in the Years 1827 and 1828* (Edinburgh, 1829), 2:177–178; Frothingham, "Memoir of Rev. James Walker," p. 454.

117. On the youth of Harvard students, see Peabody, "The Condition and Wants of Harvard College," p. 48; Walker, "Josiah Quincy," pp. 134–135; Bowen, "Eliot's Sketch of Harvard College," p. 101. Also worth noting, perhaps, is the fact that the mid-century Scottish universities were not known for educating British gentlemen so much as middle-level functionaries, however interesting their pedagogy may once have been. James Scotland, *The History of Scottish Education from the Beginning to 1872* (London, 1967), p. 331.

118. William P. Atkinson, "English University Education," *NAR* 101(October 1865):527.

119. Trollope, *North America*, p. 142.

120. Professor Colin Burke has written to me, once again, as follows: "I would support a thesis that Harvard was an educational home for a new elite in America — everything I have points to it."

Chapter 8

1. Gray, "Wayland on College Education," p. 70; Ellis, "Eliot's History of Harvard," pp. 353–354; Quincy, *Speech of February 25, 1845*, p. vi.

2. Oscar and Mary Handlin, *The Popular Sources of Political Authority* (Cambridge, Mass., 1966), p. 29; Quincy, *History of Harvard University*, 2:250–257.

3. Goodman, *The Democratic Republicans of Massachusetts*, p. 169; John Quincy Adams–Benjamin Waterhouse, July 31, 1812, in Adams, *Writings of John Quincy Adams*, 4:381; Morison, *Three Centuries of Harvard*, pp. 172, 212–214.

4. Morison, *Three Centuries of Harvard*, pp. 213–215; Quincy, *History of Harvard University*, 2:295.

5. Josiah Quincy–Daniel Webster, August 17, 1833, Daniel Webster Papers, (MHS Microfilm Edition).

6. At the suggestion of Charles Lowell, for example, the debates over student disorders in 1834 were held in executive session. John Quincy Adams, July 31, 1834, in Adams, *Memoirs of John Quincy Adams*, 9:162–163.

7. See, e.g., J. G. Cogswell–George Ticknor, February 18, 1816, in Ticknor, *James G. Cogswell*, p. 44; Gray, *Letter to Governor Lincoln*, pp. 22–25.

8. *Journal of the Massachusetts Constitutional Convention of 1820* (Boston, 1821), p. 69.

9. Thomas Motley–Nathan Appleton, 1832, Nathan Appleton Papers, MHS; Morison, *Three Centuries of Harvard*, pp. 218–219. Morison dismisses the Harvard influence over the legislature's reluctance to fund Amherst, but the Motley quotation alone would seem to suggest otherwise.

10. Gray, *Letter to Governor Lincoln*, pp. 25 ff.; *Journal of the Massachusetts Constitutional Convention of 1820*, pp. 71, 549.

11. See, e.g., Gray, *Letter to Governor Lincoln*, pp. 5–25; George W. Warren–Isaac Warren, August 11, 1827, in Thomas C. Amory, *Class Memoir of George Washington Warren* (Boston, 1886), p. 81; Charles Francis Adams, August 8, 1836, in "Extracts from the Diaries of John Quincy Adams and Charles Francis Adams," p. 35.

12. Quincy, *Speech of February 25, 1845*, p. iii; George Bancroft–Board of Overseers, January 1845, Overseer Reports, vol. 7, HUA; Daniel A. White–Josiah Quincy, February 23, 1846, Josiah Quincy Papers, MHS; Charles Francis Adams, January 16, 1845 and August 27, 1845, in "Extracts from the Diaries of John Quincy Adams and Charles Francis Adams," pp. 22, 25.

13. Joseph Story–John Brazer, April 2, 1845, in Story, *Joseph Story*, 2:526.

14. Edward Everett–Peter Chardon Brooks, July 18, 1845, in Frothingham, *Edward Everett*, p. 267.

15. For this episode, see, e.g., Boutwell, *Reminiscences*, 1:95; Fred Harvey Harrington, *Fighting Politician: Major General N. P. Banks* (Philadelphia, 1948), pp. 10–11; Morison, *Three Centuries of Harvard*, pp. 287–288.

16. Quoted in Elias Nason and Thomas Russell, *The Life and Public Services of Henry Wilson* (New York, 1969), pp. 110–111.

17. Samuel A. Eliot, "Speech Delivered in the Massachusetts House of Representatives, on the bill to change the government of Harvard College," *Boston Atlas*, May 9, 1850; Jared Sparks–Banjamin R. Curtis, April 3, 1849, Jared Sparks–Samuel Hoar, January 16 and January 27, 1851, Jared Sparks–Willard Phillips, February 2, 1851, Jared Sparks–Simon Greenleaf, February 28, 1851, Jared Sparks–Caleb Cushing, May 23, 1851 and May 1, 1852, Jared Sparks Letters, HUA.

18. Nason and Russell, *Life and Public Services of Henry Wilson*, pp. 111–112; Samuel Eliot Morison, "Francis Bowen, An Early Test of Academic Freedom in Massachusetts," *MHSP* 65(January 1936):507–511.

19. Nason and Russell, *Life and Public Services of Henry Wilson*, p. 112.

20. Morison, *Three Centuries of Harvard*, pp. 290–293.

21. Nason and Russell, *Life and Public Services of Henry Wilson*, p. 96; Boutwell, *Reminiscences*, 1:95–96; Hoar, *Autobiography*, 1:30.

22. James Walker–John Amory Lowell, February 5, 1856, James Walker Letters, HUA.

23. *Official Report of the Massachusetts Constitutional Convention of 1853* (Boston, 1853), 3:35.

24. Ibid., 3:255.

25. Ibid., 1:143; 2:28–30, 36–46.

26. Warren, *The Harvard Law School*, 2:187–200; Samuel D. Bradford, *Works of Samuel Dexter Bradford* (Boston, 1858), pp. 389–397; Pope and Loring, *Loring Genealogy*, p. 97.

27. Morison, *Three Centuries of Harvard*, pp. 292–293; Warren, *The Harvard Law School*, 2:198–200.

28. So termed by Rufus Choate and John Lothrop Motley, as quoted in John Raymond Mulkern, "The Know-Nothing Party of Massachusetts" (Ph.D. diss., Boston University, 1963), pp. 140, 229–230. Mulkern's work is an extremely useful treatment of the Know-Nothing movement and of insurgent politics generally in Massachusetts during the 1850s.

29. Bradford, *Works of Samuel Dexter Bradford*, pp. 367–375; Huntington, *Memoirs of Frederic Dan Huntington*, p. 104; Nason and Russell, *Life and Public Services of Henry Wilson*, p. 111. The local press called this a potential "Jesuit Professorship."

30. Mulkern, "The Know-Nothing Party," pp. 138–139.

31. Robert C. Winthrop, Simon Brown, Abbott Lawrence, Thomas Russell, "A Committee on the Plummer Professorship," April 11, 1855, Overseers Miscellaneous Reports, vol. 1.

32. See George Morey, Samuel Hoar, George W. Blagden, Henry B. Wheelwright, "Overseer Committee on powers, duties, and responsibilities of the President and Fellows, and of the Overseers of Harvard, more especially in reference to appointments, tenure of office, salaries and finances," January 3, 1856, "Overseer Committee on Corporation and Overseer Rules and Procedures," January 29, 1856; George Morey et al., "Committee on Relations with the Overseers," September 6, 1856; George W. Blagden, Ebenezer R. Hoar, Emory Washburn, "Overseer Committee on Separating the Theological School from the University," January 28, 1858; Francis Bassett, Philip H. Sears, Jacob Sleeper, Rollin H. Neale, J. M. Churchill, Thomas Russell, Lorenzo N. Thayer, "Overseer Committee on the 1859 Legislative Bill on the Organization of the Overseers," May 19, 1859; J. F. Clarke, James Walker, William Gray, Stephen Weld, Edward E. Hale, Darwin E. Ware, William A. Richardson, "Committee on the Overseers and the Corporation," January 1859; Francis Bassett, John Goodwin, Josiah Abbott, "Committee on the Secretary of the Overseers," June 20, 1861. These reports are all contained in Overseers Miscellaneous Reports, vol. 1, HUA.

33. Pisani, *Prince Napoleon in America*, p. 272.

34. See, e.g., Josiah Quincy, "Inaugural Address," 1829, in Louis Franklin Snow, *The College Curriculum in the United States* (n.p., 1907), p. 166; Samuel A. Eliot, "Speech Delivered in the Massachusetts House of Representatives, on the bill to change the government of Harvard College," *Boston Atlas*, May 9, 1850.

35. *Journal of the Massachusetts Constitutional Convention of 1820*, pp. 75, 545–547, 550.

36. Ibid., p. 76.

242   The Forging of an Aristocracy

37. *Report of the Massachusetts Constitutional Convention of 1853*, 3:42, 250; James Walker–Thomas Worcester, February 10, 1957, James Walker Letters, HUA.

38. *Report of the Massachusetts Constitutional Convention of 1853*, 3:42–45.

39. Ibid., 3:250–253.

40. Walker et al., *Rights and Duties of the President and Fellows*, pp. 7, 16.

41. *Journal of the Massachusetts Constitutional Convention of 1820*, p. 548.

42. "Indisputable Facts," unsigned ms., ca. 1840, Corporation Papers, HUA.

43. Quincy, *History of Harvard University*, vol. 1.

44. *Journal of the Massachusetts Constitutional Convention of 1820*, p. 546; *Report of the Massachusetts Constitutional Convention of 1853*, 1:725–726; Eliot, *Sketch of Harvard College*, pp. 156–165.

45. *Report of the Massachusetts Constitutional Convention of 1853*, 3:250.

46. Jared Sparks–Willard Phillips, February 2, 1851, Jared Sparks Letters, HUA.

47. Jared Sparks, Lemuel Shaw, James Walker, Charles G. Loring, B. R. Curtis, Samuel A. Eliot, "Harvard College Memorial," Massachusetts House Document no. 10, January 14, 1851, p. 16; Walker et al., *Rights and Duties of the President and Fellows*, pp. 24–26.

48. John Eliot Thayer, *The Last Will and Testament of John Eliot Thayer* (Boston, 1855), pp. 9, 19.

49. Mason, *Ebenezer Francis*, p. 12; [Thomas Hill ?], untitled ms., undated, Corporation Papers 1863–64, HUA.

50. "Indisputable Facts."

51. *Journal of the Massachusetts Constitutional Convention of 1820*, p. 77.

52. Gray, *Letter to Governor Lincoln*, pp. 5–6; *Report of the Massachusetts Constitutional Convention of 1853*, 3:37.

53. *Boston Atlas*, May 9, 1850.

54. Parsons, "Argument of Chief Justice Parsons on the Subject of the Visitors of Harvard College," pp. 9–15.

55. Dunne, *Joseph Story*, pp. 165–166, 171, 181; McClellan, *Joseph Story*, pp. 206, 208.

56. Dunne, *Joseph Story*, pp. 189–190; McClellan, *Joseph Story*, pp. 202–203.

57. Dunne, *Joseph Story*, pp. 170–175.

58. Ibid., p. 175; McClellan, *Joseph Story*, p. 203. For the close relations between Story and Webster, see Irving Bartlett, *Daniel Webster* (New York, 1978), pp. 81–82.

59. McClellan, *Joseph Story*, p. 228.

60. Ibid., p. 207; Dunne, *Joseph Story*, p. 188.

61. The wording is contained in the *Harvard Quinquennial Catalogue*, p. 14.

62. Joseph Story–John Brazer, April 2, 1845, in Story, *Joseph Story*, 2:526.

63. Jared Sparks–Benjamin R. Curtis, April 3, 1849, Jared Sparks–Simon Greenleaf, February 28, 1851, Jared Sparks–Caleb Cushing, May 1, 1852, Jared Sparks Letters, HUA.

64. Hoar, *Autobiography*, 1:23, 37–38, 42; Jared Sparks–Samuel Hoar, January 27, 1851, Jared Sparks Letters, HUA; Moorfield Storey and Edward W. Emerson, *Ebenezer Rockwood Hoar* (Boston and New York, 1911), pp. 4–7; Frederick H. Gillett, *George Frisbie Hoar* (Boston and New York, 1934), p. 9.

65. James Walker–John Amory Lowell, February 5, 1856, James Walker Letters, HUA.

66. Edward Everett Hale–George J. Abbot, November 22, 1845, in Robert S. Morison, "Letter Written by Edward Everett Hale," *CHSP* 4(October 1909):92–93.

67. Jared Sparks–Samuel A. Eliot, November 6, 1849, Jared Sparks Letters, HUA.

68. The basic source for Hoar's career is Storey and Emerson, *Ebenezer Rockwood Hoar*.

69. O'Connnor, *Lords of the Loom;* Henry J. Gardner–Amos A. Lawrence, March 1856, "List of delegates to American Party National Convention," February 5, 1856, Amos A. Lawrence Papers, MHS.

70. Josiah Quincy–Daniel Webster, August 17, 1833, Daniel Webster Papers, (MHS Microfilm Edition); Andrew P. Peabody–John Amory Lowell, April 25, 1862, C. C. Felton Letters, HUA.

71. Jared Sparks–Edward Everett, March 24, 1849, Jared Sparks Papers, HUA; Andrew P. Peabody–George Morey, March 7, 1862, Andrew P. Peabody–John Amory Lowell, March 28, 1862, C. C. Felton Papers, HUA.

72. Andrew P. Peabody–John Amory Lowell, March 31, 1862, C. C. Felton Papers, HUA.

73. Walker et al., *Rights and Duties of the President and Fellows*, p. 13.

74. *Report of the Massachusetts Constitutional Convention of 1853*, 3:45, 75–76, 84, 252.

75. William G. Roelker, " 'But, Gentlemen, Who Shall Oversee the Overseers?'," *Harvard Alumni Bulletin* 42(May 24, 1940):3–4.

76. Quincy, *History of Harvard University*, 2:399; William Minot–Louisa Minot, August 19, 1840, in Channing, *Minot Letters*, pp. 361–362; Joseph Story–Leverett Saltonstall, September 8, 1843, Leverett Saltonstall Papers, MHS.

77. Charles Francis Adams, April 27, 1839 and April 26, 1841, in "Extracts from the Diaries of John Quincy Adams and Charles Francis Adams," pp. 13, 43–44; Adams, *Memoirs of John Quincy Adams*, 10:467 (April 26, 1841).

78. Roelker, " 'But, Gentlemen, . . .'," pp. 7–8; Jared Sparks–Henry I. Bowditch, April 24 and April 27, 1849, Jared Sparks–Samuel A. Eliot, April 16, 1849, Jared Sparks Letters, HUA; Edward Everett, "Festival of the Alumni of Harvard," 1852, in Everett, *Orations and Speeches*, 3:114, 121; Charles Francis Adams, April 12, 1856, in "Extracts from the Diaries of John Quincy Adams and Charles Francis Adams," pp. 41–42.

79. C. C. Felton–Amos A. Lawrence, July 1860, Amos A. Lawrence Papers, MHS; C. C. Felton–[Samuel?] Osgood, May 12, 1860, C. C. Felton Letters, HUA; Thomas G. Cary, George Livermore, and Henry G. Denny–

Henry David Thoreau, December 1, 1859 and January 21, 1859, in Henry David Thoreau, *The Correspondence of Henry David Thoreau*, ed. Walter Harding and Carl Bode (New York, 1958), pp. 541–542, 545.

80. Henry Lee, Jr.–Amos A. Lawrence, October 17, 1855, Amos A. Lawrence Papers, MHS; John C. Warren, October 13, 1855, in Warren, *John Collins Warren*, 2:265–266.

81. For early Harvard Club leaders, see, e.g., Charles W. Eliot, "Club Committees," October 1855, printed flyer, Amos A. Lawrence Papers, MHS; Edward H. Ammidown–Amos A. Lawrence, January 13, 1857, Amos A. Lawrence Papers, MHS.

82. [Thomas Hill?], undated ms., Corporation Papers, HUA; Ebenezer R. Hoar–Thomas Hill, April 18, 1864, Corporation Papers, HUA.

83. "Freeing Harvard from Politics," *HGM* 14(December 1905):361–362.

84. Ebenezer R. Hoar–Thomas Hill, April 18, 1864, Francis J. Child–Thomas Hill, April 8, 1864, Darwin E. Ware–Thomas Hill, April 15, 1864, Corporation Papers, 1863–64, HUA.

85. Francis J. Child–Thomas Hill, April 8, 1864, Corporation Papers, 1863–64, HUA. Among the leaders were Thomas Hill, James Walker, Charles W. Eliot, Charles G. Loring, Charles C. Paine, Horace Coolidge, Francis E. Parker, Darwin E. Ware, Ebenezer R. Hoar, Emory Washburn, Francis J. Child, and Robert Johnson.

86. James B. Thayer, "Memoir of Hon. Darwin Erastus Ware," *CSMP* 5 (November 1897):38–39; Edes, *Annals of the Class of 1852*, pp. 66, 198; *Proceedings of the Fiftieth Anniversary of the Graduates of the Class of 1841* (Boston, 1892), pp. 54–66; John Fiske–Mary Green, August 25, 1866, in Fiske, *Letters*, pp. 151–152; Charles Greely Loring II–Justin Winsor, February 27, 1879, Charles Greely Loring Papers, Houghton Library; Emma Forbes Ware, *Ware Genealogy* (Boston, 1901), p. 260.

87. Ebenezer R. Hoar–Thomas Hill, April 18, 1864, Corporation Papers, 1863–64, HUA.

88. Charles G. Loring–Charles Eliot Norton, November 27, 1865, Charles Eliot Norton Papers, Houghton Library; Darwin E. Ware–Francis J. Child, April 8, 1864, Corporation Papers, 1863–64, HUA.

89. *Journal of the House of Representatives of the Commonwealth of Massachusetts, 1865* (Boston, 1865), pp. 37–38, 292; Edes, *Annals of the Class of 1852*, p. 198.

90. Between 1828 and 1851, thirty-three men were elected as Overseers (exclusive of ex officio members); between 1852 and 1858, fifty were elected; between 1866 and 1870, twenty-eight were elected. Information on college degrees and Corporation membership comes from the *Harvard Quinquennial Catalogue;* on wealth, from the probate courts of Suffolk, Norfolk, Essex, Middlesex, Worcester, and Bristol Counties, Massachusetts; on residence and ideology, Forbes and Greene, *Rich Men of Massachusetts* (both editions); *List of Persons, Copartnerships, and Corporations . . . in the Year 1860;* Dearborn, *Boston Notions*, pp. 302–374; William T. Davis, *History of the Judiciary of Massachusetts*

(Boston, 1900), pp. 192–287; Boutwell, *Reminiscences*, 1:119–248; Mulkern, "The Know-Nothing Party," pp. 222–231.

91. James Lawrence and Phillips Brooks, to be sure, were Episcopalians, but by now this hardly sufficed to alter the conclusion. Also worth noting is the fact that of the first nineteen Overseers elected in the three years immediately following the severance of state ties, no fewer than nine had been associated with one or more of the following: the Alumni Association, the Harvard Club, and the movement to pass the severance act of 1865. Among the nine were Charles Francis Adams, Alumni Association; James Lawrence, Henry Lee, Francis Parkman, Theodore Lyman, and Charles W. Eliot, Harvard Club; and Darwin E. Ware, Ebenezer R. Hoar, and Francis E. Parker, severance movement. Some individuals participated, as noted above, in more than one of these "causes."

92. For other instances of the severance of college and state around this time, see Whitehead, *The Separation of College and State*, which discusses Dartmouth, Brown, and Yale as well as Harvard without, however, providing the degree of analysis which would enable students to make distinctions as to consequences or correlate the trend with the rise of antebellum social stratification or mid-century radical insurgency.

Chapter 9

1. For the concept of a stabilizing cultural center with a conservative bias, see Raymond Williams, *Culture and Society* (New York, 1958).

2. On mid-century Massachusetts politics, where there is still an enormous gap in the historical literature, the best sources are probably Bean, "Party Transformation in Massachusetts"; O'Connor, *Lords of the Loom;* and Mulkern, "The Know-Nothing Party." For the occupations of Boston's state representatives, see the *Boston City Directory for 1830* and the editions of *Poole's Statistical View of the Executive and Legislative Departments of the Government of Massachusetts* covering the years 1848 to 1855. For the city officers, see Pessen, *Riches, Class, and Power*, pp. 284–288. Among city officials, the proportion of artisans and workers had increased by the early 1850s from one-fifth to one-third; among state representatives, the prtportion of lawyers and merchants fell steadily from 63 percent of the Suffolk delegates in 1848 to 22 percent in 1855, their replacements being principally doctors, ministers, and farmers in the early 1850s and doctors, ministers, and artisans or "manufacturers" in the mid-1850s.

3. The new hospitals were the Massachusetts Homeopathic Hospital (1855), the Boston City Hospital (1864), and The Carney Hospital (1865). Langtry, *Metropolitan Boston*, pp. 321–326; Edwin Bacon, *King's Dictionary of Boston* (Cambridge, Mass., 1883), pp. 95, 125–126, 315–316.

4. New institutions included the New England Historic-Genealogical Society, the Boston Public Library, the New England School of Design, and the Boston Art Club, plus certain institutions of higher education noted below.

5. The new colleges were Tufts College and Boston University, Holy Cross and Boston College, Massachusetts Agricultural College and the Massachusetts Institute of Technology.

6. Cf. Harold Wade, Jr., *Black Men of Amherst* (Amherst, Mass., 1976), pp. 3–77, passim. Black men were hardly welcomed anywhere, but more at Amherst than at Harvard.

7. The growth of Episcopalianism may be traced in the church listing of the Boston city directories for the 1850s. For the Orthodox, see, e.g., Rich, " 'A Wilderness of Whigs'," pp. 273–275. For the 1853 elite-Catholic alliance and, indeed, the closeness of hierarchy and elite throughout the early and middle decades of the century, see Donna Merwick, *Boston Priests, 1848–1910* (Cambridge, Mass., 1973), pp. 1–59.

8. For industrial dividends, see Joseph G. Martin, *A Century of Finance* (Boston, 1898), pp. 126–131, 145–149. For the decline in shipping, see Morison, *Maritime History*, p. 398. Bank directors and capitalization are provided in the Boston city directories for 1850 and 1860; the travail of the Suffolk system is covered in Wilfred S. Lake, "The End of the Suffolk System," *Journal of Economic History* 7(November 1947):183–207.

9. Alan Olmstead, *New York City Mutual Savings Banks, 1819–1861* (Chapel Hill, 1976); Sam Bass Warner, Jr., *The Private City* (Philadelphia, 1968), pp. 49–160; and Michael Holt, *Forging a Majority* (New Haven, 1969) cover selected phases of economic and political strife at mid-century for New York, Philadelphia, and Pittsburgh, respectively, and suggest, at least, trends broadly resembling those of the Boston area.

10. To determine the ranking of 1860 party activists by wealth, names obtained from Boston newspapers in October and November of that year were checked against the *List of Persons, Copartnerships, and Corporations . . . in the Year 1860*. The precise figures are as follows:

Party	Number of men	Median wealth	Average wealth
Republican	53	$28,200	$62,500
Democratic	20	27,700	48,300
Constitutional			
Union	14	27,000	75,900

The election returns from ward 6 show Lincoln with 55 percent, Bell with 35 percent, and the two Democratic tickets combined with 10 percent. *Boston Evening Transcript*, November 7, 1860.

11. Barrett Wendell–Mrs. Mary Wheelock, February 28, 1912, in Howe, *Barrett Wendell*, p. 245.

12. See, e.g., Richard M. Abrams, *Conservatism in a Progressive Era* (Cambridge, Mass., 1964), pp. 30–52, passim; Samuel Eliot Morison, *One Boy's Boston, 1887–1901* (Boston, 1962), pp. 59–60; Gerald McFarland, *Mugwumps, Morals, and Politics, 1884–1920* (Amherst, 1975).

13. This sample consisted of the 411 Bostonians who held executive or

directorial positions in an industrial (exclusive of banking or railroad) corporation which was listed with the New York Stock Exchange in 1919. Within this group, the religious affiliation was as follows: Unitarian, 43 percent; Episcopalian, 33 percent; Orthodox Congregationalist, 6 percent; other, 18 percent.

14. Robert C. Winthrop, *Memoir of the Hon. David Sears* (Cambridge, 1886), pp. 11–16. See also Eliot, "Being Mayor of Boston," p. 160, for a description of the interdenominational church built at Nahant at about the same time as the Sears initiative.

15. See, e.g., Martin, *A Century of Finance*, pp. 130–131, 148–149; Johnson and Supple, *Boston Capitalists;* William B. Gates, Jr., *Michigan Copper and Boston Dollars* (Cambridge, Mass., 1951), pp. 1–63; C. Harry Benedict, *Red Metal* (Ann Arbor, 1952), pp. 1–76; James D. Norris, *A History of the American Zinc Company* (Madison, 1968), pp. 3–71; Harold C. Passer, *The Electrical Manufacturers, 1875–1900* (Cambridge, 1953), pp. 56–57; N. R. Danielian, *A.T.&T.* (New York, 1939), pp. 40–71.

16. See, e.g., the Boston directories for commercial banks and their capitalization and directors; Whitehill, *The Provident Institution for Savings,* pp. 46–98; Irene D. Neu, "Edmond Jean Forstall and Louisiana Banking," *Explorations in Entrepreneurial History* s.2., vol. 7 (summer 1970), pp. 397–398; Gras, *The Massachusetts First National Bank,* pp. 164–186, passim; Joseph H. Taggart, *The Federal Reserve Bank of Boston* (Boston and New York, 1938), pp. 230–238, passim; Edward C. Garget, "The Influence of Legislative Regulation Upon the Relative Growth of National Banks, State Banks, and Trust Companies in New England, 1863–1924," in *The New England Economic Situation,* ed. Edwin Gay and Allyn Young (Chicago and New York, 1927), pp. 39–68; Edward W. Weeks, *Men, Money and Responsibility* (Boston, 1962); *Old Colony Trust Company* (Boston, 1915); William W. Wolbach, *The Boston Safe Deposit and Trust Company* (New York, 1962).

17. For millionaires in the Social Register, see Gabriel Kolko, "Brahmins and Businessmen," in *The Critical Spirit,* ed. Kurt Wolff and Barrington Moore, Jr. (Boston, 1967), p. 358. For the early twentieth-century industrialists, see note 13. The third-ranking city was Philadelphia, with 373 officers. The leader, New York, had more than a thousand.

18. The Massachusetts General Hospital attracted some $600,000 in private charitable funds during the 1860s alone; by 1870 it was admitting 1,700 patients a year and spending $200,000 annually, a sum greater than the total endowments of its competitors. For institutional endowments in the early twentieth century, see, e.g., *Forty-First Annual Report of the State Board of Charity of Massachusetts for the Year Ending November 30, 1919, Part 2.*

19. The late nineteenth-century institutions are best described in Nathan Shiverick, "The Social Reorganization of Boston," in Alexander Williams, *A Social History of the Greater Boston Clubs* (Barre, Mass., 1970), pp. 128–143.

20. Alfred Bowditch, *Boston Athenaeum Statement of Accounts* (Boston, 1912); "Schedule of Property, Lowell Institute, Annual Report for the Year Ending

July 31, 1925," ms., Lowell Institute Papers, Boston Athenaeum; Benson, *Massachusetts Horticultural Society*, pp. 516–518; Walter Muir Whitehill, *Museum of Fine Arts, Boston* (Cambridge, Mass., 1970), 1:10–11; Walter Muir Whitehill, ed., *Handbook of the Colonial Society of Massachusetts, 1892–1952* (Boston, 1953), pp. 1–2.

21. The growth of the Harvard endowment may be traced in the treasurers' reports, issued annually with the report of the president. By 1900 the Harvard endowment was worth approximately $8 million by conservative estimate. For postwar private funding patterns, see, e.g., Gibbs, "Gifts and Bequests," vol. 2.

22. James, *Charles W. Eliot*, 1:7–82, passim.

23. The 1890 Corporation included, besides Eliot, businessmen Edward W. Hooper, Frederick Lothrop Ames, and Alexander Agassiz; lawyers William C. Endicott and John Quincy Adams; and politician Martin Brimmer. Of this group Brimmer, Ames, and Agassiz were all millionaires, while Adams was worth half a million and the others not a great deal less.

24. Charles W. Eliot–William H. Forbes, April 21, 1881, Charles W. Eliot Letters, HUA. Among those supporting the professorships cited were rail-roadman Samuel Hooper, copper magnate Quincy Adams Shaw, and investment banker Henry Lee.

25. Charles W. Eliot–R. T. Crane, September 12, 1901, Charles W. Eliot Letters, HUA.

26. Estimated from the twenty-fifth year classbooks of the Harvard classes of 1894, 1895, and 1896.

27. The residences of Harvard graduates appear in the classbooks, which indicate that approximately 45 percent of Harvard graduates for these years lived in eastern Massachusetts, with New York a fairly distant second; for sectional origins, see, e.g., Edward S. Martin, "Undergraduate Life at Harvard," *Scribner's Magazine* 21(May 1897):531. The names of commercial bank presidents come from the Boston city directories. The noncommercial institutions analyzed include the Provident Institution for Savings, the Massachusetts Mutual Life Insurance Company (formerly the Massachusetts Hospital Life), and the Boston Manufacturers Mutual Fire Insurance Company.

28. The list of Boston millionaires represents a combination of the lists of Boston millionaires for the years 1892 and 1902 as reprinted in Sidney Ratner, ed., *New Light on the History of Great American Fortunes* (New York, 1953), pp. 9–22, 97. The derivation of the list of Boston industrialists is explained in note 13. The list of Brahmin leaders is derived from Kolko, "Brahmins and Businessmen," pp. 343–363; Jaher, "The Boston Brahmins," pp. 189–243; and Jaher, "Nineteenth-Century Elites," pp. 32–71. The names, for the record, are as follows: Charles Francis Adams, Jr., Charles Francis Adams III, Brooks Adams, Henry Adams, Alexander Agassiz, William Sturgis Bigelow, Godfrey Lowell Cabot, Thomas Jefferson Coolidge, Richard Henry Dana, Jr., Richard Henry Dana III, Charles W. Eliot, William H. Forbes, George Peabody

Gardner, John Lowell Gardner, Thomas Wentworth Higginson, Henry Lee Higginson, Francis Lee Higginson, Oliver Wendell Holmes, Jr., Gardiner M. Lane, William Lawrence, A. Lawrence Lowell, Guy Lowell, Percival Lowell, Henry Lee, Jr., Ralph Lowell, Henry Cabot Lodge, George C. Lee, John T. Morse, Charles Eliot Norton, Richard Olney, S. Endicott Peabody, Charles J. Paine, Stephen Perkins, Francis Parkman, Moorfield Storey, Quincy Adams Shaw, and James Jackson Storrow.

29. Lawrence, *Boston Dispensary*, pp. 44–45; Benson, *Massachusetts Horticultural Society*, pp. 521–523; Smith, *History of the Lowell Institute*, pp. 49–94. In the nineteenth century about fifteen hundred lectures were given at the Institute.

30. Whitehill, *Museum of Fine Arts, Boston*, 1:10–11, 213–217, 289–291, 384–386; Frederic Curtiss and John Heard, *The Country Club, 1882–1932* (Brookline, 1932), pp. 169–174; Whitehill, *The Colonial Society of Massachusetts*, p. 18. Of 403 original Country Club members, 199 were Harvard graduates.

31. Shiverick, "The Social Reorganization of Boston," pp. 130–137.

32. Barrett Wendell–Mrs. John Lowell Gardner, March 2, 1902, in Howe, *Barrett Wendell*, p. 145.

33. Everett, *On the Cam*, p. 5.

34. The story of Joseph Kennedy's rise is a classic of the era but is by no means atypical. Cf. Richard Whalen, *The Founding Father* (New York, 1964), pp. 3–77, passim.

35. Barrett Wendell–Charles W. Eliot, April 11, 1893, Charles W. Eliot Letters, HUA.

36. Charles W. Eliot–Barrett Wendell, April 15, 1893, Charles W. Eliot–Charles C. Beaman, February 16, 1889, Charles W. Eliot Letters, HUA.

37. Charles W. Eliot–C. T. Stille, January 19, 1874, Charles W. Eliot–Timothy Dwight, April, 1894, Charles W. Eliot–[?], July 21, 1899, Charles W. Eliot Letters, HUA.

38. For Philadelphia, the basic work is still Baltzell, *Philadelphia Gentlemen*. For Chicago, see Helen Lefkowitz Horowitz, *Culture and the City: Cultural Philanthropy in Chicago from the 1880's to 1917* (Lexington, Ky., 1976).

39. The phrase is from Ronnie Dugger, *Our Invaded Universities* (New York, 1974), a marvelous work which suffers only from a severe misapprehension of the class functions and business domination of the famous eastern universities, notably Harvard, which he admired above state-supported institutions such as the University of Texas, his principal focus.

Index

Adams, Charles Francis: 50, 107
Adams, Henry: 63, 97
Adams, John Quincy: 36, 112
Adams family: 52, 63
Agassiz, Louis: 65, 80–82, 85, 87, 147, 151
American Academy of Arts and Sciences: 9, 16, 19, 47, 65, 161, 163, 175
American Bell Telephone Company: 176
Ames, Fisher: 36
Amherst College: 25, 95, 97, 139, 151, 170
Andover, Mass.: 104
Andrews, William T.: 34
Appleton family: 16
Atlantic Monthly: 64, 174

Bachi, Pietro: 83
Bancroft, George: 77
Bank of England: 128
Baptists: 7, 121
Baring, Alexander: 128
Baring Brothers and Company: 4, 49, 126
Beacon Hill: 10, 15, 29, 31, 37, 44, 64, 162, 172
Beck, Charles: 65
Beverly, Mass.: 51–52
Bigelow, Jacob: 65, 113
Bond, George: 65
Bond, William: 65
Boott Mills: 39
Boston, Mass.: 10, 26–27, 29–30, 37, 39, 44, 55, 62–63, 67–68, 71, 82–83, 85–87, 91–92, 94–95, 97, 99, 102–7, 110, 113, 119, 123–24, 127–29, 131–33, 142, 147, 154,

Boston, Mass. *(cont.)*
156–58, 171, 176, 178–79; aristocracy, xi, 4, 96, 120, 159–60, 165, 181–82; business, 4–6, 9, 11, 30–32, 39–40, 45, 49, 54–55, 57, 84, 86–87, 96, 106, 127, 146, 161–62, 165, 171, 173, 175–76; civic institutions, viii, 8–13, 16, 18–21, 53, 57, 69, 89, 110, 135, 160–61, 165–68, 173–78; culture, vii–viii, xi, 7–9, 13–14, 19, 24, 40–41, 54–55, 72, 75, 135, 164–66, 174, 180, 182; elite, vii, x–xi, 3, 14–15, 23, 30, 41, 52–53, 55, 74, 85–89, 92, 97–98, 101, 106–7, 125, 130, 132, 136, 140, 153, 156, 158, 162, 166, 169, 181–82; growth, 18, 31–32, 45, 53, 160, 168, 178; lower classes, xii, 5, 11–12, 16–17, 44, 108, 117, 120–22, 135, 158, 167–71, 174, 182; politics, xii, 5–6, 31, 36–37, 40, 54, 77–79, 96, 138, 150, 170, 172; religion, 7, 30–31, 35, 98, 170, 172–73; upper class, ix–xi, 19, 21, 23, 57, 108, 113, 120, 130, 133, 137, 165, 172–73, 178; wealth, ix, 3–4, 7, 14–15, 29, 31, 45, 47, 86, 92, 152, 157–58, 175–77, 182
Boston and Lowell Railroad: 39
Boston and Worcester Railroad: 49
Boston Assemblies: 94
Boston Associates: 4
Boston Athenaeum: 8, 13–19, 22, 27, 30–32, 34, 64–65, 71, 87, 89, 107, 114, 124, 135, 144, 160–64, 166–68, 174–75
Boston Bank: 47
Boston Children's Hospital: 173
Boston College: 155

Index

Index